BIG
FOOD

BIG
FOOD

**AMAZING WAYS TO COOK, STORE, FREEZE, AND SERVE
EVERYTHING YOU BUY IN BULK**

ELISSA ALTMAN

RODALE

Printed in the United States of America
Rodale Inc. makes every effort to use acid-free ∞, recycled paper ♲.

Book design by Joanna Williams

Library of Congress Cataloging-in-Publication Data

Altman, Elissa.
    Big food : amazing ways to cook, store, freeze, and serve everything you buy in bulk / Elissa Altman.
        p.   cm.
    Includes index.
    ISBN-13 978-1-59486-087-4 paperback
    ISBN-10 1-59486-087-4 paperback
    1. Quantity cookery.   2. Customer clubs.   I. Title.
TX820.A45   2005
641.5'7—dc22   2005012688

Distributed to the trade by Holtzbrinck Publishers

2 4 6 8 10 9 7 5 3 1   paperback

RODALE
LIVE YOUR WHOLE LIFE™

We inspire and enable people to improve their lives and the world around them
For more of our products visit **rodalestore.com** or call 800-848-4735

To my late father, Cy Altman,
The Original Fresser

CONTENTS

ACKNOWLEDGMENTS

I would like to thank the following people, fressers every one of them: my mother and the reason I learned how to cook (out of self-defense), Rita Hammer; the late Clara Elice, the greatest natural cook I've ever known; the late Bertha Altman, for her Balik Fish recipe; Thelma Gordon, for making us taste everything at least once; the late Marvin Gordon; Carol and Howard Wulfson; Nina, Robert, and Russell Schwartz; Michelle Wulfson and Bill Jaeger; Harris Wulfson; Lauren and Zach London; Rick and Roberta London; Dr. Shirley Puchkoff; Robert, Steve, Vicki, Margaret, Melissa, Anna, Theresa, Jayna, and Jennifer Puchkoff; Jean Marie Cannon; Helen Winalski Turner; George and Millie Gerath; the late Ethel Zekas; Sophie and Jerry Winters; Barbara and Dick Hopkins; Betty and Hank Podolak; Bob, Ruth Ann, and Kathy Turner; and Ann and the late Alan Cassella.

To my dearest friends who tolerated me while I was writing BIG FOOD: Stevie and Porter Boggess; Lisa Feuer and Carolyn Pittis; Gale Rawson and Mike Settle; Michelle Tesser; Joey Johns and Laura Zimmerman; Linda Wells and Richard Allessio; Bonita Friedman; in Newtown, the Murphys, Turners, and Latowickis; and in Harwinton, the Romas, Mashias, Calverleys, and DeLays.

The book you are holding in your hands would never have been possible without the judicious help of Rodale editors Shea Zukowski, Miriam Backes, Margot Schupf, and Mindy Fox; and Colleen Mohyde, agent extraordinaire, who saw the necessity of BIG FOOD long before a word was written. My greatest thanks to Antonia Allegra and the staff of the Greenbrier, who continue to nurture food writers selflessly; Bobbi Mark; Jim Mellgren and Giorgio DeLuca of Dean & DeLuca; the late Laurie Colwin; Doe Coover; at *Gourmet,* Diane Abrams; Lary Bloom; at *Northeast Magazine*, Stephanie Summers, Jenifer Frank, Steve Courtney, Anne Farrow, Bob Bonn, Dave Funkhouser; Linda Giuca at the *Hartford Courant;* Kim Upton of Tribune Media Services/ *Los Angeles Times* Syndicate; Prudence Sloane; and Colman Andrews for constant inspiration. And to my dear partner and light of my life, Susan Turner: first, middle, last, and always.

INTRODUCTION

Growing up outside of New York City, I was lucky enough to be surrounded by people and food shops of every kind: on just one street, we had a butcher (from whom you could place an order by phone before picking it up or having it delivered at the end of the day, thus guaranteeing its freshness for dinner); an Asian fishmonger; a greengrocer; a Hungarian baker; a European-style deli (where you could have fresh cold cuts sliced to your specifications in quantities as small as an eighth of a pound); an Italian market specializing in imported pastas, cheeses, sauces, and breads; and a tiny dairy shop that sold only whole milk, cream, eggs, butter, and the occasional package of frozen cheese blintzes. At the far end of the street was a small Associated Grocery store, run by an older fellow named Henry. He and his dour wife, who never spoke, sold staples, which included paper products, flour, skim milk, containers of juice, dried spices dating back to the Second World War, frozen and canned foods, and bottles of soda. My mother and grandmother, who lived with us, shopped regularly from Henry, supplanting their daily excursions to one or several of the other shopkeepers on the street. Their buying patterns never changed, and every week, the staples would arrive, like clockwork, from the Associated. A grocery carton would be delivered to our home, containing three quarts of milk (one skim); two containers of orange juice; two cans of asparagus (the only vegetable I would deign to eat); two rolls of paper towels; a six-pack of Tab; and, to satisfy my youthful cravings, one small bottle of Bosco.

Every order would be placed by phone to a cheerful Henry, who would answer, "GoodMorning-AssociatedWhatCanIGetForYouToday?" And today was a very important factor in his greeting, because what one customer needed today may have been very different from what another would need tomorrow. Whole families sat down together for dinner—even in the wild 1960s—and the staples bought from Henry were completely used up by the following week, when we placed our orders again. No one ever really thought of buying large quantities of anything.

In our home, as in most, shopping was done according to need, desire, and freshness: I would come home from school, and my grandmother invariably would be standing in the kitchen, still deciding whether to make broiled fish, roast chicken, or beef stew for dinner. How would she know what to make? It would depend on what the store had in stock and what had just come in that morning. And that was that. Even in a small suburb on the outskirts of cosmopolitan Manhattan, everything was prepared according to seasonality and freshness; the only things that were ever made ahead and frozen were Mason jars filled with Italian sauces, which came to us from our next-door neighbors who had a country house upstate. They taught us to freeze tomato sauce in the summer so that, deep in the middle of winter, we'd have a luscious, fresh reminder of the fruits of warm weather. Other than that, our tiny freezer held only one thing: ice cube trays.

How did it come to pass, then, that a mere 40 years later, a large portion of the American population—upward of 40 million people, in fact—would, in a nation so stolidly rooted in agriculture, the family farm, and the independent, entrepreneurial store owner, do their food shopping once or twice a month at a mammoth discount club . . . a gigantic airplane hangar-size establishment big enough to house the Queen Elizabeth II, where they could buy a package of paper towels large enough to be used as an end table, cedar lawn furniture, 48 pairs of Jockey shorts, enough antiperspirant to keep you dry for the next 80 years, a vat of your favorite shampoo, the odd cashmere sweater, a wide-screen television, enough toothpaste to keep the 101st Airborne smiling from ear to ear, and enormous quantities of whatever kind of food you might ever possibly desire during the course of your lifetime, from dried shiitake mushrooms to imported, salt-packed Italian anchovies, from immense tubs of organic yogurt and huge bags of fresh red bell peppers, to the fillet of beef that ate Cleveland—all at astoundingly good prices?

The answer is, in one word, time.

No one has time anymore; we have no time to shop, no time to get the car washed, no time to buy a ream of computer paper. We're overextended, hyperconnected, overdrawn, overrushed, driven to exhaustion; we cut corners, talk while we drive, drive while we talk, talk while we walk, work while we fly, and eat on the run. So what better way to satisfy the needs of a relentlessly busy population than to give us the phenomenon that is discount club shopping, where we cannot only take care of all of our families' needs under one roof, but also take care of them to the extent that we don't have to go out shopping every day, every week, or every 2 weeks?

We Americans are known the world over as cultural groundbreakers, as revolutionaries, as entrepreneurs who like to do things our own way; we blaze trails that are sometimes popular, sometimes not, but invariably copied and followed all the world over. And when we generally do something, we tend to do it really *big*, which is exactly why discount club shopping is so appealing: the bigger the product, the longer it will last; the bigger the product, the bigger the discount, and the bigger the savings. Buy big enough, and you will actually have a bigger amount of time left to take care of the other things in life that pull you in every direction.

But when you're talking about food, big can also be wasteful, particularly if you don't use up everything you buy; with the best of intentions firmly in hand, you can wind up throwing away half of what you bring home, along with the money that went into buying it in the first place. And the sheer size of *big* can be unhealthy. For example, our fast-food restaurant portions have gotten much bigger over the years, and while the result is perceived value—you can get a supersize fries *and* a supersize shake *and* a supersize burger for less than the cost of a package of skinless, boneless chicken breasts—the health implications are startling. In a nation that now counts a poor diet and obesity as the second curable cause of death behind tobacco use, portions are not the only things that are getting dramatically bigger: we are.

But the fact is that we simply cannot throw the baby out with the bathwater: buying *bigger* can indeed be *better* if we learn how to buy in bulk and use everything we bring home over the course of a reasonable amount of time. Buying in bulk can save us great quantities of time, money, and energy if we plan our shopping trips and endeavor to use everything we buy in quantity, from meat to cheese and everything in between. Very often, however, we also buy what can be prepared and eaten quickly, and sometimes these choices aren't the healthiest. So while we're busy budgeting and buying and planning and saving, if we can also manage to stop thinking of food as fuel but rather something to be savored and enjoyed—even when we are at our absolute busiest—*big* can and will be healthy, healthful, delicious, simple, and intensely creative. All we need is a realistic, workable game plan and an evolving shift in mindset that will forever revolutionize what we do with the food that we bring into our home kitchens in immense quantities—how we cook it, store it, and serve it to our families.

IS BIG FOOD RIGHT FOR YOU?

Look around your kitchen. Open the refrigerator; poke around in the icebox, past the freezer-burned sausage links and that unidentifiable container of weird, oddly colored frozen sauce (perhaps it's pesto?) that you dated in Magic Marker 3 years ago, back when you were trying to be organized. What's staring back at you? Can you identify any of it? If you can, do you know how old it is (if you don't count that strange, dated sauce)? Do you know, off the top of your head, how long a frozen chicken will last before it becomes inedible and something you shouldn't even feed to the squirrels, much less your family?

Take a peek inside your pantry. How many half-eaten packages of pasta are there? Can you remember why exactly you bought that family-size box of barley groats and the gallon can of chicken stock? Are you afraid to open it because then, of course, you'll use maybe half a cup, and the can is too big to fit into the fridge or the freezer?

Now think about your family: How do they eat? What do they eat? If your family is comprised only of you and one other person, think about your partner's likes and dislikes, and take a gander at the overwhelming multitudes of stuff gazing back at you from the depths of the fridge, partially eaten by the two of you, and now probably growing enough mold to produce penicillin for the eastern seaboard. If you have a few kids running around—maybe heading out to Little League practice or Girl Scouts or music lessons before racing home to do homework, shove some food down their craws, watch some television, and get to sleep—how do you feed them? If you're working 9 to 5, time is probably of the essence: your family wants to eat, and odds are they don't have the patience to sit around while, exhausted and bleary-eyed, you throw off your coat and make blanquette de veau from scratch. As if you had the energy to. So, by necessity, both they and you turn to that sort of glorified fast food that, as if by magic, somehow manages to leap off your local supermarket shelves and into your shopping cart because it requires perhaps nothing more than the addition of chopped meat, is "easy to serve," and fills everyone up quickly. This is not food; it's fuel.

Now think about your shopping habits. How often do you run to the market: Once a week? Twice a week? Twice a month? Of what you buy and bring home, how much do you actually wind up eating? How much goes bad before you even have a chance to cook it? How much do you throw out, both in terms of food and money?

If you were able to buy big quantities of ingredients and use it all—absolutely all of it—to create delicious, simple, healthy, home-style meals that your family craved and actually even requested . . . and you managed to do it all at a great savings, would you do it?

Chances are the answer is a resounding *yes*. If it is, BIG FOOD is here to be your guide.

BIG FOOD: A NEW WAY TO SHOP, A NEW WAY TO COOK

As a food professional, I honestly miss the days of shopping at Henry's little store in Forest Hills, next door to the butcher and the baker. For me, daily food shopping trips to those smaller, local markets are a wonderful luxury that hearken back to a slower, friendlier time; they continue to be a way of life in places like Italy, France, and Spain, where some shoppers wouldn't even think of going to a large discount market. But these days, daily shopping is a very unfortunate impossibility for most Americans; as we've seen, work, school, chores, orthodontists, carpooling, and life just plain interfere. Our schedules account, in part, for a phenomenon that is distinctly American: a food shopping extravaganza that entails clearing the minivan of half-broken toys and empty coffee cups, driving it to the supermarket, and shoehorning it full of everything you think your family might eat for 2 weeks, after which you'll repeat the entire highly

organized, mechanized, downright sterile process.

But when the discount shopping club experience emerged a few years ago, it forever changed the way most of us think about buying food: just visit a Costco, BJ's, or Sam's Club on any given weekend, and watch the crowds gathering around the immense meat cases and the huge sides of Atlantic salmon. Are they thinking about what to do with an entire side of beef once they get it home, or are they simply considering the staggeringly low price per pound? This is not a comment on wastefulness: it's simply a fact of human nature. We like big stuff. We think we're getting more for less, and with a large fridge and perhaps an extra freezer, we are: the savings to be had buying food this way are staggering. That is, if we use all we buy.

And if, like me, you shop at these discount clubs, you've been there. Oh, the savings! Oh, the fabulous discounts! Oh, the gray, freezer-burned, foot-long, 8-pound half fillet that falls out of the icebox and onto the floor, bereft and forgotten, 10 months after you brought it home! You struggle to remember when you bought it, and why. Was it for a party? Or was it the simple hope that you'd be able to feed yourself and your family well at a discount? You calculate the cost of the relatively minuscule portion that you actually ate versus what you're throwing out, and are horrified to discover that it was about what you'd pay for six thick sirloins in a regular supermarket. The minute that fillet disappeared into the bowels of your freezer, your so-called savings disappeared with it.

Gigantic buckets of dried shiitake mushrooms that seemed like such a good idea at the time; enough boneless and skinless chicken breasts to feed the lower 48; an entire Atlantic salmon fillet from an entire Atlantic salmon; a 72-ounce can of chicken broth that, once opened, will go bad in 5 days; a doorstop-size round of Cheddar that will begin to rot the minute you slice into it; 12 pounds of potatoes, some sprouting eyes; 4 pounds of Florida oranges; 24 lemons; a 32-ounce can of brand-name tuna fish that you couldn't possibly use up at once (so you just leave it in your pantry, where it will sit, unopened, for years); an Army surplus-size jar of mixed bean salad in a murky, unrecognizable vinaigrette; a box of pasta big enough to keep a mob of marathoners running for a month.

These sorts of items are what buying in bulk is all about: the bigger the food, the bigger the discount, the bigger the savings. But if you're like most people who shop at these wonderful discount establishments, unless you're throwing a shoestring wedding for 300, you'll rarely use more than an immediate, smaller portion of anything for yourself and your family—and then have to figure out how to store the rest of it. The savings disappear, and the discount becomes more meaningless with every passing day that the immense can of tuna doesn't get opened or the remaining 64 ounces of chicken stock get poured down the drain.

How, then, can you rely on bulk food to feed your family well—the kind of wonderful, home-cooked dishes that real people eat—without eating the same thing three nights in a row or losing a veritable henhouse of chicken to freezer burn? How to use all of those delicious things you brought home in mouthwatering, wholesome, home-cooked dishes without bending over backward to duplicate the architecturally perfect, hypergourmet fantasy meals we see on television?

This is where BIG FOOD comes in.

A NEW WAY TO SHOP

Whether you do your shopping at a discount club the size of a football field, at a high-end market packed with artisanal cheeses, a local supermarket, or a combination of all three, good shopping skills are the very first key to savings, and ultimately to cooking and eating well. It doesn't really matter whether you're bringing home a 3-ounce tin of Beluga caviar that was on sale or a really big, really inexpensive peasant-style cut of pork-Boston butt; if you buy too much, or if you don't plan ahead of time what you're going to do with that caviar or that pork butt, or how you'll store it for the long haul, it'll wind up being tossed out, at least in part. And waste, whether you're talking about something extravagantly expensive or prized for its frugality, is a great leveler.

In the coming chapters, you'll have an opportunity to reconsider your shopping habits, to learn how to best plan your bulk shopping trips in accordance with what your family likes and doesn't like, or even what kind of diet you may or may not be on. You'll learn how to be financially prudent just by thinking ahead, so that even if you're not sure what exactly you'll want for dinner on a Wednesday 2 weeks away, you'll have many varied options waiting for you at home, in your fridge, your pantry, or your freezer. BIG FOOD will take you by the hand and show you how to think differently when you step inside a discount club; it will show you how to make the most of what is available at these vast stores, how to use everything you buy, and how to safely store what you don't immediately need.

A NEW WAY TO COOK

Twenty years ago, I cancelled a gift subscription to a well-known food magazine because its recipes always assumed that the reader would have, for example, 4 cups of homemade veal demiglace in the freezer, or an entire 2-ounce white truffle from Alba, just waiting to be shaved over homemade pasta. Round about the same time, restaurants all over America began serving architecturally magnificent dishes that were actually physically challenging to eat but were such stunning works of art that you felt guilty just slicing into them: one

establishment in California presented each diner an edible chocolate piano at the end of a meal. Coming from a musical family, I was vaguely horrified, and I don't recall whether I started dessert by breaking off its little semisweet legs, or ripping out and gnawing on its white chocolate strings . . . all 88 of them.

> "If food is not simple, it is not good."
> —Richard Olney, *Simple French Food*

Fast-forward to the present day: we're now surrounded and subsumed by 24-hour-a-day gourmet cooking TV shows promising that even the marginal home cook can prepare astounding feats of vertical, gourmet cookery; the most basic strip-mall supermarket in, say, Kansas, sells the kind of gourmet products that were once available only in high-end luxury stores. The message is clear: everyone can now prepare gourmet-style, architecturally influenced food; the subtext says that we should strive to do this if we are going to call ourselves cooks.

But in reality, not everyone should make this their goal (that's what fancy restaurants are for). The home kitchen is meant to be

exactly that—homey, and nourishing to both body and soul. And in response to the fancy food and fancy meals that now abound and leave us wowed but unsatisfied and often downright hungry, most of us really do long for a return to simple, basic cooking. Whether it's a peasant-style rustic soup that your grandmother made in Italy, France, Germany, or Beijing, or the meat loaf your aunt from New Jersey threw together from a combination of chopped meats, simple, home cooking is best and, assuming it's not swimming in lard, often healthiest as well. Heaven knows, it's the most delicious way to cook, necessitating only the most basic of skills, the most basic of ingredients, and the most straightforward of desires that we all possess, no matter who we are or where we live: to eat well.

As we now know, BIG FOOD is about planning and saving, and

> BIG FOOD assumes nothing about your kitchen skills beyond three facts: you can follow straightforward directions; you want to save money; and you want to feed your family luscious, healthy, and wholesome meals that are meant to be eaten, not photographed.

shopping and storing the way our more prudent forebears most likely did. But it's also about a return to a kind of cooking that assumes nothing about your kitchen skills beyond three facts: you can follow straightforward directions; you want to save money; and you want to feed your family luscious, home-style meals that are meant to be eaten, not photographed. BIG FOOD will also guide you through certain very basic techniques that will forever change the way you cook anything you bring home: it will explain to you, for example, why a less expensive, fattier cut of meat is often the most delicious when prepared well; why it's best when braised for a few hours and allowed to render its fat; and why the leftovers stay more tender longer (and therefore freeze very well). It will guide you through the process of turning slow-cooked meals into easy-to-serve, fast left-overs. It will show you how to store food that has been cooked or is still uncooked, and give you optimal storage-life expectancies in both the refrigerator and the freezer. It will provide gentle guidance in the often confounding area of wine matching—but, like the relatively inexpensive ingredients used in the recipes, no wine will cost more than $12 a bottle. It will ask you to take stock of everything you have purchased at a discount club, and then consult the BIG FOOD Action Chart (see page 278), which will show you at a glance what your options might be for those ingredients. BIG FOOD will simplify the way you feed yourself and your family; it will streamline the way you plan your shopping trips, the way you cook, and how you save.

Go ahead: splatter BIG FOOD. Stain it. Crack its spine. Flag its pages. Dribble sauce on it. Write in it. Take it on shopping trips. Keep it on your kitchen counter, near the fridge. BIG FOOD is meant to be referred to again and again by all of us who want to reap the bene-fits of shopping at the clubs; it will show you how to be more creative and prudent in the kitchen, using large quantities. But even if you never set foot inside a discount club, and instead enjoy the luxury of shopping at the kind of high-end markets we all love but few of us have access to, it will still be a "must-have" addition to your kitchen library (or what I like to call your "cookshelf") because it will show you how to think differently about the way you plan your shop-ping trips, the way you cook for your family and use everything you buy, and the way you eat.

BIG FOOD: A NEW WAY TO THINK

If you're reading these words, odds are that you are part of the Average American Family consisting of two working adults, 2.5 children, and a dog, and you are, without question, keeping an eye on expenses. Even the wealthiest folks among us prefer not to spend frivolously, es-pecially where food is concerned. Yet at the same time, no matter who we are or where we live, most of us are dedicated to feeding our families well—offering delicious, wholesome meals that provide nu-trition, flavor, and economical bang for the buck, which is why bulk shopping is so enticing in the first place. But because most families today are also on the small side (how many of us sit down to dinner every night with our children, both sets of grandparents, and maybe an aunt or uncle thrown in for good measure?), bulk food shopping for any meal other than the biggest dinner party just doesn't make good fiscal sense. Leftovers invari-ably wind up being too huge to use and eventually go the way of that poor, aforementioned fillet the size of Cleveland.

The guiding principle behind BIG FOOD is simple: use everything you buy and bring home in creative, healthful, delicious meals. It will show the bulk shopper—that's all of us who would like to take advantage of the food prices at discount shopping clubs or simply want to buy in larger quantities—how to reap the real financial and culinary rewards that buying BIG has to offer, without pouring even the smallest portion of those rewards down the drain or into the trash compactor. BIG FOOD will take you by the hand and show you how to think differently during a shopping trip; it will show you how to make the most of what is available at these vast stores, how to use everything you buy, and how to safely store what you don't immediately need. BIG FOOD will show you that you need not feed yourself and your family the same thing 4 days in a row in order to "use everything up." BIG FOOD is the ultimate kitchen companion for the home cook, showing you how to prepare quality meals with skill, fearlessness, and the kind of natural-born creativity that we all have and that can be applied to any cooking situation, while never straying into the often frightening gourmet vertical food territory. It is more than a guidebook: it's a concept, an idea, a thoughtful way of living, eating, and saving at a most peculiar time in our history when it is entirely possible to buy one organically grown, fresh tomato for 4 dollars and one huge, filling, prefabricated, and really unhealthy four-course meal for 2 bucks. BIG FOOD will help you plan, organize, save money and time, and then create what will become your own family's new classics.

BIG FOOD is designed for you, the new, American family cook who shops and prepares meals in an entirely fresh, exciting, delicious, and thrifty way.

THE GUIDING PRINCIPLES: HOW BIG FOOD WORKS

BIG FOOD insists on no rules and regulations; there are no musts or shoulds involved in this delicious way to eat well and save money. Instead, it begins with the highly sensible and simple-to-understand theory that if you buy in bulk and actually use what you buy, your shopping trips will be fewer and your savings greater, and you'll have more time to prepare wonderful, tasty, healthful meals with what you bring home and what you wind up freezing. It is meant as a guidebook, a framework, a jumping-off point for you and your family to create your own ways of using everything you buy in bulk.

But BIG FOOD is even more than that: it's a broader, more universal concept, a new way of thinking about how you take time to feed yourself and your family in this busy, busy life that we all lead. It borrows from our practical past—when families literally "put away" the fruits of their labor by canning vegetables or froze enough fresh venison for an entire winter, or salted and dried cod to preserve it for a Friday night meal—and marries it to the way we live and feed ourselves and our families today, and to the necessity of saving money while eating well, which are not, contrary to popular belief, mutually exclusive constructs. When you step into a discount club, your options, like the quantities you buy, are enormous: you can choose between very inexpensive, oversize bags of pork rinds and 8-pound tubs of vegetable shortening, or you can choose between the mammoth package of delicious pork tenderloins and the 6-gallon metal drum of extra virgin olive oil. What's the difference here? The pork rinds may outlive the tenderloin in shelf life, and you can use the shortening, but not the olive oil, for baking as well as cooking. But in the long run, the lean and healthy tenderloins will provide several luscious and wholesome dinners, lunches, and even breakfasts. The olive oil will go the distance in glazes for fish, chicken, and steak; in light and lemony pasta sauces; as a spicy dipping oil for boiled shrimp or crusty, peasant-styie bread; and as a fragrant, drizzled finale to a stockpot-full of rustic Italian vegetable soup so hardy that it can be served as a main course to the most ravenous among us, the leftovers frozen for another quick and filling meal months later.

BIG FOOD is also about choice: *your* choice. As someone who is choosing to buy in bulk, you are choosing to save money. You are making a conscious decision to feed your family well for less. You are choosing not to go the fast-food route, and instead reaching into your freezer for an individual portion of homemade Chicken Potpie, which you can pop into the microwave for a quick dinner before you run to your reading group or pick up your daughter from a late soccer practice.

Ultimately, all BIG FOOD asks of you is that you slow down a little and take the time to think—even if it's just once a month—about what you buy, how you might cook it, and how you might store and later prepare the surplus. It looks to the sumptuous, filling, healthy, and easy-to-prepare worlds of Mediterranean cooking as a basic culinary springboard, but also includes the home-style favorites that we all know, love, and crave every once in a while, that come from as far away as Asia and as nearby as your grandmother's Iowa farmhouse kitchen. BIG FOOD is about you—the new, American home cook.

—Elissa Altman
April 2005

TAKING STOCK

BIG FOOD SHOPPING ADVICE

When I was a child growing up in Forest Hills, New York, I bore witness to a spectacularly odd shopping style that still confounds me to this day: my grandmother had the peculiar habit of buying what was on sale—*anything* that was on sale. Okay, so maybe that isn't odd in and of itself; chances are that we all try to shop that way. But if the butcher had marked down, say, a huge batch of tripe (aka beef stomach lining), that's what grandma brought home. And that was strange.

So it wasn't a surprise when multiple jumbo-size cans of lackluster, squishy Brussels sprouts (which I hated more than having my teeth drilled without novocaine, and which likely possessed no nutritional value whatsoever) showed up one day, after our local grocer had marked the cans down to three for a dollar. Deviled ham, which we all detested because of its high salt content and metallic flavor, arrived in its own delivery carton after one of her fateful shopping excursions: like the sprouts, it was a canned good, which meant that it had a shelf life of at least 10 years and a half-life of at least a million, like plutonium. And it was a meat, so, according to my grandmother, it was packed with the protein that would build strong bones. And when Chock full o'Nuts coffee went on sale, Grandma bought her weight in it, even though we were tea drinkers. When I left to go to college many years later, the Brussels sprouts, deviled ham, and coffee were all still there, clogging up the works in an overstuffed hallway coat closet because we had no room left in the cupboards, thanks to the things that we really did like to eat.

As an adult, I've discovered that this is actually the way many of us shop: we buy large quantities of what's on sale, whether we need it or not, because we simply cannot resist the lure of a potential savings. And though many older folks shop this way because, perhaps, they lived through the Great Depression or the shortages of war, what they often don't realize is that they're hoarding food—food that they generally don't even eat—for the proverbial rainy day. Ironically, there is no better way to throw out hard-earned money than to buy food that ends up going bad in the fridge or gathering dust and clogging up cupboards, closets, and basements.

Ingrained habits are inevitably passed on and tough to break, and this is where our national genetic memory becomes a powerful force in our shopping habits, no matter what our age. When we do our shopping at a discount club, buying whatever is on sale because we simply can't resist a bargain, a *big* bargain, is a dangerous prospect because at these establishments, pretty much everything is on sale and everything is huge, often posing storage problems that cause the food to go bad fairly quickly. We become what I like to call big-food junkies, buying every big, sale-priced item we can find. It is the nature of the big-food junkie to never say no to a bargain, despite lack of space or perhaps even money. Still, most of us never get our brains around the fact that

we will incur the savings only if we actually endeavor to use what we buy . . . everything that we buy. But how many of us really know how to do this?

THE BIG-FOOD JUNKIE: THE SAGA OF BETH

BIG FOOD was a mere glimmer in my eye one day when I lived in New York City, where most people cannot buy food in bulk because they just don't have the room to store it. When your apartment is the size of a glorified shoebox and the only sensible place to keep your sweaters is in your stove, buying, say, 18 rolls of toilet paper or enough ground turkey to get you through the winter is impractical. But that didn't stop my friend Beth, who has lived for the past 12 years in a studio apartment that's the size of a one-car suburban garage. One evening, while we were sitting on the floor around her antique pine coffee table and eating Chinese takeout, I looked over at her dining-room table and realized why we weren't sitting at it instead: there were six 20-pound burlap sacks of basmati rice stacked underneath it, like sandbags trying to stave off a flood. Beth is in the medical field, so I thought perhaps she was using all

of it in some kind of experiment. She wasn't. She was just buying in bulk at a new discount club in New Jersey because it was so much cheaper—and more fun—to shop that way.

Years later, I was back in New York and visiting Beth again; we ate Chinese takeout from the same local establishment, while sitting on the floor around that same coffee table. I peered underneath the dining-room table again: five bags of rice remained; only one had been used in all that time. Beth had spent approximately $46 eight years prior in an effort to save money, but she'd eaten (if you divide $46 by six bags) only $7.66 worth. New York City real estate is highly valuable, I told her, and she would have been better off just renting out the space under the table taken up by the rice.

Later that evening, I discovered a flat of 24 cans of plum tomatoes stowed away in her bathtub (she removed them every morning before her shower); a 5-pound, barely gnawed-on block of Cheddar living in the back of her fridge (much of it covered with a sort of green, chenillelike fuzz), along with a 12-pound brisket and a 3-pound bag of fresh, microwavable spinach. "Beth, what are you going to do with all of this?" I asked. She shrugged.

"I'll do something . . ." she said, and it became clear to me that she had no plans for the stuff that she brought home in bulk. I went on to tell her that night, after I opened her freezer door and 8 pounds of half-used, half-wrapped, gunmetal-gray, freezer-burned hamburger meat fell at my feet, "Beth, you are a junkie: a big-food junkie."

The guiding principle behind BIG FOOD is to use everything that you buy in bulk.

ARE YOU A BIG-FOOD JUNKIE?

As we've seen, the guiding principle behind BIG FOOD is to use everything that you buy in bulk . . . absolutely everything. And, as we'll see, a very big part of BIG FOOD is also learning how to choose what you buy wisely and (unlike Beth) having a plan for it all before you get it home, so you'll actually want to eat everything you bring into your kitchen. I'm not talking about what to do with an enormous, family-size package of freeze-dried macaroni and cheese;

I'm referring to jumbo packs of chicken, meat, and fish; gigantic tubs of yogurt and olive oil; and multipound bags of fresh vegetables and fruit. These are good ingredients, and with some planning, you can learn how to use them all up—without having to eat the same thing night after night.

Sometimes human impulse sort of takes over our brains and turns us into the Mr. (or Ms.) Hyde of the food aisles. This has happened to me on several occasions; for example, the time that I discovered a wonderful fruit called a Meyer lemon in my supermarket in Connecticut. Meyer lemons are a cross between a mandarin orange and your garden-variety lemon and, until recently, were very hard to come by outside of California. There they were, perfectly arranged; there was still snow on the ground, but their lovely golden-yellow hue whispered sweet, summery nothings to me. The price per pound was excellent, and in the amount of time it took to look at them, I was a goner. I envisioned vast Moroccan-style tagines of couscous, chicken, olives, and preserved Meyer lemons; great, soothing vats of avgolemono, a deliciously soothing, easy-to-make Greek lemon-and-egg soup. I con-

jured up quaint little pots of home-made Meyer lemon curd to spread on toast in the morning. I dreamt of candied Meyer lemon slices perched atop a sinfully rich, flourless, dark-chocolate tart, much in the way I dreamt I'd be tall, thin, and fluent in five languages if I only owned that stunning pair of brown suede Manolo Blahnik mules I saw at Neiman Marcus for $500.

So I bought the lemons. Eight pounds of them.

"Are you with a restaurant?" the checkout clerk asked me.

"No, they're just for me," I replied.

And they were just for me and my family, which is comprised of exactly two adults, a large dog, and two cats (the latter of whom do not eat lemons of any variety).

The refrigerated shelf life of a Meyer lemon is approximately 2 weeks, and sure enough, 2 weeks later, my glorious lemons grew hard, unattractively crusty, dry, and furry, and completely inedible.

So I threw them out. Seven pounds of them.

I am not ashamed to admit that I used to be a big-food junkie; I was really no better than my friend Beth, whose story you read earlier. But instead of sacks of basmati rice (which, if kept well-sealed in a cool, dark place—say, under a dining room table—will last just this side of indefinitely), I tended to buy things that go bad very quickly, so you have to use them right away, or freeze (and inevitably forget about) them: gigantic pork tenderloins; those wonderful Meyer lemons; blood oranges; three huge, shrink-wrapped chickens; a 10-pound bag of Vidalia onions. Several guilt-ridden weeks later, when I had to throw out the stuff because it had gone bad, I realized that I had to actually think about what I was going to buy before I bought it. I had to organize. I could buy in bulk, but I had to learn to do it carefully, with a plan firmly in hand before going shopping. The revelation has since saved me a small fortune.

As the adage goes, every giant leap begins with one small step: mine involved evaluating everything that was in my refrigerator, freezer, and pantry. It doesn't matter if you're a regular discount club shopper or a plain old supermarket shopper: the purpose of the following exercises is to see how much you buy and how much you spend versus how much you actually use. When you figure this out, you'll be well on your way to mastering the art of BIG FOOD shopping. And, I assure you, it's easier than you think.

UNDERSTANDING YOUR BUYING STYLE

The first step in understanding your buying tendencies is also the first rung on the ladder toward forever revolutionizing the way you shop. The exercise on the opposite page is designed to force you to come face-to-face with the contents of your kitchen, to evaluate what you eat and what you buy and then not finish, and to determine how much money, on average, you spend on quantities of food that you wind up tossing into the trash. I like to think of it as an absolute purging of your food-buying soul. And though it may seem like work in the beginning,

EXERCISE NUMBER ONE:
UNDERSTANDING YOUR FOOD BUYING HABITS

1. Clear off all of your kitchen counters and your kitchen table.

2. Open your refrigerator and remove everything . . . absolutely everything. Don't be afraid that the contents will go bad while you're performing this exercise; you'll be finished long before they'd come to room temperature. Reach into those little nooks where you keep the cheese and the butter. Empty out the salad crisper and the contents of the meat drawer. Be relentless. Put on rubber gloves and a surgical mask if necessary.

3. Now separate the contents before you into the following categories. Once you have everything out in plain view, make your own list. If you have other categories and/or foods that reflect your particular diet, taste, or traditions, add them to your list.

A. Cheeses
- American
- Swiss
- Imported (Brie, Parmesan, mozzarella, etc.)
- Processed cheese foods (such as Velveeta)
- String, crumbled, shredded, and similar cheeses

B. Dairy
- Eggs and egg substitutes
- Milk, cream, half-and-half
- Sour cream
- Cottage cheese
- Butter
- Margarine and butter substitutes, including spreads

C. Cured, Processed, or Sliced Deli Meats and/or Poultry
- Smoked ham
- Smoked turkey
- Smoked chicken
- Roast beef
- Bacon
- Prosciutto
- Mortadella
- Capicola
- Spam

D. Vegetables and Salad Greens
- Lettuces, including fresh spinach
- Fresh herbs
- Onions
- Asparagus
- Carrots
- Tomatoes
- Garlic
- Peppers
- Cabbage
- Squash
- Parsnips
- Sturdier greens (kale, mustard greens, chard, etc.)
- Broccoli
- Cauliflower

E. Fresh fruit
- Apples
- Citrus (lemons, limes, oranges, grapefruits)
- Pineapple
- Melon (honeydew, watermelon, cantaloupe, etc.)
- Bananas
- Berries (strawberries, blueberries, raspberries)

F. Fresh Meat
- Poultry (chicken or turkey)
- Pork
- Beef (ground or whole)

- Veal
- Lamb

G. Fresh Fish or Shellfish
- Salmon
- Tuna
- Whitefish
- Halibut
- Shrimp
- Scallops
- Tilapia
- Snapper
- Trout

H. Smoked Fish
- Smoked salmon
- Smoked whitefish
- Smoked trout

I. Packaged Goods
- Peanut butter
- Jams and jellies
- Prepared tomato sauce
- Pickles
- Condiments (mustard, mayonnaise, ketchup, hot sauce, steak sauce, etc.)
- Other (capers, olives, anchovies, sardines, tomato paste)

J. Leftovers (pastas, soups, meats, etc.)

you'll find that the long-term benefits are priceless.

This exercise is like that horrible day when you finally decide to go to the gym after a decade away and they make you get on the scale. Or you step in front of the mirror, stark naked, and you wonder who that is staring back at you.

It's brutal. It's real.

It's an absolute purging of your food-buying soul.

To begin, you'll need nothing more than a yellow legal pad, an indelible marker, a few heavy-duty garbage bags, and an hour or two by yourself. (When you do this exercise, no one will want to be in the house anyway once you tell them what you're doing, so that one precious hour alone will appear as if by sheer magic, even if you have a house full of cranky kids and a spouse who's usually glued to the television.)

EVALUATING WHAT YOU HAVE, HOW LONG YOU'VE HAD IT, AND WHETHER YOU SHOULD KEEP IT (OR DONATE IT TO SCIENCE)

Your next task is to roughly determine the age of every item that was once in your fridge and is now sitting on your kitchen counter. The good news is that this isn't as taxing as it might seem, because nearly every packaged product (including sliced deli meats, cheeses, and fresh meats and poultry) is stamped with either a "Use By" or "Sell By" date, thus making this step relatively simple. The bad news is that if you've unearthed a large, discount club–size tub of sour cream or yogurt that is dated April 1, and the day you remove it from the fridge is February 1, chances are that it's almost a year old. And everyone knows that sour cream and yogurt—unlike fine wine—do not age well. Furthermore, if you've also removed leftovers from your fridge, it's entirely probable that they are not dated: the only way you can tell how old they are is if you remember exactly when you originally ate them, or if they're covered in green or white fuzz.

Using the list that you created above, next to each item, write down the approximate date that you think you either bought it or, if it's a leftover, made it. There's no need to be exact here: all you want to come away with is a general sense of how old the contents of your fridge are. Now, write down the price of each item next to the date. If the price isn't marked, just venture a guess.

Everything that's old, bad, moldy, fuzzy, slimy, or just plain unrecognizable gets tossed into the trash bag. As you throw each item out, draw a thin line through it on your list. What are you left with? If you have a cooler drawer filled with fresh fruit and vegetables plus some ripe, well-wrapped cheeses; reasonably new containers of cottage cheese, sour cream, and yogurt; meat, pork, and poultry that's a maximum of 3 days old; and fish that's no more than a day and a half old, you're doing well. If, however, you have thrown out everything but that lonely box of baking soda in your now echoing fridge, you need some help in shopping and storing cold products. The final step in this exercise is to add up the dollars and cents of the items you've crossed off. What does it come to? Write down this number and put it aside for the moment.

EVALUATING THE CONTENTS OF YOUR FREEZER

Complete the exercise on the opposite page. Again, if you're able to actually figure out what you're looking at, you're ahead of the

EXERCISE NUMBER TWO: EXAMINING THE DEEP FREEZE

Now comes the fun and challenging part of Taking Stock. Very few of us know what lurks in the depths of our freezers, behind the gnarly ice-cube trays and the grayish-white, indescribable meat that may or may not be chicken. But either way, most of us operate under the assumption that freezing food—any food—will keep it fresh and make it last a long, long, long time, which is a very good thing when you're buying in bulk and keeping an eye on your budget. Made too much spaghetti sauce? Freeze it. Too much chicken soup? Freeze it. Bought a wagonload of ground chuck? Freeze it, freeze it, freeze it.

Guess what?

Nothing could be further from the truth.

Freezing doesn't keep food fresh indefinitely, and anyone who has experienced the vaguely mildewed, old-sweat-sock-like taste of freezer-burned meat or chicken understands this fact. By the time you're done with this exercise, you will appreciate the necessity of learning how to wrap and date food for freezing, as well as being aware of its freezer life span.

1. Open your freezer, and remove everything . . . absolutely everything, and again, put it out on your kitchen counter.

2. If you've labeled and dated your freezer's contents, congratulations. You're ahead of the game. If you haven't, this may be a little more difficult than cleaning out your fridge: once stuff is frozen under layers of foil or plastic wrap or encased in Tupperware, things can get a little murky.

3. Assuming you are able to tell the breakfast links from the pork chops, separate the contents of your freezer into the following categories and make a list of what you have.

A. Frozen Sauces, Soups, Stocks

B. Chicken
- Breasts
- Thighs, wings, drumsticks
- Liver
- Bones, gizzards
- Whole chickens

C. Beef
- Steaks (strips, tenderloins, fillets)
- Stew meat
- Roasts
- Ground meat

D. Pork
- Chops
- Roasts
- Loins
- Stew meat
- Ground meat

E. Lamb
- Chops
- Shanks
- Leg
- Stew meat
- Ground meat

F. Veal
- Roasts
- Chops
- Stew meat
- Ground meat

G. Sausages or Sausage-Type Links or Patties

H. Fish
- Shrimp
- Scallops
- Salmon
- Tuna
- Whitefish (halibut, pike, red snapper, tilapia)

I. Vegetables
- Peas
- Broccoli spears
- Corn
- Spinach
- Carrots
- Mixed vegetables

J. Bread, Bagels, Pizza Dough, etc.

K. Milk

L. Ice Cream, Sherbet, Frozen Yogurt, etc.

M. Leftovers

game. As you did in the previous exercise, and using the list you created earlier (along with any additional items), check off every item that corresponds to what you found in your freezer. Next to each item, write down the approximate date that you think you either bought it or made it. As you did above, don't worry about being exact: all you want to come away with is a general sense of what's in your freezer, and its approximate age and condition. Pricing the contents may be a bit more difficult than in the previous exercise, but generally, you should be able to get an idea of what you use and what you throw away.

Now, anything that's unrecognizable, blue (or gray) with freezer burn, or coming out of its wrapper and exposed to air—or fish that once was fresh, or that you have frozen yourself for longer than a week—gets tossed out. As you throw each item out, record its approximate price and cross it off your list. What are you left with, and how old is it? Do you remember why you bought it: because it was on sale, or for a party or special occasion? Now that you have it out of the freezer, think about your plans for it, and write them down too. Realistically, will they happen if they haven't happened already? Now add up the total cost of the food you've just thrown out and add it to the amount you came up with in the previous exercise.

EVALUATING THE CONTENTS OF YOUR PANTRY

Using the same technique as you did before, create a list that reflects the contents of your dry storage. Again, feel free to add to the one on the opposite page based on your own family's likes and dislikes. Next to each item, write its approximate date; if it's open, try to remember when you last used it. And again, scribble down its price.

If you have duplicate items—say, six cans of chicken stock or two bags of unbleached flour of the same variety—write down how many of those items you have and how many are opened at the same

---

THE TRUTH ABOUT FREEZING FISH

Yes, it is a good thing to eat fish: it's an excellent source of lean protein; it's packed with the fish oils (omega-3s) that the medical field promises will do good things for our collective hearts; it takes to broiling, baking, steaming, sautéing, roasting, and grilling in a way that little else does; you can choose full-flavored fish (bluefish or salmon) or mild-flavored (cod or trout); and it's perfect for a very quick, light, weeknight dinner, pan-seared atop some salad greens. But the one thing that's difficult about fish is that it doesn't freeze well. Why?

When you buy fish at either your local supermarket or a discount shopping club, odds are it has already been frozen and then completely thawed prior to it being put out for sale. Freezing anything before you cook it changes its chemical structure; when you thaw it completely (be it fish or chicken or meat), it should never be refrozen, which is in essence what happens when you take home, say, a 6-pound salmon fillet that's been previously frozen and thawed, and you refreeze it. The primary concern: food safety. Any previously frozen item that has been thawed completely doubtless contains its fair share of microbes that can only be done away with by thorough cooking. Additionally, frozen fish becomes mealy in texture and utterly lackluster in flavor. So don't refreeze raw fish once you get it home! Plan ahead and pick out some delicious things to do with all of it during its relatively short life span: poach it, grill it, steam it, sauté it, broil it, and then turn the cooked leftovers into crispy fish cakes, protein-rich salads, or tasty Asian-style burgers. The only exception to this rule is shrimp: bags of cooked, frozen shrimp are a great treat to have on hand, and they will last as long as 6 months in your freezer in a resealable freezer bag. Uncooked frozen shrimp have a slightly shorter life span—approximately 3 to 6 months—but again, never, ever refreeze raw shrimp that you've already defrosted once.

EXERCISE NUMBER THREE: COMING OUT OF THE CLOSET

For most of us who are lucky enough to have one, a pantry can be heaven-sent: a well-designed, thoughtfully executed pantry can hold all of your canned and dry goods in full view, where you can see and reach them easily. It can be effortlessly organized to hold flours, grains, and pastas on one shelf, cereals on another, and canned items on yet another. And those of us who don't have the luxury of a pantry generally make do with standard kitchen cabinets, a rearranged coat closet, or even a corner of the basement.

But the minute that storage space—wherever it is—begins to overflow with huge quantities of things that you opened and used once, or perhaps not at all (exotic spices? barley groats? chickpea flour? four bags of half-finished dried pasta? canned fruit cups from 1968?), you'll be unable to see the stuff that you do use all the time, so you'll wind up buying it again and again, like any good big-food junkie. Or, not sealed tightly, it will go bad before you have the opportunity to use it up: out it will go, along with the savings you thought you were incurring when you bought it. So, what to do?

1. Evaluate your canned and dry good storage the same way you did the contents of your freezer and your refrigerator.

2. Remove everything you have tucked away in your pantry/basement/closet/cabinet, get it all out in full view, and separate the contents into the following categories:

A. Cereals
- Instant hot cereals (wheat, instant oats, instant Irish oatmeal)
- Long-cooking hot cereals (steel-cut oatmeal)
- Boxed dry cereals

B. Grains
- Flour (unbleached, bleached, Wondra, whole wheat, chickpea)
- Cornmeal
- Polenta or grits
- Masa harina
- Barley
- Quinoa
- Couscous
- Flaxseed
- Millet

C. Rice
- Brown
- White
- Converted
- Jasmine
- Sticky
- Basmati
- Wild
- Short-grain (risotto or sushi)

D. Canned Goods
- Tuna
- Tomato paste
- Tomatoes
- Soups and stocks
- Beans (uncooked, baked)
- Chili, stew, etc.
- Miscellaneous (such as condensed or evaporated milk)

E. Pasta

F. Crackers (saltines, whole wheat, water crackers)

G. Dried Beans (white, garbanzo, navy, black)

H. Dried Spices

I. Bread Crumbs

time. (My downfall here: bread crumbs. I generally have three open canisters, all half empty.) In the case of dried spices, if you've had it longer than a year, it goes straight into the trash; anything else that has not been well-sealed or is open to the air in any way should be tossed out. As you purge, make sure you cross off the corresponding item.

What are you left with?

If you have plenty of canned soups, beans, tomatoes, stews, reasonably new spices, and grains (pastas and rice included) that your family uses as staples, congratulations (so long as you don't have as many canned tomatoes as our friend Beth did). But if your trash bag is filled with large quantities of dry goods that were partially used, and only as recently as last year, chances are that you could use some help in the shopping and dry-storage department.

THE BIG FOOD BOTTOM LINE

You have now gone through and evaluated the contents of your refrigerator, freezer, and pantry. What trends have you noticed? Do you have an overwhelming amount of stuff to throw out? How frightening an experience was it? Did it remind you of being in science lab, way back in high school? Are you considering ordering a dumpster from the local hauling company? What is the average age of the contents of your freezer? How much of it was unwrapped or partially wrapped? How many open boxes of cookies or crackers are lining the shelves of your pantry? How much do you estimate you've thrown out, in dollars and cents?

Looking at the three lists you've drawn up, you should now be able to determine what your shopping tendencies are, if you have an inclination to duplicate products because you forget what you already have, if you buy too much of something your family doesn't particularly like, or if you purchase something just to use it once. When you're planning on buying in bulk to save your proverbial dough, none of those three scenarios is prudent.

THE BIG FOOD SHOPPING TRIP

The next step in the process toward becoming a practical BIG FOOD shopper, a successful saver, and, in actuality, a better cook (no matter how or where you shop) is to firmly understand the basics—the building blocks—of restocking your cold and dry storage with products that you buy in bulk. Now that you've cleared out the cabinets, the fridge, and the freezer, it's time to make the most important choices you'll face in the process of relearning how to shop, plan, and cook from quantities that you buy in bulk. The *staples* that you choose to buy in bulk, if stored well, will go the distance for months; they will form the foundation for anything you cook from the coming pages, be it elegant or simple (or simple *and* elegant), Italian, Asian, Eastern European, American, Latin American, or Middle Eastern. Virtually all of the recipes in BIG FOOD use these staples as a springboard; even the most basic condiments that we take for granted, such as mustard, ketchup, and mayonnaise, can be reworked, reflavored, and stored well to give you an edible wardrobe of culinary choices. These recipes and techniques will follow; in the meantime, first things first.

When you purchase staples, choose items that can be reworked, reflavored, augmented, and stored well in order to create an edible wardrobe of culinary choices. Brownies, cookies, Twinkies, Devil Dogs, and potato chips are not staples.

BUYING STAPLES FOR YOUR REFRIGERATOR

Certainly, tastes change; moreover, no one wants to eat the same thing every night. And dietary restrictions preclude some of us from eating certain things, like pork products or shellfish. But the most basic basics are unquestionable necessities in the kitchen. Every refrigerator should contain the following items, all of which can be purchased in bulk-size quantities:

- Eggs (1 to 2 dozen, depending on number of household members)
- Egg substitutes or liquid egg whites

- 2 percent milk (buy 2 gallons: one for your fridge, one for your freezer)
- Unsalted (sweet) butter (buy 2 packages; place two sticks in your fridge and the balance in the freezer)
- Cream cheese (regular or low-fat)
- 1 large container of mayonnaise (regular or low-fat)
- 1 large container of plain yogurt (regular or low-fat)
- 2 large wedges of good-quality cheese (1 hard, for grating, such as Parmesan, Locatelli Romano, or Cheddar; and 1 softer, such as queso blanco, Gouda, or Brie)
- 1 bag of 6 to 8 limes
- 1 bag of 6 to 8 lemons
- 1 pound of any of the following: salt pork, thick-sliced bacon, slab bacon, turkey bacon, vegetarian bacon

This list, as always, can be amended to reflect your personal tastes: if you don't like limes but prefer oranges, buy oranges—just make sure that they are suitable for eating, cooking, and juicing. If your family doesn't eat eggs, consider egg substitutes (also available in a freezable version), which can be used to make everything from luscious frittatas, scrambles, and omelets to glazes for lamb and pork.

THE (OH SO SIMPLE) ART OF STOCKING YOUR FREEZER

Filling the freezer with essentials can be a tricky endeavor if you don't own the sort of gigantic thing typically used for storing huge portions of freshly hunted meat. Still, we've come a long way since the old days. Modern refrigerators used to cordon off just a tiny sliver of a space, which was referred to as an icebox (because it was literally just large enough to hold a couple of trays filled with ice cubes). But today, as more people discover the glories of bulk shopping, refrigerators (and the freezers inside them) are getting larger and larger. In fact, some fridges even have bottom drawers big enough to freeze an entire venison or two. It is imperative to understand what your freezer essentials need to be; otherwise you run the risk of overstocking the freezer—or understocking it.

But beyond the issue of space, we also have to consider what makes a good "freezable" staple (unfortunately, the answer isn't always ice cream) because, frankly, some things freeze well and some things don't. In the coming pages I will provide you with the information you'll need to understand how long you should freeze everything from meat to soup to bread, before you lose it to freezer burn. Generally speaking, simple is best. A necessity or staple on an ingredient list is almost an afterthought, and freezer staples are no different: you should always have them on hand, so you don't have to think about them at the end of a busy day.

Fill your freezer with:

- Unsalted butter
- 2 percent milk
- 6 ice cube trays: 2 clear, 2 of one color, and 2 of another

Freeze leftover canned stock in colored ice-cube trays (so you don't accidentally drop a cube of meat stock into a glass of scotch). Adding a cube of frozen stock to sauces, soups, or stews provides an easy punch of flavor.

And that's all. Why so easy? Because your freezer will eventually be filled with BIG FOOD leftovers, along with meats, poultry, sauces, compound butters, soups, stews, and everything else that you will make from the ingredients you buy in bulk. So now . . . on to your pantry.

THE BIG FOOD PANTRY

Consider the BIG FOOD pantry to be like an artist's palette; all of the main colors are there—blues, reds, yellows—and they can absolutely stand on their own. But blend them together, and a veritable encyclopedia of shades, moods, and hues becomes yours, to use as your mood strikes. Likewise, BIG FOOD pantry staples: if you stock your pantry with the basics, you give yourself the foundation to make nearly every dish in this book, along with all the other ones you'll create on your own. In the coming pages, we'll learn how to take BIG FOOD pantry basics like olive oil and flavor them with fresh herbs, garlic, and citrus fruits; how to dress up ordinary mayonnaise and butter and use them on everything from a simply broiled piece of fish to fresh-baked bread and leftover chicken. You'll also find out how to augment ordinary mustard and ketchup with different kinds of BIG FOOD spices and other condiments, from

honey to horseradish, for use as glazes, marinades, and sandwich spreads. And canned tomatoes will easily evolve into sauces, stews, and even cold soups. All it takes to use all of your BIG FOOD pantry items is a little forethought and some creativity, which we all have.

The following list is sort of a rough guide to filling your pantry. It contains the necessities that I believe we should all have but is by no means set in stone. If you detest white vinegar, substitute another mild variety, like rice vinegar. If you prefer crushing your own canned tomatoes, buy them whole and crush them in the can. If you like traditional American-style hot-dog mustard better than Dijon, by all means, use it. And if the very thought of soaking dried beans makes you shudder, buy the canned variety (although their texture is softer and their flavor is, by comparison, blander). Just endeavor to use absolutely all of each staple before stocking up again.

The BIG FOOD pantry contains:

- Canned plum tomatoes, crushed or whole (the Italian, or San Marzano, variety is sweetest)

- Canned black or green olives (unstuffed)
- Canned tuna (preferably Italian-style, packed in olive oil)
- Canned or jarred anchovies
- Dijon mustard
- Ketchup
- Soy sauce or tamari sauce (preferably low-sodium)
- White vinegar
- Balsamic vinegar
- White wine vinegar
- Red wine vinegar
- Apple cider vinegar
- Extra virgin olive oil
- Vegetable oil
- Unflavored cooking spray
- Maple syrup
- Light coconut milk
- Hot sauce
- Pearl barley
- Basmati rice
- Long-grain white rice
- Short-grain white rice
- Dried white beans

- Dried black beans
- Dried garbanzo beans
- Unbleached, all-purpose flour
- Cornmeal
- Pastas: spaghetti (or a similar long variety), penne (or a similar tubular variety), and ditalini (or a small, tubular style)
- Kosher salt
- Stocks: chicken, beef, vegetable
- Saltines or a similar cracker
- Dried spices and herbs: basil, black peppercorns, chili powder, garlic powder, ginger, lemongrass, mint, onion powder, oregano, paprika, parsley, red pepper flakes, rosemary, sage, thyme

Now, looking at the BIG FOOD pantry staples list, questions will inevitably come up. Why saltines? Because, as most American Southerners know, they make arguably the tastiest, lightest crumbs, perfect for creating crisp coatings. Coconut milk? A can or two will enable you to turn leftover chicken, shrimp, beef, a side dish of vegetables, and some steamed rice into a delicious, simple curry; add it to chicken stock along with lemongrass and a few chilies, and you've got a Thai-influenced sweet-and-sour soup. Anchovies? Anchovies are the cilantro of fish: a lot of people like them, and just as many people utterly detest them. But at the end of the day, there is no better way to create a flavor-packed, healthy sauce that can be used on hot or cold pasta, as a cold vegetable dip, or a salad dressing than by pounding a couple of anchovies together with a little garlic, kosher salt, olive oil, lemon juice, and fresh basil. Your guests—who may even dislike anchovies on pizza or in salads—will wonder where that fabulous briny flavor is coming from. And stored properly, that sauce, dip, or dressing will last for days in the refrigerator.

BIG FOOD, as we've seen, is all about choices—making the right choices about what to do with what you bring home in bulk, whether it's an enormous can of chicken stock, a mammoth box of crackers, or several pounds of frozen shrimp. But it's also about thinking ahead, planning, and saving what you bring home in terms of both food and money, as well as learning how to store what you buy, how to cook it, and how to keep the leftovers or create luscious, secondary meals.

A WORD ABOUT DRIED SPICES AND HERBS

The ancient practice of drying spices and herbs for out-of-season use is one of the many gifts our forebears gave us: the Egyptians did it, as did the Mexicans, the Africans, the French, the Italians, and even the Colonial Americans. But unlike our ancestors, many of us refuse to acknowledge the fact that dried spices do not last indefinitely—in fact, they don't really last longer than a year. My own mother-in-law has powdered sage in her spice pantry from 1955, so if you, like her, have anything that has lost its fragrance, resembles green sawdust, or was packaged when Eisenhower was in office, replace it! (Better still: make your own. More on that later.)

Dried spices are a wonderful way to pump up flavor in deepest, darkest winter, when fresh spices can be hard to come by (unless you live in a temperate area, like California, where herbs often grow wild on the side of the road). Moreover, buying dried herbs and spices in bulk is a terrific way to learn how to combine them to make your own customized blends that can then be stored in your pantry for quick and easy use: Asian, Mediterranean, Indian, Cajun, and seasoned salt blends are extremely easy to put together, and tremendously flavorful.

TOOLS THAT NO ONE SHOULD BE WITHOUT

Carpenters, doctors, lawyers, painters, plumbers, musicians, and business people—all have tools that enable them to accomplish their missions. Without a plunger or a drain snake, a plumber can't do his or her job. Without a guitar or a piano, a musician might be sunk. No canvas or brushes, and a painter might as well hang it up. The same thing is true for home cooks, particularly those of us who shop at discount clubs and bring home large quantities of food to feed to our reasonably small families. If we don't learn how to keep and use what we've got, we've lost the point of the whole discount shopping exercise; this necessitates learning about the actual tools that will enable us to do our jobs.

Many years ago, my grandmother brewed coffee, tea, and, often, chicken soup in the same small glass percolator that sat directly on the stove. She had one pan for broiling meat, and another for braising stuffed cabbage or making meatballs. Her stockpot boiled water for pasta but wasn't right for stew, which was cooked in something that she called a schissel—a flatter, squatter soup pot with two handles. Nearly every pot she owned had a plastic handle that, sooner or later, melted to some degree.

Grandma's refrigerator storage techniques included double-wrapping in plastic wrap and reusing the plastic tubs that had once contained store-bought coleslaw or potato salad: these were the pre-microwave days, so she didn't concern herself about reheating directly in the storage container. And if a lid had mysteriously gone missing, she simply stretched a piece of wax paper over the top of the vessel and secured it in place with a (usually red) rubber band.

Today, we home cooks are offered such an astonishing array of cooking tools, storage containers, plastic wraps, and freezer wraps that the whole subject borders on the dizzying: What can go into the oven? What's suitable for freezing, or reheating in the microwave? Is it dishwasher-safe? Will it discolor? Will its plastic lid melt? How hard is it to keep cast iron clean? Is expensive French copper the best cookware that money can buy? Why? Is heavier always better? Do I really need that olive pitter, that pizza cutter, or those cannoli forms?

The first thing to consider when you're "tooling up" is that it pays, again, to choose well. Just as BIG FOOD asks you to learn to prepare any number of dishes from the things you buy in bulk, it also suggests that you avail yourself of tools that will do double duty. For example, a small, inexpensive electric coffee grinder can also grind spices or nuts, and a rolling pin can be used to pound meat in a pinch; for that matter, so can an empty wine bottle. (Likewise, if you're cooking in an unfamiliar kitchen and need a rolling pin, just flour a wine bottle.) Large freezer bags can be used to store "hard" leftovers such as chicken or chopped meat; they also make the cleanest tool for marinating meat or chicken, and they're wonderful for storing soup, particularly when space is at a premium in your freezer or your fridge. Vegetable peelers of differing shapes can peel carrots, potatoes, or parsnips; they can also shave long, wide strips of Parmesan to lay atop pasta or a salad, or even chocolate as a garnish for a steaming cup of hot cocoa.

TOOLS FOR STORAGE

Because being a successful bulk-food buyer depends so heavily on how you store your purchases (not to mention your leftovers), I'm going to begin this list in a way many might think of as being somewhat backward: rather than leading off with pots and pans, let's focus on storage tools and how to use them. The best news about storage tools is, of course, that they can also all be bought in bulk at a discount club.

Plastic Storage Bags

I always recommend purchasing heavy-duty ziplock freezer bags instead of the old-fashioned variety with twist ties (the latter of which make terrific cat toys). The reason is simple: the older kind leak because holes somehow form in them; and even if they stay intact, whatever is inside invariably migrates to the outside of the bag. (This is one of the great mysteries of home economics, right after where single socks go when you do the laundry.)

Heavy-duty freezer bags are a perfect vehicle for storing both in the fridge and the freezer. If your fridge is packed and you suddenly find yourself with a gallon of soup, you can pour it into a freezer bag and (with the air pressed out) bend it into a shape that will allow it to go where you need it to go, which is something you can't do with a bowl or a hard plastic container. Freezer bags also work beautifully when you're marinating chicken, pork, fish, or any kind of meat: prepare the marinade, pour it into the bag, add the meat, press

out the air, zip up the bag, toss it around to coat, and place it in your fridge for however long it must marinate. When time's up, take out the meat and toss out the bag. It's that simple.

Freezer bags are also a great way to store leftover pastas, salads, and roasted potatoes waiting to be turned into potato salad; they also create a nearly perfect barrier around plastic-wrapped cheese.

Every kitchen should have:

- Resealable quart freezer bags
- Resealable gallon freezer bags
- Resealable 2-gallon freezer bags

Plastic Wrap

Plastic wrap is one of those items that come in all sorts of styles and variations: to cling or not to cling? Microwavable or not? Colored or clear? Heavy-duty or thin? First things first: never buy colored plastic wrap. Your leftover creamed spinach will appear to be brown even if it's fresh; you won't be able to tell your cod from your chicken breasts or your sliced pork loin. So forgo it, even if it's on sale. Second: if anyone ever gives you one of those supposedly simple and reusable circular plastic wraps

edged with elastic (meant to go over bowls), politely say no, unless you happen to need an extra set of shower caps. Simply put, they do not create an airtight seal on anything (not even your hair) and are therefore unsuitable.

When you're faced with a wall of plastic wrap, the best thing to do is try a few varieties, and when you find one you like, stick with it. I prefer heavy-duty wrap—nothing fancy—and I buy it in bulk. Finally, learn how to use it.

The idea behind plastic wrap is to create a seamless barrier between the outside world and your food, which, ideally, should not be touched by air (unless it is cheese—more on that later). Even if what you're wrapping is misshapen, simply do the following:

1. Pull off an appropriate length of plastic wrap, and lay it flat on a clean surface.
2. Set your foodstuff squarely in the middle of it.
3. Fold one side over the foodstuff, and pull it as taut as you can.
4. Repeat on the other side, and pull it taut.
5. If you are storing for the long haul (a few days) or planning

to freeze the food, repeat the process with a second layer, wrapped in the opposite direction. Pop the whole thing into a freezer bag and *date it*.

If you're bringing home good cheeses, bear in mind that they prefer a humid, somewhat moist environment. Wrap a hard cheese tightly in plastic wrap and change the wrapping every few days. Softer cheese can be wrapped in wax paper, and then more loosely wrapped with plastic wrap. And always store your cheese in the produce section of your fridge.

Face it: you're busy running after the kids, or working, or both. Who has the time or the inclination to accurately *remember* the age of leftovers? Hence, the importance of dating. Equip yourself with a few Sharpie markers, and date your leftovers so that you can safely determine how old they are—and when you've got to toss them out or wind up in the emergency room. It sounds compulsive, but the practice of dating your leftovers is a lifesaver and will become habit rather than something you have to force yourself to remember to do.

Plastic Storage Containers

If you're like me, you collect storage containers, and inevitably lose or misplace the lids. What happens then? You wind up stretching the above-mentioned plastic wrap over the plastic containers and voilà: the food inside goes bad. Why? Because plastic wrap doesn't stick to plastic, unless one of them is Scotch tape.

These days, humongous sets of storage containers can be had for very little money, so it pays to stock up and buy sets that are composed of every size and shape. These, too, can be dated: just write on some fabric first-aid tape stuck on the container; when you're ready to clean the container, remove the tape.

When it comes to buying plastic storage containers, heed my advice: they do not last forever. If they become stained or retain an order, toss or recycle them, and replace them.

Aluminum Foil

I grew up in the 1960s, in a home where aluminum foil was thought to be a cure-all with magical properties second only to penicillin. My mother loved the stuff so much that she wrapped virtually every-thing in it; in our house, aluminum foil was like a slipcover for food. It was everywhere, and in my mother's house, it still is.

But, like pretty much everything else, aluminum foil is better used for certain things than others: wrapping anything that is even remotely acidic (like foods that have been cooked with tomatoes, wine, or vinegar) in foil is problematic because the acid in the food will react with the metal. Instead, use foil to wrap nonacidic foods for a short time.

I like to use foil for cooking in an ancient, very healthy French method called *en papillote*, or "in an envelope." Lay a long piece of foil on a clean, flat surface, and place on it a piece of fish or chicken, some vegetables, spices, and a dot or two of butter (or a drizzle of olive oil). Pinch the ends together, create an airtight tent over the food, and poke a few holes in the foil with a fork. Put the package in a hot oven or grill, and in a short time you'll have a steaming, stunningly delicious amalgam of flavors cooked in their own juices. Nothing could be easier and no cleanup faster (except when you grill).

Again, when you buy aluminum foil, certain choices have to be made: nonstick or not, heavy-duty or standard weight. My recommendation is to always forgo the nonstick style (that's what olive oil or cooking spray is for) and opt for the plain old heavy-duty variety. It will tear less frequently and will hold up to cooking in the oven or on the grill.

TOOLS FOR COOKING

Over the years, more has been written about pots and pans and kitchen tools than nearly any other food-related subject. Today, glimmering kitchenware shops abound, beckoning us to purchase things that promise to turn us into better cooks. And while better cooks just don't get born overnight, having the right tools for the job does indeed make cooking a lot easier, in the same way that having the right storage materials and understanding how to use them is a necessity when learning how to use everything you buy in bulk.

When it comes to cooking tools, I believe in keeping it simple and adhering to a few basic rules of thumb:

- Buy the best quality you can afford, learn to take care of it,

and you'll have it for years.
- Buy what will do double duty.
- Buy only what you need, even if you are blessed with enough storage space to go wild in a kitchenware shop. This means no copper turbot poachers or those strange little rubber tubes that promise to remove the outer papery layer of garlic with ease (that's what the flat of a knife is for).

Every kitchen should be stocked with . . .

- Knives: Look for high-quality models that offer balance and weight, and hold their edge. Buy three: a paring knife, a 6-inch utility knife, and an 8-inch chef's knife. Keep them sharp, and never, ever put them in the dishwasher or let them sit in the sink. Instead, rinse them with soapy water, dry them well with a dish towel, and put them back in their knife block, where they will live happily for the next 40 or 50 years, until you pass them on to your grandchildren.
- Shears: Good-quality kitchen shears will enable you to do everything from butterflying a chicken to removing the strings from a rolled leg of lamb. Do not let your

When you go out knife shopping, make sure to purchase ones that have a "full tang." No, we're not referring to the orange-flavored instant breakfast drink the Apollo astronauts sipped through a plastic tube; having a full tang simply means that the knife is constructed of a single piece of tempered steel that runs the full length of the handle. The result is incomparable balance, quality, and sturdiness.

child use them in place of safety scissors.

- Sauté pans: You'll need three, all commercial-grade, and free of any plastic handles that preclude you from popping them under the broiler to brown something quickly. The small one, at 6 inches, is ideal for making one omelet, pounding a chicken breast, frying an egg, or sautéing a small quantity of diced mushrooms. The next size, at 8 or 12 inches, will be used for sautéing larger quantities of chicken or quickly pan-searing a pork tenderloin before popping it into the oven, which you'll be able to do with aplomb because the pans will be ovenproof. And finally, one straight-sided, ovenproof, 5-quart sauté pan with a cover will allow you to make a plethora of one-pot stews, braises, or pasta sauces, or a mess of sautéed greens. Make sure all your pans are of a heavy weight. It's true: Heavier pans are better than lightweight ones because they distribute heat more evenly and therefore cook food more evenly.

• One stockpot or Dutch oven: An 8- or 12-quart stockpot can be used for everything from boiling water for pasta, to making soup, to serving as an ice bucket if you left yours in your college dorm room back in the 1970s. A Dutch oven is usually shorter and squatter, and can do all of the above in addition to being indispensable for making chili, braising an entire chicken, cooking up a batch of stuffed cabbage, or making a pot roast either in the oven or on top of the stove. If you opt for the Dutch oven, be brave and go for the enameled cast iron. (Yes, it's heavy, but you may not have to renew your gym membership if you use it often enough.)

• Saucepans: You should have at least two, one small one (1½ quarts) and one larger (2 to 3 quarts). They should also be ovenproof.

• Cutting boards: It used to be that every home owned only one, and it was wood. Nowadays, heavy-duty plastic—not wood—is thought to be much more sanitary. Pick out three in different colors, and remember to use the same one every time for pork or beef, another for chicken and fish, and the third for aromatics like garlic, onions, and vegetables. Wash them in very hot, soapy water, or pop them in the dishwasher. Wooden cutting boards, provided they're of rock-hard maple or bamboo, should also be scrubbed thoroughly after each use and dried well to avoid cracking and buckling, whereupon you can use them to serve a lovely selection of cheeses.

• Immersion blender: Also called a stick blender, this gadget is one of the handiest, and every kitchen should have one. Plug it in and puree soups, vinaigrettes, or spreads in the container you prepared them in.

KEEPING WHAT YOU COOK, STORING WHAT YOU DON'T

One of the primary tenets of BIG FOOD is that if we are going to use everything we buy in bulk, we also have to learn how to store it, which we've discussed. When you're

<aside>

TO STICK OR NOT TO STICK

My first set of pots and pans was bought for me by my father, who believed that those made with a nonstick coating were the best in terms of ease of care (simple to clean) and health (less oil or fat needed for cooking). And while he was mostly right, he was also partly wrong.

Nonstick pans are definitely easier to clean, and, yes, you can use a bit less oil or fat to cook in. However, not all nonstick pans are created equal; the less expensive variety tend to be very thin and flimsy, and are therefore not suitable to cooking at high temperatures, which is what you do when you sauté or brown on top of the stove or in the oven. In addition, they often require special utensils designed not to scratch the nonstick surface and thereby deposit it into your food. Today, higher-quality nonstick pans are available in nearly every good kitchenware shop. If you prefer nonstick, buy the best you can afford, but keep in mind the following when you use them:

• They do not tolerate heat as well as traditional pans and should be replaced the minute the surface begins to peel or crack.

• Do not reduce the amount of oil or fat you would normally use; otherwise, whatever you are cooking will not sear, brown, or sauté properly.

</aside>

dealing with something like the aforementioned six zipped burlap bags of basmati rice that Beth, the original big-food junkie, kept under her dining-room table, storing is simply a matter of space.

But storage is a very real health

issue too, and so it's vitally important to learn—and remember—how long you can safely keep different foods under refrigeration or in the freezer. Contrary to popular belief, not everything has the same "shelf" life. And not everything freezes indefinitely. It's easy to tell when things like salad greens have turned and it's time to replenish, but it's not immediately apparent when it comes to meat, eggs, poultry, or fish—that is, unless it is really old or "off" and you can tell with just a sniff.

In addition, many people automatically assume that leftovers, having been cooked already, keep forever under refrigeration. My stepmother and my mother-in-law, both New Englanders, firmly believe that they can take a roast out of the oven and let it sit at room temperature for hours—literally hours—because it's been cooked. In fact, nothing could be further from the truth. Both scenarios result in one nasty, evil thing that happens to food with the ticking of the clock: the growth of bacteria. And when it comes to food, that's one gnarly enemy. I needn't go into detail.

Properly storing fresh foods like poultry, fish, and meat, and even canned goods, seems to be a conundrum for many of us; even something that has been wrapped perfectly, as though it were a priceless gift from Tiffany, can go bad. The trick is to know its life expectancy in the refrigerator, the freezer, and even the pantry, and to use it during that time.

But if you are in doubt, throw it out.

Each recipe contains information about how long to store the key ingredients you've brought home to help you understand what your cutoff point is, whether you're dealing with something that should be frozen, or just refrigerated. There's also a handy chart in the back of the book that summarizes the life expectancy of every dish. Eventually, this will become second nature, but until it does, refer to it frequently.

YOUR BIG FOOD FUTURE

The idea of forever changing the way you shop for food, store it, create delicious secondary meals from it, and ultimately save quite a bit of money is an exciting one; and in this chapter, we've come to understand that in order to do all of these things, we have to get our brains around our habits, and realize that what we bring home to feed our families needs to be planned for ahead of time and stored prudently so that we use as much of it as we can, without repeating anything several days in a row.

Now that we're equipped with new knowledge and the proper tools, it's time to get to work in the BIG FOOD Kitchen. As you thumb through the following pages, you'll find each recipe begins by identifying what you've brought home (no matter how many pounds of it may be staring at you from your countertops). When choosing recipes, you might also want to take a quick look at the BIG FOOD Action Chart at the end of this book so you can see the other dishes that share common ingredients. To further help you see how the recipes interrelate, look for the primary and secondary labels at the top of each recipe. Primary dishes will give you the building blocks for creating delicious new dishes from your leftovers (which are politely referred to as Secondary dishes); just make sure to look at the yield information carefully as you may sometimes need to make extra in order to use it in another dish.

THE
BASICS

HOW TO MAKE EVERYDAY ESSENTIALS GO THE DISTANCE

One of the primary tenets of BIG FOOD is that when we shop for food in bulk, we need to *augment* the staples that we bring home, thus turning them into storable, delicious condiments that you will then use time and again. This will forever change the way you shop and increase the way you save, and you'll be adding to your recipe repertoire all the while.

For example, there is no need to purchase a giant container of barbecue sauce that will go bad by the time only half of it is gone when we can make our own from a few essential BIG FOOD staples (ketchup, cider vinegar, spices, and molasses). Likewise, ottoman-size vats of chicken stock will rarely be used up by a family of four before the stock goes bad in the refrigerator. What to do? Augment it with Asian spices like ginger and star anise and store it correctly, so that by adding rice noodles and vegetables, you've got an Asian noodle soup ready to go on a cold night when you've come home late from work.

Of everything you might bring home in bulk from a discount club, the basics often prove to be the most challenging because, really, just how much mayonnaise or butter can one family eat unless, say, they're the Brady Bunch? But armed with a plan of action and a list of possibilities, you can transform that huge jar of mayo into an assortment of other delicious condiments, from garlicky aioli to wasabi dressing. Sweet butter will be reborn as a lemon-and-herb compound butter that can be frozen for months and sliced as you need it, to top a filet mignon or enrich a sauce with incomparable flavor. In BIG FOOD BASICS, we'll cover everything from olive oil to Dijon mustard and dried spices. You will be amazed by how much you can do with simple, packaged staples and condiments, and in no time, you'll put them to work.

WHAT TO DO WITH IT

- Decant some oil into several very clean, airtight, heatproof glass bottles and store in a dark, cool place in your pantry, away from heat or sunlight.
- Store infused and specialty oils (such as nut oils) in the refrigerator.

HOW LONG IT WILL LAST

- Unflavored EVOO will last approximately 6 months.
- Flavored EVOO will last approximately 2 to 3 weeks, refrigerated, depending on the infusion. Garlic-infused EVOO should be used promptly; otherwise, store it in the refrigerator for up to 3 days.

ADDITIONAL SERVING RECOMMENDATIONS

- Drizzle Basil-Infused EVOO on pizza, poached chicken breasts, and grilled meats.
- Drizzle Rosemary-and-Lemon-Infused EVOO on shrimp, lamb, and mild white fish, such as cod or halibut.
- Drizzle Spicy Red-Pepper Olive Oil on pastas.
- Add drained black olives to Spicy Red-Pepper Olive Oil (they'll keep, refrigerated, up to 10 days).

BIG FOOD INFUSED OLIVE OILS

Mixing extra virgin olive oil (which I'll refer to as "EVOO") with fresh herbs, sun-dried tomatoes, garlic, and/or even lemon is a time-honored tradition. The resulting infusion provides a punch of concentrated flavor to even the simplest dishes. Certainly, the kind of EVOO you use for these condiments (as well as for dressings and sauces) affects the flavor: some Italian varieties (Tuscan, for example) are dark green and peppery; others, like EVOO from the south of France, are more flowery and herbaceous.

BASIL-INFUSED EXTRA VIRGIN OLIVE OIL

Basil and olive oil are two parts of a culinary trinity that may also include lemons, garlic, tomatoes, and a host of other delicious comestibles too numerous to mention. In late August, when basil is at its peak and just about to flower, I use it to make a deliciously flavored olive oil that can be drizzled on fish, pastas, vegetables, or chicken, or used as a dip for a good, crusty bread. Remember to store flavored oils in the refrigerator and let them come to room temperature prior to using. Use this one within 14 days.

1   large bunch fresh basil, leaves separated from stems (Genovese, Thai, purple, or a combination)
     Extra virgin olive oil

Optional: *Dried whole chili pepper, garlic cloves, lemon zest*

> They look so beautiful, don't they—all those rustic bottles of oil that you see in kitchen stores and magazines, stored on fancy stainless-steel shelves above well-used ranges. Guess what? Those oils are not being used for consumption, and they never will be, because nothing turns oil rancid faster than light and heat. Keep your oils away from the stove, unless, of course, they're in the pan.

1. Carefully wash and dry basil leaves.
2. Place leaves in a tall, clear, glass bottle. Add chili pepper, garlic, and zest at this point, if using.
3. Cover with extra virgin olive oil. Seal, and shake gently.

ROSEMARY-AND-LEMON-INFUSED EXTRA VIRGIN OLIVE OIL

Follow the recipe as above, but substitute 8 to 10 sprigs of fresh rosemary and $\frac{1}{2}$ cup of lemon zest for the basil.

SPICY RED-PEPPER OLIVE OIL

Follow the recipe as above, but substitute 3 or 4 whole dried chilies for the herbs.

BIG FOOD COMPOUND BUTTERS

In moderation, there simply is no substitute for butter: it is consummately creamy and luscious. It melts like absolutely nothing else, and it provides a flavor that cannot be duplicated, whether it is spread on fresh bread; used to enhance a light, lemony sauce for fish; or drizzled on grilled meat before slicing. Many of us are under the impression that butter will keep indefinitely in the freezer; in fact, it will keep from approximately 6 to 9 months, depending on the brand you buy (some have more preservatives than others). But whatever brand you choose, a wonderful way to use your bulk butter is to create flavorful compound butters and freeze them for later use.

BIG FOOD HERB BUTTER

2	sticks unsalted butter, at room temperature
2	tablespoons each: chopped fresh parsley, sage, and thyme

Waxed paper

Lay a 9-by-11-inch sheet of waxed paper on a clean, dry surface, and place the butter in the middle of it.

Place an equal-size piece of waxed paper on top of it, and roll it into a 7-inch circle, using a rolling pin.

Remove the top layer of waxed paper and add herbs. Replace the waxed paper, and incorporate by rolling it out again to a thickness of 1/2 inch.

Remove the top layer of waxed paper and, using your hands, seal the butter in the waxed paper. Form into a log, and refrigerate for up to 3 weeks. Freeze for up to 4 months.

BIG FOOD LEMON BUTTER

Add a tablespoon of grated lemon zest (page 184) to the herb butter.

Yields 1 cup

Salted butter is a by-product of the days when salting was the only way to preserve perishables. If you must have salted butter—and I don't recommend it both because of its metallic flavor and because inevitably you'll make a mistake and bake something sweet with it (revolting!)—begin with a good-quality unsalted butter, and prudently sprinkle a bit of coarsely ground kosher salt directly on whatever it is you're buttering.

WHAT TO DO WITH IT

• Remove four sticks from the package.

• Put two sticks in the coldest part of your refrigerator for later use, and set aside two sticks for this recipe.

• Date and freeze the balance, double-wrapped in plastic, labeled, and dated.

HOW LONG IT WILL LAST

• Wrapped well, unsalted butter will last up to 2 weeks, refrigerated; compound butters will last up to 10 days, refrigerated.

• Unsalted butter will last 6 to 9 months in the freezer; compound butters will last up to 4 months in the freezer.

ADDITIONAL SERVING RECOMMENDATIONS

• Slice rounds of herb butter to lay atop roasted fillet of beef.

• Spread lemon butter on fish, chicken, or pasta.

• Rub a roasting chicken or turkey all over with either butter.

- **Leftover pieces of cheese: Stilton, Swiss, Cheddar, Asiago, Brie, Camembert, Parmesan, Pecorino Romano, Manchego, Gorgonzola, queso blanco**
- **Garlic**
- **Inexpensive dry white wine**

WHAT TO DO WITH IT

- Cut larger pieces of cheese into 1-inch cubes.
- Grate harder cheeses (Parmesan, Pecorino Romano, queso blanco, Asiago).

HOW LONG IT WILL LAST

- Kept in an airtight crock in your refrigerator, Fromage Fort will last up to 10 days.

ADDITIONAL SERVING RECOMMENDATIONS

- Spread on slices of crusty bread, and toast under the broiler until the cheese is bubbling.
- Spread on rounds of French or Italian bread, as an accompaniment to a salad.
- Serve as you would a dip, with sides of crackers and cut-up fresh vegetables.

FROMAGE FORT

The scenario: The discount club had a sale on cheese, and a little while ago, you bought a wide variety, the dregs of which are now clogging up the works in your fridge. What to do? Literally translated as "Strong Cheese," Fromage Fort is a delicious, traditional cheese spread suitable for serving on crackers or toasted bread, or folding into a cooking omelet. Made from whatever leftover cheeses you have available, white wine, and garlic, it is perfect for the kind of spur-of-the-moment gatherings that happen so frequently during the summer. Blended together in a food processor, the spreadable result will amaze even the most finicky guests, who will demand to know exactly what it is and where you bought it.

1½	pounds leftover cheese, cubed or grated	Kosher salt and freshly ground black pepper
2	garlic cloves, peeled	
½	cup inexpensive dry white wine	

Pulse cheese and garlic in a food processor until pulverized. Add wine by the quarter cupful, pulsing after each addition, until smooth and creamy. Add salt and pepper, if necessary, to taste. Refrigerate for 2 hours. Serve cold.

Yields approximately 3 cups

When making Fromage Fort, it is always a good idea to include a variety of cheese textures: a combination of soft and runny (Brie, Camembert) with dense and smooth (Cheddar, Swiss) makes for a more consistent spread.

BIG FOOD AIOLI

It's probably a rare occasion when ordinary mayonnaise conjures up images of the south of France; most of us just think of it as a binder for tuna or chicken salad—but as far as mayo goes, there's much, much more. Rich and redolent of garlic, BIG FOOD Aioli can be created using store-bought mayonnaise; kept in an airtight container, it can be used on everything from fresh grilled fish or steamed shrimp, to the cold boiled beef you have leftover from Pot-au-Feu (page 48). Make it as garlicky as you can stand it.

BASIC AIOLI

4	tablespoons mayonnaise (low-fat or full-fat)	3	garlic cloves, peeled and finely minced
			Juice of 1 lemon

In a small bowl, whisk together mayonnaise, garlic, and lemon juice until well blended.

Yields approximately ¹/₂ cup

WASABI MAYONNAISE

For those of us who love a little zip in our food, nothing beats wasabi—that deceptively mild-looking, incendiary light green Japanese condiment that is responsible for more tearing eyes and running noses than a late-night screening of *Casablanca*. This flavorful mayonnaise is a delicious way to add a powerful punch of Asian flavor to otherwise mild dishes, from cold poached salmon to boiled shrimp.
- Add 1 teaspoon prepared wasabi and a dash of toasted sesame oil to 4 tablespoons of mayonnaise.

SOUTHWESTERN MAYONNAISE

Rich with the spicy Tex-Mex flavors of ancho chili, cilantro, and lime, this mayo turns ordinary diced chicken breasts into something unforgettable. Dollop it into the center of a quesadilla stuffed with leftover chicken, make a luscious salad with it, use it in place of plain mayo, or try it as a dip for grilled shrimp.
- Add ¹/₂ tablespoon chopped fresh cilantro, 1 teaspoon ancho chili powder, and the juice of 1 lime to 4 tablespoons of mayonnaise.

WHAT YOU HAVE ON HAND
- **1 large jar of mayonnaise, low-fat or full-fat**
- **Garlic**
- **Lemons**

WHAT TO DO WITH IT
- Set aside 4 tablespoons of mayonnaise for this recipe, and store the balance in its original container in the refrigerator for up to 1 month.

HOW LONG IT WILL LAST
- Stored in an airtight container in the refrigerator, BIG FOOD Aioli will last up to 5 days.

ADDITIONAL SERVING RECOMMENDATIONS
- Serve as a dip for cold leftover beef or chicken.
- Serve as a sauce for poached fish.
- Spread on rounds of lightly toasted French or Italian bread.

BIG FOOD COCKTAIL SAUCE

Dollop it on oysters, or dip cold Spiced Shrimp Boiled in Black Beer (page 152) into it; no matter how you look at it, cocktail sauce is an American favorite, but it certainly doesn't have to be ordinary. I love a cocktail sauce that marries the spice of prepared horseradish, the sweetness of ketchup, and the tart tang of lemons. The following version can be spiced up or down, as you like it.

½	cup ketchup	¼	teaspoon Tabasco sauce
1	tablespoon packaged white horseradish (mild or spicy)	¼	teaspoon Worcestershire sauce
	Juice of 1 medium lemon		

Combine ketchup, horseradish, lemon juice, and Tabasco and Worcestershire sauces in a mixing bowl. Serve with cold, boiled shrimp or freshly shucked oysters.

Yields ³/₄ cup

BIG FOOD BARBECUE SAUCE

Some like it hot, some like it sweet, and some like it tangy and smoky. Either way, this barbecue sauce is a wonderful way to use the large quantities of ketchup and vinegar you've lugged home from the discount club. Brush this lip-smacking sauce directly onto roasting or grilled chicken breasts or pork chops for a quick taste of summer. Better still, if you have some time on your hands, layer it over our BIG FOOD Dry Rub for the most tender, luscious ribs this side of the Whistle Stop Café.

2	cups ketchup	$1/2$	tablespoon ancho chili powder
$1/4$	cup blackstrap molasses	1	tablespoon dry mustard
$1/4$	cup soy sauce	1	teaspoon garlic powder
$1/4$	cup cider vinegar	2	teaspoons onion powder
$1/4$	teaspoon Tabasco sauce	1	tablespoon liquid smoke
2	tablespoons dark brown sugar		

In a medium saucepan set over low heat, combine ketchup, molasses, soy sauce, vinegar, Tabasco, and brown sugar. Stir frequently, until sugar is completely dissolved. Add chili powder, mustard, garlic powder, onion powder, and liquid smoke. Blend well, and heat very gently for 15 minutes.

Remove from heat and pour into a heatproof, airtight glass jar.

VARIATIONS

• Add 1 tablespoon of apricot preserves to the sauce while it is heating, for a fruitier flavor.

Yields approximately 3 cups

WHAT TO DO WITH IT

• Set aside 2 cups of ketchup for this recipe; the balance will keep in its original container in the refrigerator for up to 3 weeks.

HOW LONG IT WILL LAST

• Refrigerated in an airtight container, this sauce will keep for up to 2 weeks.

- 1 large jar of French Dijon, dark German, or spicy Polish mustard

WHAT TO DO WITH IT

- Divide mustard into smaller, airtight containers, and store in the refrigerator for up to 1 month.

HOW LONG IT WILL LAST

- Flavored mustards will last, refrigerated in airtight containers, for up to 2 weeks.

How to choose when you're staring at gigantic tubs of French Dijon, dark German, spicy Polish, and good old American ballpark-style deli mustards? Favoritism wins out, but it also pays to experiment. Here's a basic rule of thumb:

- If you prefer a more textured, deeper flavor, stick to German-style mustard, which generally contains whole mustard seeds.
- If your plan is to augment mustard with flavors such as maple syrup, honey, horseradish, fruit jam (such as apricot), or fruit essences such as raspberry or strawberry, start with something relatively mild, like French Dijon.
- If you're planning on enjoying mustards primarily with sweeter-flavored meats (such as bratwurst, cold sliced steak, lamb, or pork), go with something flavorful that has more of an edgy bite to it, like Polish mustard.

American deli-style ballpark mustard, because of its extremely intense flavoring, generally doesn't take very well to augmenting. Enjoy it with franks and wursts, and on sandwiches served on fresh multigrain bread.

BIG FOOD FLAVORED MUSTARDS

Mustards have come a very long way since the days when they did little more than drip down the front of your shirt at a baseball game. Today's supermarkets offer a dizzying array of the delicious condiment, and it's a good thing, because mustard can be used as a wonderful low-calorie, low-fat sauce to accompany cold chicken, lamb, pork, or beef.

MAPLE HORSERADISH MUSTARD

This peculiar-sounding condiment is a great combination of deeply sweet and spicy, but not too hot. It's particularly delicious with ham and bratwurst.

Combine 1 cup Dijon mustard with 2 tablespoons prepared horseradish (mild or spicy, your choice) and 2 tablespoons Grade B dark maple syrup.

HONEY MUSTARD

A favorite owing to its smooth texture and tangy sweetness, honey mustard was the condiment of choice in the 1980s and 1990s: it's easy to understand why. Enjoy this version with sliced fresh turkey breast and fresh salad greens, rolled together in a wrap.

Combine 1 cup Dijon or German mustard with $1/4$ cup clover honey. For a smooth consistency, pulse quickly in a food processor.

WASABI MUSTARD

Combine 1 cup Dijon mustard with 2 teaspoons prepared wasabi. Enjoy it as a spicy dip for fried shrimp or calamari.

HERB MUSTARD

Combine 1 cup Dijon mustard with $1/2$ teaspoon each dried tarragon and parsley. Blend with 1 teaspoon mayonnaise, and enjoy it on mild, broiled fish.

Yields approximately $1^1/_2$ cups

BIG FOOD DRY SPICE MIXES

If you shop at discount clubs, you've seen them: quart-size plastic containers of dried spices that seem like such a good idea! Imagine—enough dried basil to keep your pasta sauces tasty for the next few years. It's a nice thought, but unfortunately, dried spices actually don't last much longer than a year; after that time, they lose their potency and flavor, and are as good as sawdust.

One of the best ways to get the most out of flavorful bulk spices is to combine them to make exciting spice blends. Stored correctly, they'll provide you with a simple and quick way to create Asian, Mediterranean, and American Southern dishes, and you'll easily use up everything you've brought home.

BIG FOOD MEDITERRANEAN SPICE BLEND

1 tablespoon each:

- Dried basil
- Dried oregano
- Dried thyme
- Dried rosemary
- Dried fennel seed

Place ingredients in a glass jar with a tight-fitting lid. Shake until well blended.

Yields 1/3 cup

WHAT YOU HAVE ON HAND

- **Dried basil**
- **Dried oregano**
- **Dried thyme**
- **Dried rosemary**
- **Dried fennel seed**

WHAT TO DO WITH IT

- Set aside the quantities called for in the recipe, and store the balance in their original containers in a cool, dark location. Replace after 1 year.

HOW LONG IT WILL LAST

- BIG FOOD Mediterranean Spice Blend will keep for 1 year in a cool, dark location.

ADDITIONAL SERVING RECOMMENDATIONS

- Use in all BIG FOOD recipes calling for Mediterranean Spice Blend.

- Dried ginger
- Garlic powder
- Crushed black peppercorns
- Crushed white peppercorns
- Allspice
- Star anise
- Cloves
- Fennel seed
- Ground cinnamon

WHAT TO DO WITH IT

- Set aside the quantities called for in the recipe, and store the balance in their original containers in a cool, dark location.

HOW LONG IT WILL LAST

- BIG FOOD Asian Spice Blend will keep for 1 year in a cool, dark location.

ADDITIONAL SERVING RECOMMENDATIONS

- Use in all BIG FOOD recipes calling for Asian Spice Blend.

BIG FOOD ASIAN SPICE BLEND

Spicy, sweet, savory, and packed with the fragrant, earthy aromas of the far eastern kitchen, this blend is delicious massaged into everything from pork tenderloin and roasts to chicken. Heat the spice blend in a dry cast iron pan prior to using it, for even stronger taste.

1	tablespoon ground ginger
1	tablespoon garlic powder
$1/2$	tablespoon crushed black peppercorns
$1/2$	tablespoon crushed white peppercorns
1	teaspoon ground allspice
2	whole star anise
1	teaspoon ground cloves
$1/2$	tablespoon fennel seed
$1/4$	teaspoon ground cinnamon

Grind all ingredients together in a food processor or a clean coffee grinder. Store in a clean glass container for up to 1 year.

Yields $1/4$ cup

BIG FOOD DRY RUB

A sweet, hot, spicy, salty, utterly unctuous blend that will tenderize ribs, chicken, beef, and pork, this dry rub smells like a Kansas City barbecue joint in midsummer. Sprinkle it on ribs, refrigerate them overnight, and oven roast them the next day, using BIG FOOD Barbecue Sauce (page 37) to baste.

1	cup raw sugar (Turbinado)	2	tablespoons lemon pepper
½	cup paprika	1	tablespoon freshly ground black pepper
¼	cup kosher salt	1	tablespoon dried sage
¼	cup garlic powder	2	teaspoons dried thyme
¼	cup onion powder	2	teaspoons dry mustard
¼	cup celery salt	1	teaspoon cayenne pepper
¼	cup chili powder		

Pour ingredients into a medium Mason jar with a tight-fitting lid. Shake for 1 minute to blend.

VARIATIONS

- Increase any of the ingredients to vary sweetness, spiciness, or saltiness.
- Substitute maple sugar for raw sugar.
- Substitute brown sugar for raw sugar.
- Add 1 teaspoon of curry powder (mild or hot) to the mix.

Yields approximately 3 cups

WHAT YOU HAVE ON HAND

Large containers of dried spices:

- Onion powder
- Garlic powder
- Celery salt
- Chili powder
- Ground black pepper
- Thyme
- Cayenne pepper
- Sage
- Kosher salt
- Paprika
- Sugar

WHAT TO DO WITH IT

- Set aside the quantities called for in the recipe, and store the balance in their original containers in a cool, dark location.

HOW LONG IT WILL LAST

- This spice rub will last up to 6 months stored in an airtight container in a cool, dark location.

ADDITIONAL SERVING RECOMMENDATIONS

- Rub on Oven-Barbecued Pork Spareribs (page 262).
- Rub on Oven-Barbecued Pulled Chicken with Spicy Apricot Sauce (page 180).

WHAT TO DO WITH IT

- Set aside 2 (28-ounce) cans of Italian-style tomatoes, crushed or whole.

- Set aside 2 large onions; store the balance in a mesh bag, in a cool, dark location, away from potatoes or fruit.

- Set aside 2 large carrots for this recipe; store the balance in your salad crisper.

- Set aside 2 large stalks of celery for this recipe; store the balance in your salad crisper.

- Set aside 2 garlic cloves for this recipe; store the balance in a cool, dark location.

BIG FOOD MARINARA SAUCE

My first morning on the job at New York's famed Dean & Deluca found me peering over the shoulder of my late colleague Mark Alton, who was preparing marinara sauce in an enormous stockpot set over a small propane burner in the middle of the store. By the time the store opened its doors 2 hours later, a quarter of the sauce had disappeared on hunks of fresh bread, right down the gullets of a dozen salivating employees. Elemental and easy to store, this classic recipe, which is adapted from Mark's, is The Little Black Dress of tomato sauces. Simmer sausages in it, toss it with pasta, ladle it over a roast, or dab a little behind each ear. It's that good.

2	tablespoons extra virgin olive oil	2	(28-ounce) cans Italian-style crushed or whole tomatoes, preferably San Marzano
2	large onions, peeled and finely chopped		
2	large carrots, peeled and finely chopped	1	teaspoon sugar
		1/2	teaspoon red pepper flakes
2	large celery stalks, finely chopped	1	tablespoon dried basil or 2 tablespoons minced fresh
3	garlic cloves, peeled and finely minced		Kosher salt

Optional: 1/2 cup dry red wine

Heat oil in a large saucepan or Dutch oven over medium-low heat, until rippling but not smoking. Add onions and carrots, and cook until softened, 6 to 8 minutes. Add celery and garlic. Cook until softened, about 5 minutes, stirring frequently to ensure that vegetables don't brown.

Add tomatoes and their juice; if using whole tomatoes, use a fork or a potato masher to gently break them up. Stir well to blend, increase the heat to medium, partially cover, and cook for 30 minutes, stirring frequently. If sauce seems too thick, add up to ½ cup of wine.

Add sugar, pepper flakes, and half of the basil. Stir, partially cover, and cook for an additional hour.

Add the remaining basil, season to taste with salt, and serve hot. Or, cool completely to prepare for storage. (You can do this quickly by filling your sink with ice cubes and setting the pot in it so that the ice comes halfway up the sides of the pot. Stir several times while sauce cools.) Ladle cooled sauce into freezer-proof containers and refrigerate or freeze.

Yields 2 quarts

HOW LONG IT WILL LAST

- Stored in an airtight container, this sauce will last up to 5 days in the refrigerator and up to 6 months in the freezer.

ADDITIONAL SERVING RECOMMENDATIONS

- Use for pizzas, pastas, and anything else that calls for tomato sauce.

BIG FOOD STOCKS AND SOUPS

> "A good cook is never apologetic about leftovers."
> —Jacques Pepin

When it comes to the world of BIG FOOD, making stocks and soups is one of the most natural ways to use everything that you bring home from a discount club shopping trip: they are easy to make, extremely satisfying to eat, and freeze exceptionally well. In the coming pages, you'll learn how to make a basic tomato soup that will evolve into a hearty Pasta e Fagiole—a wonderful vehicle for white beans (canned, fresh, or leftover), canned tomatoes, and any small pasta; the consommé left over from hearty Pot-au-Feu will enjoy a second life as Mushroom and Barley Soup; Traditional Jewish-Style Chicken Soup will provide you with the ingredients to later make quesadillas or pastas.

STORING STOCKS AND SOUPS

Before we jump into stock and soup recipes, here are a few basic rules of thumb:

• Skim as much fat and froth as possible off stocks and soups while they're cooking, and cool them down completely and quickly prior to freezing. That way, they will last longer and stay fresher, and you may avoid any bacterial issues.

• Let a cooled stock "rest" overnight in the refrigerator; remove fat the next morning. This will make it clear, lower in fat, and fresher tasting. Prepared stocks packaged in a paper carton can be frozen, unopened, in the carton.

• Prepared or canned broths and stocks should be frozen in labeled, dated, ice cube trays, heavy-duty freezer bags, or airtight plastic containers.

• Chicken and most meats should be removed from stocks and soups and refrigerated or frozen separately. Soups that contain sausage or smoked meats can be frozen in their entirety.

• Carrots become mealy after an extended time in the freezer. Remove them from soups and stews prior to freezing if you plan to store them for more than 3 months.

Beef-Based Soups

Rich, hearty, and deeply flavorful, beef-based soups have an unmistakable rusticity to them that is unique; chicken soup might be soothing and even crave-worthy, but beef-based soups always seem to conjure up thoughts of roaring fireplaces and coziness during blustery snowstorms. In the heat of the summer, no one ever says, "Gee, I'd love a good cup of mushroom and barley soup right around now." Gazpacho, yes. Beef broth, no.

The beauty of beef-based soups is that they all begin with the same element that provides a very intense flavor: beef stock, which is not only available everywhere in bulk but is probably one of the most "thrown out" purchases most of us make. We buy a lot to use a little, and the rest winds up going bad unless we freeze it, which many of us often forget to do until it's too late. So in this section, I've started off with a traditional Pot-au-Feu, which essentially *creates* its own beef stock (or consommé) that can either be enjoyed as part of the dish itself, or strained and then frozen for use in other beef soups.

I have not included a BIG FOOD Beef Stock recipe here because the likelihood of you buying meat with the express purpose of making stock from it is probably slim. If, however, you *do* have a hankering to try your hand at beef stock, replace the quantity of chicken in BIG FOOD Basic Chicken Stock with lean meat, such as top round, and meaty bones or short ribs. Roast the bones at 450°F for 10 minutes, and then proceed with the balance of the recipe.

Chicken-Based Soups

Herbert Hoover's 1925 campaign slogan, "a chicken in every pot," still resonates today: chicken—no matter if it's whole or in parts—is associated with some of the world's most comforting soups. Whether you hail from France, Mexico, Italy, Asia, or the Bronx, odds are you either have, had, or know a grandmother who has offered sustenance with the aid of this most popular of birds.

Making soups from the chickens you buy in bulk on your discount shopping excursions is a spectacular way to use what you bring home, whether you have a hankering for Traditional Jewish-Style Chicken Soup (aka Jewish Penicillin); spicy Mexican Chicken Soup with Vegetables, Chili, and Lime; or Italian Tortellini en Brodo (which will also use up those big bags of tortellini that are available in bulk). But the real benefit to making chicken-based soups is that you'll end up with leftover luscious, tender, flavor-infused chicken meat that you can then use in salads, quesadillas, and sandwiches, or even minced together with scallions, chilies, ginger, lime, and peanuts, and then rolled up in Boston lettuce, Vietnamese-style.

No matter what kind of chicken soup you're making, it's always a good idea to remove the bird, or parts, once the soup is done, let it cool, pull the meat from the bones with your fingers (neatness doesn't count here), and store any extra meat, double-wrapped, freezer-bagged, and dated, in the refrigerator or freezer. I like to make my soups with an extra whole chicken brought home from the discount club. The final dish ends up much more flavorful, and I have the added benefit of having a whole bird's worth of extra meat on hand for secondary dishes. The possibilities are endless.

Vegetable-Based Soups

It's August, and farm stands all over America are exploding with fresh tomatoes, zucchini, garlic, corn, cucumbers, red peppers, peas, and fresh herbs. Or, conversely, it might be December, and you've discovered a treasure trove of fresh vegetables at your local discount club—unfortunately, they're all wrapped together, so you're stuck buying a lot more than you need. And everyone knows that fresh vegetables don't last very long. Is it money thrown away? Absolutely not.

Vegetable-based soups are an ideal way to make the most out of fresh veggies at any time of year: refreshing, chilled Gazpacho travels well; Tuscan Bread Soup calls not only for fresh or canned tomatoes but leftover, day-old bread; and *Zuppa di Cannelini*—which combines canned tomatoes, packaged vegetable stock, virtually any kind of Italian-style sausage, chopped escarole, and canned white beans—is hearty enough for a main course and a cinch to throw together, and it freezes perfectly for months.

A WORD ON HOMEMADE VEGETABLE STOCK

Making your own vegetable stock is a nice thought. It really is. All those peelings and shavings and choppings and cuttings have to go somewhere! Why not back into the pot, if not into the compost bin? A noble, frugal, and thoroughly judicious idea.

However, while many of us even in suburbia do have compost piles—these days, places somewhere out in the backyard where we can take a bowl of cuttings and peelings and add it to the thriving mix on a daily basis—few of us have the space or the inclination to save our peelings and keep a saucepan of vegetable stock simmering on the back burner all day (or all week, like our ancestors did), and just keep adding to it. Unlike homemade beef stock and chicken stock, which are relatively simple to make and yield other delicious leftovers like boiled beef or chicken, vegetable stock is a tough nut. Therefore, it's perfectly reasonable to always buy it packaged, which, in all honesty, is what I do. Find one of good quality that's low in sodium and low in fat, and endeavor to always keep one package in the fridge, one in the freezer, and some in an ice cube tray. You'll use it for enhancing flavor in soups, poaching chicken, and even boiling rice.

- 8 pounds of top round, chuck, brisket, or short ribs
- 4 pounds of chicken breast, ribs and skin attached

WHAT TO DO WITH IT

- Divide uncooked meat in half. Double-wrap one half in plastic; place in a freezer bag, label, date, and refrigerate for up to 3 days, or freeze for up to 3 months.
- Divide uncooked chicken in half. Double-wrap one half in plastic; place in a freezer bag, label, date, and refrigerate for up to 3 days, or freeze for up to 4 months.

HOW LONG IT WILL LAST

- The strained consommé from Pot-au-Feu will last 3 days refrigerated, and 6 to 8 months frozen.
- Cooked meat and poultry will last for 3 days refrigerated.
- Cooked poultry can be double-wrapped and frozen for up to 3 months. Reheat it in soup, or allow it to thaw completely in the refrigerator before using (otherwise it will become stringy). Frozen cooked meat should be thawed completely in the refrigerator before using.

PRIMARY
POT-AU-FEU

In deepest winter, there is perhaps no more satisfying a meal than Pot-au-Feu. A quintessential BIG FOOD dish, traditional Pot-au-Feu calls for simmering a variety of meats, poultry, and marrow bones along with vegetables, and then serving the whole shebang in separate courses: you have the resulting consommé first, and then the sliced meats and vegetables with a variety of accompaniments, like cornichons. I've limited us to beef and chicken breast, but by all means, if the mood strikes you, go with as many of the time-honored ingredients as you'd like. My favorite way to enjoy Pot-au-Feu leftovers is also the simplest: the meat sliced thin and served cold, with a hearty dollop of BIG FOOD Aioli (page 35), or with prepared horseradish sauce, a few cornichons, and some thick toasted slices of French bread spread with a fine layer of unsalted butter.

4	pounds top round, chuck, brisket, or short ribs	2	medium celery ribs, peeled and cut on the bias into 2-inch pieces
2	pounds whole, skinless chicken breasts	2	medium parsnips, peeled and cut on the bias into 2-inch pieces
8	whole cloves	2	garlic cloves, peeled but otherwise left whole
2	medium white onions, peeled and quartered	5	whole black peppercorns
4	medium leeks, white portions only, outer woody leaves removed, rinsed well, and sliced in half, lengthwise	10	thyme sprigs
		10	parsley sprigs
		2	bay leaves
2	medium carrots, peeled and cut on the bias into 2-inch pieces		Kosher salt and freshly ground black pepper

Optional: *2 pounds beef bones, tiny new potatoes*

Place beef, chicken, and beef bones, if using, in a large (8- to 10-quart) stockpot. Insert 4 cloves into each onion. Add onions to the pot, along with leeks, carrots, celery, parsnips, garlic, and peppercorns.

Tie thyme, parsley, and bay leaves together with kitchen twine. Add to the pot.

Cover with cold water, and place over medium-high heat. Bring to an active simmer for 30 minutes, and then reduce the heat to low (the soup should be barely "sputtering"). Simmer covered, skimming foam from the surface regularly, until meat is fork-tender, about 4 hours.

If you are serving this dish immediately, transfer meat and chicken to a platter, cover with foil, and keep warm in a low oven. Discard beef bones, if used.

Carefully remove vegetables and herbs. Discard herbs, and set vegetables aside to cool.

Strain broth through a very fine mesh strainer into a bowl, and season with salt and pepper. If you are not serving this dish immediately, refrigerate broth overnight, remove the fat, and proceed with the recipe or with storage.

To assemble the dish:

1. Boil potatoes, if using, until soft.
2. Slice chicken and meat; place on a large platter, surrounded by the carrots, leeks, celery, and potatoes.
3. Serve broth as a first course, followed by the platter of meats and vegetables.
4. Pass the condiments (see "Additional Serving Recommendations").

Serves 4 to 6

Fattier cuts of beef tend to jell when refrigerated, but fear not. This luscious, flavor-packed by-product can either be sliced and removed, or reheated along with the meat.

ADDITIONAL SERVING RECOMMENDATIONS

- Serve skimmed consommé as an appetizer, and sliced cold meats and vegetables as a main course, with the following accompaniments:
  - Cornichons
  - Toast points with sweet butter
  - Kosher salt
  - Grainy mustard
  - Horseradish
  - Tiny steamed potatoes tossed with a small pat of butter and some chopped fresh parsley

SECONDARY DISHES

- *Mushroom and Barley Soup (page 50)*
- *French Onion Soup with Melted Gruyère (page 54)*
- *Asian Chicken-Stuffed Lettuce Rolls (page 168)*
- *Quesadilla of Chicken, Chilies, Tequila, and Lime (page 182)*
- *Beef sandwiches, on warm rye bread with mustard*

MUSHROOM AND BARLEY SOUP WITH FROMAGE BLANC CROUTONS

This soup—which is thick enough, really, to be called a stew—sprang to life after one particularly memorable BIG FOOD shopping experience that left me with an immense tub of fresh mushrooms and a gigantic plastic container of dried wild mushrooms (shiitakes, in my case) that I was certain I was going to have kicking around for the rest of my life. Dense with the rich flavors of the earth, this soup can double as a main course. Use the leftover beef consommé from your Pot-au-Feu or a packaged low-sodium beef stock for the base. You can thin out the finished soup to your liking with water or stock, if desired.

WHAT YOU HAVE ON HAND

- 2 pounds of fresh mushrooms (button, cremini, baby bella, oyster, or a combination)
- Large container of dried mushrooms
- Packaged stock, beef or vegetable, or leftover consommé from Pot-au-Feu (page 48)

WHAT TO DO WITH IT

- Divide the fresh mushrooms in half. Poke a large freezer bag with about 10 fork holes on both sides; add mushrooms, press out excess air, seal, and store in salad crisper.
- Store the container of dried mushrooms in a cool, dark pantry.

HOW LONG IT WILL LAST

- Fresh mushrooms will last, refrigerated, approximately 3 to 4 days.
- Dried mushrooms should be used within 18 months.
- Mushroom and Barley Soup will keep in the freezer for 6 months.

SOUP:

1	loosely packed cup dried wild mushrooms	1	pound fresh mushrooms, sliced (button, cremini, baby bella, oyster, or a combination)
3/4	cup good-quality dry red table wine		
2	tablespoons extra virgin olive oil	4	cups water
1	medium onion, peeled and roughly chopped	4	cups beef stock or vegetable stock
2	carrots, peeled and roughly chopped	1	cup pearl barley
1	celery stalk, roughly chopped	1/2	teaspoon dried sage
1/2	cup peeled and minced shallots		Kosher salt and freshly ground black pepper
2	garlic cloves, peeled and minced		

Optional: Fresh parsley sprigs, Madeira

CROUTONS:

1	plain (not sourdough) baguette or loaf of French bread	1/4	cup fromage blanc or softened goat cheese
2	garlic cloves, peeled and sliced in half		

This recipe is suitable for vegetarians; replace the beef stock with vegetable stock, and proceed as directed.

FOR THE SOUP:

Place dried mushrooms in a mixing bowl and cover with wine. Set aside.

Heat oil in a large stockpot, until rippling but not smoking. Add onion, carrots, celery, shallots, and garlic. Cook until softened, about 8 minutes. Add fresh mushrooms, and stir well. Cook until mushrooms begin to release some of their liquid, 8 to 10 minutes. Add water and stock, and bring to a simmer.

Strain dried mushrooms through a fine sieve to rid them of any excess dirt, and reserve the soaking liquid. Add dried mushrooms to stockpot, along with their soaking liquid. Add barley and sage. Stir, cover, and simmer until barley and all vegetables are cooked, about 1 hour.

FOR THE CROUTONS:

Ten minutes before serving the soup, slice baguette into ½-inch rounds. Rub each slice (top and bottom, or to taste) with cut-side of garlic cloves. Spread one side of each slice of bread with a thin layer of fromage blanc. Toast, cheese-side up, under a broiler until golden brown, about 5 minutes.

Season soup to taste with salt and pepper. Serve hot in warm bowls or crocks, topped with Fromage Blanc Croutons and a light drizzle of Madeira and parsley sprigs, if using.

Serves 6

Fromage blanc is a boon for cheese fanatics who are watching their fat intake. Made from skim milk, it contains no fat or cholesterol, but has the full-fat flavor of luxurious mascarpone combined with sour cream.

Pulverize a cup of dried mushrooms in a food processor to create an earthy rub for roast chicken. Store in a tightly sealed container or a well-sealed, heavy-duty freezer bag in a cool, dry place.

ADDITIONAL SERVING RECOMMENDATIONS

• Serve as a soup course, or as a main course accompanied by a salad and thickly sliced country-style bread.

WHAT YOU HAVE ON HAND

- 6 pounds bottom round, rump, or chuck; or short ribs (or leftovers)
- 1 small sandwich ham (approximately 1 pound), or ham ends
- 2 large bunches of fresh beets
- Large bag of onions
- Large head of cabbage
- Canned white beans
- Beef stock or consommé (page 46)

WHAT TO DO WITH IT

- Set aside 3 pounds of the beef or beef ribs for this recipe. Double-wrap the balance, seal in a freezer bag, date, and store for 3 to 6 months.
- Separate 8 medium beets from their greens; wrap greens loosely in a paper towel and place in a resealable bag. Refrigerate for up to 2 days. Wash and dry the beets, place in a baking dish, and roast at 400°F until fork-tender. Cool, remove skin, and dice.
- Slice the cabbage in half, remove the core, and cut the leaves into thin strips. Reserve 3 cups for this recipe, and store the balance in a large freezer bag in the refrigerator for up to 4 days to use in salads.

PRIMARY/SECONDARY

ELENA'S UKRAINIAN BEEF BORSCHT

I've never been wild about borscht, that is, until my friend Elena insisted that I try her mother's hot beef borscht: it changed my mind forever. Richly aromatic, this dish offers a delightfully flavorful way to use up extra beef stock, as well as odds and ends of stewing meat that you might have leftover from Pot-au-Feu, or other braised or boiled meat dishes. In addition, this dish calls for cuts of meat that are readily available at discount clubs and larger supermarkets but are generally overlooked, such as small sandwich ham (ham ends can also be used).

3	pounds beef roast: chuck, brisket, or bottom round
1	small sandwich ham or ham ends (prosciutto or pancetta ends work just as well)
4	celery stalks, coarsely chopped
3	carrots, peeled and cut on the bias into 1-inch pieces
2	medium onions, peeled and chopped
2	whole garlic cloves, peeled
1	tablespoon fresh flat-leaf parsley or 1/2 tablespoon dried
1	bay leaf
8	medium beets, roasted, peeled, and cut into 1/2-inch dice
3	cups thinly sliced cabbage
1	(28-ounce) can whole Italian-style tomatoes, with juice
1	(16-ounce) can white beans, with liquid
4	tablespoons fresh lemon juice
	Kosher salt and freshly ground black pepper

Optional: Fresh dill, sour cream, leftover or packaged beef stock to replace half the water

If using leftover boiled beef for this recipe, replace the water (or half-water/half-stock mixture) with all beef stock, either leftover or packaged. This will make up the flavor difference between the cooked meat you are using versus the fresh meat that adds flavor as it cooks in the soup.

Place beef, ham, celery, carrots, onions, garlic, parsley, and bay leaf in a large saucepan, and cover with cold water. (Alternatively, use half water and half leftover or packaged beef stock.) Bring to a boil, skimming the froth off the surface.

Reduce to a simmer, and add beets, cabbage, and tomatoes. Cover and cook until beef and vegetables are fork-tender, about 2½ hours.

Stir in beans and lemon juice, replace cover, and simmer 20 minutes more. Season to taste with salt and pepper, and serve hot, topped with fresh dill sprigs and sour cream, if desired.

Serves 6 to 8

THE ART OF ROASTING ROOT VEGETABLES

Dry-roasting root vegetables (beets, turnips, and rutabagas, for example) is a simple way to bring out their natural sweetness and makes them easy to peel. Preheat oven to 375°F; place root vegetables on a heavy-duty baking sheet, and roast until fork-tender. (This will take anywhere from 45 minutes to 1½ hours, depending on the size of the vegetables.) Remove from the oven, and when cool enough to handle, peel the skins off the vegetables with a knife or vegetable peeler, and proceed with the rest of your recipe.

HOW LONG IT WILL LAST

- Elena's Ukrainian Beef Borscht will keep, refrigerated, for up to 5 days. It will keep in the freezer for 6 months.

ADDITIONAL SERVING RECOMMENDATIONS

- Let cool, refrigerate overnight, reheat over low heat the next day, and serve as directed.

PRIMARY/SECONDARY

FRENCH ONION SOUP WITH MELTED GRUYÈRE

Soothing and rich, this country-style French peasant soup is a longtime favorite that is a meal in a bowl. There are dozens of variations on this recipe, but the simplest is what I always return to. Enjoy this when you've lugged home an enormous mesh bag of onions and have a lot of good leftover or canned beef stock on hand. The red wine and garlic both work to increase flavor.

6	tablespoons (³/₄ stick) unsalted butter	1	cup good-quality red table wine
6	large yellow onions (Vidalia or Spanish), peeled and thinly sliced		Kosher salt and freshly ground black pepper
1	garlic clove, minced	6–8	¹/₂-inch slices of French bread, toasted
1¹/₂	tablespoons unbleached, all purpose flour	1	pound Gruyère cheese, grated coarsely
2	quarts leftover or packaged beef stock		

If you can't find Gruyère, substitute any of the following cheeses: French Comté, Swiss, Emmentaler, raclette, or Jarlsberg.

Melt butter in a large, heavyweight stockpot or Dutch oven over medium-low heat. Add onions and garlic. Sauté, stirring regularly, until onions are golden, about 45 minutes.

Sprinkle flour over onions, stir well, and cook for another few minutes, until the flour begins to take on the golden color of the onions.

Add stock and wine, cover, and gently simmer for 45 minutes. Season to taste with salt and pepper. (The soup is freezable at this point.)

Preheat broiler. Place slice of toasted bread in the bottom of each soup bowl, add 1 tablespoon of cheese to each, and ladle soup over all.

Divide the remaining cheese evenly among the bowls. Place bowls on a baking sheet, and brown under the broiler until cheese is melted and bubbling, 5 to 7 minutes.

Serves 6 to 8

Never store onions together with potatoes! Doing so will cause the spuds to react to the natural ethylene gas produced by the onions. The result: quickly rotted potatoes.

ADDITIONAL SERVING RECOMMENDATIONS

- Serve in sturdy, ovenproof soup crocks that are tough enough to be popped under the broiler to melt the cheese. Accompany with sliced French bread and a green salad with a mild dressing.

WHAT TO DO WITH IT

• Set aside 2 chickens for this soup. Double-wrap the third in plastic, place in a dated freezer bag, and freeze for 3 to 6 months.

HOW LONG IT WILL LAST

• This chicken soup (without noodles) will keep, refrigerated, for up to 4 days. Add freshly cooked noodles to the dish as you reheat leftovers.

• Without the noodles, this soup will freeze for 6 months.

• Cooked chicken from the soup should be refrigerated and used within 3 days, or skinned, frozen, and used within 3 months.

PRIMARY

TRADITIONAL JEWISH-STYLE CHICKEN SOUP

I was at school in Boston, studying for finals and felled by the flu, when I called my grandmother to ask for her chicken soup recipe.

"First," she said thoughtfully, "get a chicken."

My suggestion to you echoes hers, with one small change: these days, I actually use two smaller birds for my soup, which gives it intense flavor and provides extra meat for leftovers. The addition of dill, parsnips, carrots, and celery gives this soup its memorable and sweet flavor, which conjures up memories of Friday nights around the dinner table. Remember to boil the noodles separately and add them to the soup judiciously; otherwise, you'll have chicken noodle stew (which isn't so bad either).

2	(3-pound) chickens, giblets removed and reserved		2	celery stalks, cut on the bias into 1-inch pieces
1	medium onion, peeled and quartered		½	cup fresh dill, divided
3	medium carrots, peeled and cut on the bias into 1-inch pieces			Kosher salt and freshly ground black pepper
2	medium parsnips, peeled and cut on the bias into 1-inch pieces			

Optional: 1 pound egg noodles, boiled separately and cooled under cold water

Rinse chickens thoroughly and pat dry. Place onion quarters in a large stockpot, set chickens on top, and fill the pot with cold water to cover the birds. Bring to a boil over high heat. Reduce to a medium simmer, and add carrots, parsnips, celery, giblets, and ¼ cup of the dill. Cover and cook for 2 hours, repeatedly skimming the surface to remove froth. Add the remaining ¼ cup dill, season broth to taste with salt and pepper, replace cover, and continue to cook for another hour.

Carefully remove the chickens (they will fall apart, and this is okay) from the pot, and set aside on a platter to cool. Remove the giblets and discard. Once cool, pull the chicken off the bone, and proceed with one of the following options:

- Return chicken to the soup along with half the cooked noodles, and reserve the balance of the noodles for leftovers
- Return half to the soup and set the other half aside for secondary recipes
- Set the chicken aside for secondary recipes, and add only the noodles

Serves 6 to 8

ADDITIONAL SERVING RECOMMENDATIONS

- For a family-style meal, bring this soup to the table in a porcelain tureen and spoon it out carefully, serving everyone some chicken, vegetables, and broth.
- If you like a clearer broth, remove the vegetables and chicken from the pot, then strain the broth twice through a fine mesh strainer and back into another pot. Refrigerate up to 4 hours or overnight, skim fat, add back the vegetables and chicken, and reheat.

SECONDARY DISHES

- *Quesadilla of Chicken, Chilies, Tequila, and Lime (page 182)*
- *Grilled Vegetable Salad with Chicken and Pine Nuts (page 88)*
- *Asian Chicken-Stuffed Lettuce Rolls (page 168)*
- *Fettucine with Lemon Chicken, Parmesan, and Wine (page 184)*

PRIMARY

BIG FOOD BASIC CHICKEN STOCK

Many purists argue that homemade chicken stock is better than anything you can buy in a store, but these days, the quality of the packaged kind is often very good, so preparing it from scratch may seem like a waste of time. It really isn't, especially if you do your shopping at a discount club, or if you need your stock to be low in salt or fat because of dietary concerns. By making homemade chicken stock, you are in control of the amount of salt, fat, herbs and spices, and chicken that goes into it. Four pounds of chicken parts will yield a tasty, rich, and robust stock. You can also strain it, and strain it again, and enjoy it as a warm and comforting mug of clear broth when your world gets a little too big for its britches. When you run low, you can blend your homemade stock with the packaged kind, if need be. What makes BIG FOOD stock so special? Simple: it uses double the quantity of chicken that most stock recipes call for, resulting in a concentrated chicken flavor that can be used as a base for a multitude of delicious recipes.

4–6	pounds chicken parts or 2 (2- to 3-pound) whole chickens, cut up
4	large celery stalks, cut into 3–4 pieces each, leafy tops included
3	large carrots, cut into 3–4 pieces each
2	large unpeeled onions, quartered
1	head of garlic, cloves separated but unpeeled
2	tablespoons whole black peppercorns

Place chicken, celery, carrots, onions, garlic, and peppercorns in a large (8-quart) stockpot. Add cold water to cover. Bring to a low boil, and cook for approximately 4 hours, repeatedly skimming foam off the surface.

Remove from heat, carefully remove chicken parts and vegetables, and set aside. The meat can be skinned and used in any recipe calling for leftover chicken. Discard the vegetables. Cool stock completely (you can speed up this process by placing the pot in a sink filled with ice water).

Pour cooled stock through a fine mesh strainer into another container, and refrigerate overnight. Remove fat from the surface. Stock is now ready to be used in recipes or frozen for later use.

Yields approximately 5 quarts

When buying chicken parts to make stock, be sure to buy less expensive pieces, such as backs and necks, which yield tremendous flavor.

TORTELLINI EN BRODO

So mind-bogglingly simple to make from leftover chicken soup or packaged stock, this tasty traditional Italian soup uses up both stock and those wonderful frozen tortellini that are available in bulk and are a terrific addition to your freezer staples. They cook quickly in soup, and are delicious simply tossed with a bit of butter, chopped sage, and freshly grated Parmesan. Try adding them to BIG FOOD Rustic Tomato Soup (page 64).

| 3 | quarts leftover BIG FOOD Basic Chicken Stock (opposite) or packaged | 2 | cups frozen tortellini of any variety |

Optional: *Freshly grated Parmesan cheese, 2 tablespoons ribboned fresh basil (page 81)*

Heat the stock in a medium saucepan, until gently simmering. Add the tortellini, and continue to simmer until all the tortellini rise to the surface, about 6 minutes. Serve in shallow bowls with a sprinkling of Parmesan and basil, if using.

Serves 6 to 8

ONION + CARROT + CELERY = CULINARY HEAVEN

In France, it's called the *mirepoix*; in Italy, the *battuto* (or, when it's cooked, a *soffrito*, which is also what it's called among Spanish cooks). What, exactly, is it? Call it what you will; I call it The Culinary Holy Trinity, and it's a wise home cook who learns that it forms the basis for nearly everything in the kitchen (except dessert).

Whether it be a soup or a stew or a sauce that you make, slowly cooking together onions, carrots, and celery will give you a remarkable base of flavor.

WHAT YOU HAVE ON HAND

- **Leftover BIG FOOD Basic Chicken Stock (opposite)**
  or
- **4 quarts packaged chicken stock**
- **A 2-pound bag of frozen tortellini**

WHAT TO DO WITH IT

- Set aside 3 quarts of chicken stock for this recipe.
- Set aside 2 cups of frozen tortellini for this recipe, and freeze the balance in a heavy-duty freezer bag for up to 2 months.

HOW LONG IT WILL LAST

- Tortellini en Brodo is simply pasta cooked in simmering clear broth. The broth will keep in an airtight container in the refrigerator for up to 3 days, or freeze for 6 to 8 months.

SECONDARY

ASIAN CHICKEN SOUP WITH GREENS

This quick and easy soup gets its unmistakable flavor from the highly aromatic star anise, a spice commonly used in Asian cooking and one of the main ingredients in Chinese five-spice powder (and no relation to the cloying anise used to flavor licorice). Enjoy this soup as is or with the addition of Asian noodles, dumplings, chicken, or shrimp, which can be cooked in the broth as you make the soup. Freshly grated or ground ginger and packaged lemongrass—an herb long thought to be a stress reducer—add a sweet, spicy, and calming flavor to the dish.

1	tablespoon canola oil
3	scallions, roughly chopped
2	garlic cloves, peeled and thinly sliced
2	tablespoons freshly grated ginger or 1 tablespoon ground
8	cups prepared or leftover BIG FOOD Basic Chicken Stock
2	whole star anise
1	tablespoon soy sauce
1/2	pound leftover chicken meat, preferably breast, thinly sliced
1	(1/2-pound) bunch baby bok choy, washed and sliced into bite-size pieces

Heat oil in a large saucepan over medium-high heat, until rippling but not smoking. Add scallions, garlic, and ginger. Stir, reduce heat to medium, and cook until softened, about 3 minutes. Add stock, star anise, and soy sauce. Bring to a very gentle simmer, cover, and cook for 30 minutes. Add chicken and bok choy, cover, and simmer gently for another 25 minutes. Remove star anise, ladle into bowls, and serve.

VARIATIONS

- Substitute shrimp, Asian dumplings, or wide Asian noodles for chicken. Adjust cooking time accordingly.
- Serve over cooked, leftover white rice, or soba noodles, for a heartier dish.
- Add $\frac{1}{2}$ cup of light coconut milk, a dash of red pepper oil, 1 tablespoon of dried lemongrass, and the juice of one lime for a sweet-and-sour, Thai-flavored version.

Serves 6 to 8

WHAT TO DO WITH IT

- If you're making this soup from a combination of water and packaged stock, set aside 2 quarts of the stock for the recipe, and freeze or store the balance.
- If you're using a combination of packaged stock and leftover broth, combine enough to give you 2 quarts, and freeze the balance.
- If using fresh chicken, you'll need approximately 3½ to 4 pounds; double-wrap and freeze any that's left.

HOW LONG IT WILL LAST

- This soup will last 3 to 4 days refrigerated, and 6 months frozen.

PRIMARY/SECONDARY

MEXICAN CHICKEN SOUP WITH VEGETABLES, CHILI, AND LIME

This soup, which is based on chef Rick Bayless's delicious Mexican ranch-style chicken soup, can be strained and served as a golden broth with a lime wedge and a little chopped cilantro. I prefer it heartier and filled with the vegetables that are readily available in bulk everywhere from discount stores to farmer's markets. Make it quick, with packaged stock or leftover chicken stock, or from scratch, with an additional fresh or frozen whole chicken (or parts). Enjoy it with a warm white corn tortilla and an icy Mexican beer.

1	(4-pound) whole chicken, giblets removed and reserved	1	teaspoon dried thyme
1	large white onion, peeled and diced	2	medium firm tomatoes, diced
6	garlic cloves, peeled and smashed	2	medium carrots, peeled and cut on the bias into 1-inch pieces
4	bay leaves	½	cup chopped fresh cilantro
2	jalapeño peppers, seeded and chopped	2	fresh ears of corn, kernels cut from the husk, or 1 cup frozen corn kernels
1	teaspoon dried marjoram		Juice of one lime
			Kosher salt

Optional: 1 to 2 quarts chicken stock, leftover or packaged; cilantro sprigs

Place chicken and giblets in a large saucepan or Dutch oven, and cover with cold water (or cover with half water and half chicken stock, if desired, for richer flavor).

Bring to a boil, then reduce to a simmer. Skim the froth. Add onion, garlic, bay leaves, jalapeño, marjoram, and thyme. Cover partially and cook for 1 hour. Carefully remove chicken and giblets; set aside to cool. Discard giblets.

Add tomatoes, carrots, and cilantro to the pot. Cover and continue to simmer for 30 minutes. While the vegetables cook, pull chicken meat from bones.

Return chicken to the pot, add corn and lime juice, and season to taste with salt. Serve hot, topped with cilantro sprigs, if desired.

VARIATIONS
• Add 1 (16-ounce) can of posole to the hot finished soup.

Serves 6 to 8

When making fresh chicken soup of any kind, store the soup and the chicken separately; it will be easier to defat the broth.

ADDITIONAL SERVING RECOMMENDATIONS

• Serve the chicken separately, wrapped up in warm white corn tortillas and sprinkled with chopped chilies and salsa.
• Serve everything together, as a stew.
• Float strips of sliced corn tortillas on top.

PRIMARY

BIG FOOD RUSTIC TOMATO SOUP

A perfect place to begin talking about vegetable-based soups is the equally loved and maligned tomato soup. I'm not ashamed to admit that I used to eat a bowl almost every day after school, straight out of the can. It was years before I tasted the real thing, and once I made it myself, I realized that 1) it was a snap, and 2) it could be varied in any number of ways, then stored for months.

This rustic version uses canned tomatoes and their juice (although you can use the freshest of fresh tomatoes, or a combination of the two), and blends them with sautéed onions, garlic, and basil, all of which are natural companions to tomatoes. Cold and chunky with the addition of some cucumber and vinegar, the soup becomes refreshing gazpacho. Warm with fresh summer vegetables, a dollop of fresh pesto, and a grating of Parmesan, and you've got a light summer minestrone.

2	tablespoons extra virgin olive oil
1	medium carrot, peeled and diced
1	large yellow onion, peeled and diced
2	garlic cloves, minced
4	cups canned tomatoes with their liquid or 5 cups fresh tomatoes, peeled, seeded, and chopped, with their liquid
1	cup vegetable stock
2	tablespoons chopped fresh basil leaves or 1 tablespoon dried
	Kosher salt and freshly ground black pepper

Optional: *Dash of sugar*

In a large saucepan over medium heat, heat oil until rippling but not smoking. Add carrot and onion, and cook until softened, about 5 minutes (do not brown). Add garlic, stir, and cook for 3 minutes.

Add tomatoes and their juice, and combine thoroughly, cooking until tomatoes soften and fall apart, 8 to 10 minutes. Add stock, cover, and simmer for 10 minutes. Add basil, cover, and continue to simmer for 20 minutes more.

Season to taste with salt and pepper. If the soup is bitter, add a dash of sugar. Serve hot, or refrigerate overnight and reheat for more intense flavors.

VARIATIONS

- For a smoother, creamy soup, omit the basil, and purée in a blender or using an immersion blender. Add $1/4$ cup heavy cream to 1 cup of the warm soup, stir well, and return to the blender. Purée again, and serve.
- For a spicy version, add 1 teaspoon red pepper flakes along with the basil.

Serves 6 to 8

Although it is wonderful to use fresh, ripe tomatoes in season, it's equally wonderful to use good-quality canned tomatoes when good fresh ones are unavailable. Many canned tomatoes are of top-notch quality these days because they're packaged at their ripest. Look for any labeled San Marzano: these lovely plum tomatoes are among the sweetest and meatiest available; have fewer seeds; and are lower in acid, higher in sugar, and worth their weight in gold when making soup or sauce.

If you buy your canned tomatoes whole, crush them yourself in their own liquid by using the back of a fork or a flat potato masher.

ADDITIONAL SERVING RECOMMENDATIONS

- Serve hot with fresh pesto, garlic croutons, or grated cheese.
- Serve chilled with a drizzle of good-quality extra virgin olive oil.

SECONDARY DISHES

- *White Bean Soup with Escarole and Sausage (page 66)*
- *Tuscan Bread Soup (page 68)*
- *Pasta e Fagiole (page 70)*
- *Traditional Gazpacho (page 72)*

WHAT YOU HAVE ON HAND

- 1 (28-ounce) can or 12-can flat of crushed or whole Italian-style plum tomatoes
  or
- 28 ounces of BIG FOOD Rustic Tomato Soup (page 64)
- Italian-style sausages, preferably sweet
- BIG FOOD Basic Chicken Stock (page 58)

WHAT TO DO WITH IT

- Set aside the amount of canned tomatoes needed for this recipe; freeze the opened balance in a dated plastic container for up to 6 months. Store unopened cans in a cool, dark location, and use them within a year.

HOW LONG IT WILL LAST

- Refrigerated, this soup will last 3 to 4 days; frozen, it will last 6 to 8 months.

SECONDARY

WHITE BEAN SOUP WITH ESCAROLE AND SAUSAGE

"Zuppa di Cannellini con Scarola."

I don't speak a word of Italian except for that one line, and when I say it, I'm automatically transported back to a lovely villa in the Tuscan hamlet of Rappalano Terme. One morning, the groundskeeper presented us with a gift of fresh figs, wild flowers, fig leaves, and a jug of local wine. He had wanted to offer us something, so he went out foraging, and there were the original fruits of the earth, right under his nose. This recipe was born virtually the same way: My cupboard was bare but for a few cans of white beans, vegetable stock, sausage links, a can of tomatoes, a packaged quart of chicken stock, and a head of escarole. The rest is history. Use whatever kind of sausages you might have in the freezer (although not Cajun or andouille), replace the prosciutto with a small end of ham that's been cubed, or go all vegetarian and omit the meat (or replace it with meatless sausage) and use vegetable stock, along with spinach, kale, or chard instead of the escarole. The best part of making this dish: it's better the next day, and even the day after that.

2	tablespoons extra virgin olive oil
1	large Spanish onion, peeled and diced
2	medium carrots, peeled and diced
2	celery stalks, diced
2	garlic cloves, minced
1/2	cup minced prosciutto, or leftover ham
2	(1- to 1 1/2-pound) bunches escarole, leafy greens roughly chopped, white portions discarded
1	tablespoon freshly ground black pepper
1	tablespoon fresh ribboned basil, or 1/2 tablespoon dried

4	Italian-style chicken, pork, or turkey sausages (preferably sweet), sliced into 1-inch pieces, on the bias
2	(12-ounce) cans cannellini beans
1	quart leftover BIG FOOD Basic Chicken Stock, packaged chicken stock, or vegetable stock
1	(28-ounce) can crushed Italian-style tomatoes, or a combination of canned tomatoes and leftover BIG FOOD Rustic Tomato Soup
	Kosher salt
	Fresh Parmesan cheese for grating

Optional: Fresh pesto, extra olive oil for drizzling

Heat oil in a large (8-quart) stockpot over medium heat, until rippling but not smoking. Add onion and carrots, and cook until vegetables begin to soften, about 6 minutes (do not brown). Add celery, garlic, and prosciutto; stir well.

Reduce heat to low and cook for 15 minutes. Add escarole, pepper, and basil. Stir well, and cook until escarole is cooked down and any liquid has evaporated, 8 to 10 minutes.

Add sausage and beans. Stir well, heating the meat and beans through, about 6 minutes.

Add stock, stir, bring to a boil, and immediately reduce to a simmer. Cover and cook for 20 minutes. Remove cover, add tomatoes, stir well, and bring to a boil. Reduce to a simmer and cook 20 minutes more.

Season with salt to taste and top with freshly grated Parmesan cheese. Add a dollop of pesto and drizzle with olive oil, if desired. Serve hot with a hunk of fresh, country-style bread.

Serves 6

If dietary laws (or just your diet, for that matter) restrict you from using pork products, skip the prosciutto or ham and use Italian-style chicken, veal, turkey, or meatless sausage instead of the pork.

If you're making this dish using leftover BIG FOOD Rustic Tomato Soup, reduce the amount of onion, carrot, and celery by half.

SECONDARY

TUSCAN BREAD SOUP

If you think you see a pattern here, you're right: many Italian recipes are quintessential BIG FOOD dishes. One recipe or basic ingredient (like bread or tomatoes) can be used over again in any number of ways: the cost savings is tremendous; the taste, delicious. This peasant-style recipe, which came to me from the great Tuscan chef Pino Luongo, is designed to use up the prior day's stale bread. If you think that your bread is "too" fresh (or soft, and will fall apart under the hot soup), pop it into the toaster or under the broiler, just to crisp it up and give it body.

2	cups torn pieces stale white or Italian bread
2	cups vegetable stock, at room temperature
2	tablespoons extra virgin olive oil
2	garlic cloves, thinly sliced
1	(28-ounce) can crushed Italian-style tomatoes; or a combination of canned tomatoes and leftover BIG FOOD Rustic Tomato Soup; or all leftover soup; or 3 pounds ripe, fresh tomatoes, chopped

1/2	cup tightly packed basil leaves, roughly chopped
	Kosher salt and freshly ground black pepper

Optional: Dash of sugar

Place stale bread in a large bowl and pour stock over it, making sure that all the bread is saturated. Set aside.

In a large saucepan, heat oil until rippling but not smoking. Add garlic and cook over medium heat until honey-colored.

Add tomatoes, increase the heat to medium-high, and cook, stirring frequently, until liquid is expelled and tomatoes are softened, about 8 minutes. Add basil and stir well.

Squeeze all of the liquid out of the soaked bread, and add bread to the soup. The soup should be stewlike. If it is too thick, add spoonfuls of vegetable stock to achieve desired consistency. Season to taste with salt and pepper, adding sugar if bitter, and serve hot.

VARIATIONS
• Add a dash of balsamic vinegar to the cooking tomatoes for heightened flavor.
• Add a pinch of red pepper flakes to the cooking tomatoes.

Serves 6

PASTA E FAGIOLE

WHAT YOU HAVE ON HAND

- 1 (28-ounce) can or 12-can flat of crushed or whole Italian-style plum tomatoes
  or
- 28 ounces of BIG FOOD Rustic Tomato Soup (page 64)
- Any small pasta (elbows, dittalini, alphabet letters, stars, pastina)

WHAT TO DO WITH IT

- If using canned tomatoes, set aside the amount needed for this recipe, and freeze the balance in a dated plastic container for up to 6 months; store unopened cans in a cool, dark location and use them within a year.

HOW LONG IT WILL LAST

- This soup will last, refrigerated, for up to 4 days, and will freeze for 6 months, beans, pasta, and all.

This is a delicious, hearty soup that can be made in less than an hour. The small tubular pasta (or tinier pasta, like orzo, baby shells, stars, alphabet letters, or elbows) will bring you back to your childhood. Add a slice or two of rustic garlic bread and a salad, and call it dinner.

3	tablespoons extra virgin olive oil
1	medium carrot, peeled and diced
1	medium onion, peeled and diced
1	celery stalk, diced
2	garlic cloves, peeled and minced
1	(28-ounce) can crushed Italian-tomatoes and their liquid or a combination of canned tomatoes and leftover BIG FOOD Rustic Tomato Soup, or all leftover soup
2	cups vegetable or chicken stock
1	(12-ounce) can cannellini or garbanzo beans, drained
2	sprigs fresh rosemary, or ½ tablespoon dried
½	pound small pasta (dittalini, tiny shells, stars, or alphabet letters), cooked according to package instructions and drained
½	cup fresh basil, chopped, or 2 tablespoons dried, plus more for garnish
	Kosher salt and freshly ground black pepper to taste

Optional: Dash of sugar, extra olive oil for drizzling, freshly grated Parmesan cheese

In a large saucepan, heat oil over medium heat, until rippling but not smoking. Add carrot, onion, and celery; cook until well softened, 8 to 10 minutes. Add garlic and continue to cook for 3 minutes.

Add tomatoes and their liquid; cook until tomatoes begin to break down, about 8 minutes.

Add stock, beans, and rosemary; bring to a boil. Reduce heat to a simmer, partially cover, and cook until flavors blend, about 15 minutes.

If the soup is too thick at this point, add 2 tablespoons water or stock.

Add cooked pasta and basil and stir. Season to taste with salt and pepper. If soup is bitter, add sugar.

Ladle into bowls, drizzle with olive oil and top with freshly grated Parmesan cheese, if using. Serve hot.

Serves 6

OVEN-ROASTED TOMATO SOUP

It's August, and you cannot restrain yourself from stopping at the local farm stand: the tomatoes are fresh, ripe, and absolutely luscious. So you buy 3 pounds. What to do now? Roast!

Roasting tomatoes maximizes the fruit's natural sweet and nutty flavor. For this recipe, I never bother seeding or peeling the tomatoes, which get pulverized with the use of my immersion blender. If you prefer your soup without seeds, strain it through a fine mesh sieve before serving.

1½	tablespoons extra virgin olive oil, divided	½	teaspoon freshly ground black pepper, divided
3–4	pounds fresh tomatoes, cut into ¼-inch slices	1½	tablespoons peeled and minced shallots
½	teaspoon sugar, divided	½	cup vegetable stock (or chicken, or beef)
½	teaspoon salt, divided		

Optional: *Extra olive oil for drizzling, freshly grated Parmesan cheese for garnish, pesto, Fromage Blanc Croutons*

Preheat oven to 300°F.

Lightly grease a heavy-duty baking sheet with ½ tablespoon of the oil. Lay tomatoes in a single layer on the sheet. Sprinkle with half of the sugar, salt, and pepper. Turn tomatoes over and repeat. Roast for 30 minutes, turning tomatoes frequently, until they begin to brown. Remove from oven and transfer to a mixing bowl.

Heat the remaining 1 tablespoon oil in a medium saucepan until rippling but not smoking. Add shallots and cook until softened, about 5 minutes.

Add tomatoes and stir well. Add stock, bring to a simmer, and cook for 10 minutes.

Using an immersion or traditional blender, purée the soup until smooth. Return soup to saucepan, add salt and pepper to taste, and reheat.

Serve hot, with a drizzle of olive oil and a sprinkle of Parmesan, if using. Top with a swirl of pesto and Fromage Blanc Croutons (page 50), if desired.

Serves 4 to 6

WHAT YOU HAVE ON HAND

- **3 to 4 pounds of fresh tomatoes, any variety except green**

WHAT TO DO WITH IT

- Plan to have roasted tomato soup in deepest, darkest winter, when the rest of the world is eating potatoes and root vegetables.

HOW LONG IT WILL LAST

- This soup will last 4 days in the refrigerator, 6 to 8 months in the freezer.

SECONDARY

TRADITIONAL GAZPACHO

There is possibly no more refreshing a soup on a hot summer's day than this one. I like mine spicy, and generally add more garlic and Tabasco sauce than this simple recipe, which was passed down to me by my dear friend and home cook extraordinaire Stephena Romanoff, calls for. During the warmer weather, when tomatoes are in season, I make this in great quantities and store it in my refrigerator, in a covered glass pitcher.

1	(28-ounce) can crushed Italian-style tomatoes, pureed in a blender; or 1 quart low-salt vegetable juice; and 1½ pounds chopped fresh tomatoes or 28 ounces leftover BIG FOOD Rustic Tomato Soup	4	medium tomatoes, peeled, seeded, and finely chopped
	Juice of 1 large lemon	1	large cucumber, peeled, seeded, and finely chopped
		3	garlic cloves, minced
2	medium green bell peppers, seeded, ribbed, and chopped	2	tablespoons extra virgin olive oil
		1	tablespoon red wine vinegar
1	medium onion, peeled and finely diced		Tabasco sauce
			Kosher salt

In a large bowl, stir together pureed tomatoes and lemon juice. Add peppers, onion, chopped tomatoes, cucumber, garlic, oil, and vinegar. Season to taste with Tabasco and salt, and stir well. Chill for at least 1 hour before serving.

VARIATION
- Add 2 seeded, ribbed, and puréed sweet red peppers to the soup.

Serves 6

One of the easiest, fastest ways to make this quasi-traditional dish is to use vegetable juice in addition to canned or fresh tomatoes.

For a thicker soup, add more fresh, chopped tomatoes.

HOW TO PEEL AND SEED A TOMATO

Not as difficult a task as it sounds, peeling and seeding fresh tomatoes results in a smoother consistency and cleaner taste.

1. Fill a medium saucepan with water, and bring it to a rapid boil. Fill a large bowl with ice water, and put it to the side.
2. Cut an X in the stem end of each tomato, and gently lower each into the boiling water.
3. After 30 seconds you will see the skins loosen and pull back from the fruit; quickly remove the tomatoes and plunge them into the ice water.
4. Wait a moment or so before slipping the skins off. To seed, cut the tomatoes in half and scrape out the seeds with a spoon or your finger.

ADDITIONAL SERVING RECOMMENDATIONS

- Serve Traditional Gazpacho in tall, chilled water glasses, with a garnish of chopped cucumber and onion.
- Garnish with chopped fresh basil, chopped fresh mint, or minced red onion.

PRIMARY

CORN AND CRABMEAT CHOWDER

Necessity is the mother of invention, which is exactly how this thick, heavenly, simple-to-prepare chowder came to be, after I discovered large cans of backfin crabmeat lurking in the recesses of my local discount club's refrigerated case. Sweet and spicy, with flavors reminiscent of the eastern shore of Maryland, this late summertime treat (which is definitely not for dieters!) can be made anytime of year with frozen corn.

$\frac{1}{2}$	cup unsalted butter	1	(1-pound) can backfin or lump crabmeat, or 1 pound fresh crabmeat, cleaned
$\frac{1}{2}$	cup Wondra flour		
2	cups half-and-half or heavy cream	2	cups corn kernels, fresh or frozen
$1\frac{1}{2}$	cups whole milk	1	jalapeño pepper, minced
$\frac{1}{2}$	cup vegetable or chicken stock		Kosher salt and freshly ground black pepper
1	small sweet onion (such as Vidalia), peeled and minced		

Melt butter in a heavy-bottomed saucepan over low heat. Drizzle flour in little by little, stirring constantly with a whisk, until the consistency is that of a thick cream and mixture coats the back of a spoon. Do not let the mixture take on any color. If you do not need the full $\frac{1}{2}$ cup of flour, do not use it all.

Add half-and-half and milk, stirring until very smooth, about 8 minutes.

Add stock and onion, stir well to combine, bring to a low simmer, and cook for 10 minutes. If soup appears too thick, thin to desired consistency with more stock, or water.

Add crabmeat, corn, and jalapeño. Bring to an active simmer, cover, and cook until crabmeat is heated through and the corn is tender, 8 to 10 minutes. Season to taste with salt and pepper.

Serve hot, in warmed bowls, spooning out lumps of crabmeat with a slotted spoon and pouring the chowder over them.

VARIATIONS

- Add crumbled, well-cooked bacon, prosciutto, or pancetta to the milk mixture.
- Substitute peeled and cleaned baby shrimp for crabmeat.
- Substitute leftover lobster meat for crabmeat.
- If making this dish with fresh crab, add large pieces of shell to the chowder to enrich the soup base; remove the shell prior to serving.
- Spike with cayenne pepper or Tabasco.

Serves 6

Congratulations! You've just made what we call in my family a fauxroux! "Terrific!" you say. "What exactly is a fauxroux?"

A fauxroux ("froo," which rhymes with *clue*), is a time-tested way to thicken soups, chowders, sauces, and gravies; in fact, it's a primary step in the creation of a sort of quasi-béchamel sauce, which (believe it or not) we are all familiar with, thanks to dishes like mac and cheese and traditional lasagna Bolognese. The making of a fauxroux is not hard: it just needs a little bit of attention to ensure that it doesn't cook or go brown (and if it does, you've got the beginnings of a traditional Cajun roux, which is one of the basic ingredients in jambalaya).

1. In a heavyweight pot, heat unsalted butter slowly, over low heat.
2. Slowly drizzle in flour, stirring well until it absorbs all the butter. Do not let this combination color.
3. Drizzle in milk, and stir briskly, until smooth.

This "sauce" can be flavor-enhanced with wine or herbs to make a delicious accompaniment to chicken, fish, and even beef dishes.

ADDITIONAL SERVING RECOMMENDATIONS

- Sprinkle with chopped scallions and fresh parsley, and serve hot in rustic-style, ovenproof crocks.

SECONDARY DISHES

- *Spicy Corn and Black Bean Cakes (page 104)*
- *Spicy Southwestern Corn, Crab, and Black Bean Salad (page 82)*

PRIMARY

COLD POTATO SOUP WITH ROASTED GARLIC AND ROSEMARY

We've all seen those mammoth bags of Idaho potatoes at our local discount clubs; invariably, they all seem to sprout eyes before we use them (especially now, since the advent of low-carb diets). This very simple, eminently traditional "vichyssoise" will give you a gloriously easy way to use your spuds; the roasted garlic gives it a nice (and unexpected) nutty kick. Make it a day in advance to allow the soup to chill and the flavors to blend.

1	large head garlic
1	teaspoon kosher salt, plus extra for seasoning
	Freshly ground black pepper
2½	tablespoons extra virgin olive oil, divided
4	leeks (woody green leaves removed), cleaned well and thinly sliced into rings

2	tablespoons fresh rosemary sprigs, or 1 tablespoon dried
4	medium Idaho or russet potatoes, peeled, cubed, and placed in ice water
4	cups vegetable or chicken stock
1	cup whole milk or half-and-half
	White pepper

Preheat oven to 400°F.

Slice the pointed end off the head of garlic, season with salt, black pepper, and ½ tablespoon of the olive oil. Wrap in aluminum foil, and roast until soft and lightly golden brown, 30 to 40 minutes. When cool enough to handle, squeeze the flesh of each clove into a bowl; set aside.

In a heavy-bottomed saucepan, heat the remaining 2 tablespoons oil over medium-low heat, until rippling but not smoking. Add leeks and rosemary, and cook until softened, about 10 minutes. Add roasted garlic and stir well to combine.

Add potatoes, stock, and 1 teaspoon salt; bring to a boil for 5 minutes. Reduce to a low simmer, cover, and cook for 30 minutes.

Purée soup until smooth. Place milk in the saucepan, add soup back, and bring to a boil for 1 minute. Season to taste with salt and white pepper. Let cool, and refrigerate overnight. Adjust seasoning if necessary before serving.

Serves 6

To prevent potatoes from discoloring as you peel, dice, or grate them, have a large bowl of ice water waiting nearby. After you prepare each potato, slip it into the bowl. This will prevent your spuds from oxidizing and turning gray.

ADDITIONAL SERVING RECOMMENDATIONS

- Make it *veddy, veddy* fancy by serving it out of a china tureen.
- Go for a more rustic presentation and serve in stoneware crocks.
- Enjoy it out of chilled glasses, each garnished with one large, boiled, cold shrimp curling over the rim of the glass.

BIG FOOD SALADS

"A salad is an abused, neglected thing. Everyone laughs when the waiter in *Ninotchka* says to Greta Garbo, who has ordered a plate of chopped greens, 'Madame, this is a restaurant, not a meadow.'"
—Laurie Colwin

Gone are the days of lackluster iceberg "salads" covered with your mother's attempt at home-made Russian dressing (ketchup and mayo, mixed together in stained Tupperware), or those hapless bowls of wilted lettuce leaves weighted down by veg-etable oil—and way too much of it. Today, salads can be anything from a simple combination of fresh greens and herbs drizzled with a mild, lightly piquant vinai-grette, to cold, leftover sliced meats tossed with flame-roasted vegetables and a dash of white wine vinegar, to a combination of finely chopped leftover chicken breast, crumbled bacon, and blue cheese. In the following pages, you'll learn how to think of salads as a wonderful way to use up everything you bring home: left-over bread and tomatoes will be reincarnated as the dazzling and very traditional Italian Panzanella, which actually gets better with age. Leftover salmon that has been grilled, roasted, or poached will be reborn as a cold salmon curry with grapes and walnuts, suitable for serving to friends who've stopped by for an im-promptu lunch (or, for that matter, a fancy one); leftover Tuna Salad Niçoise, a healthy salad made with olive oil instead of mayonnaise, makes a divine Pan Bagnat—a French-style salad in a sandwich that's been pressed thin under a weight, refrigerated overnight, and then allowed to come to room temperature before serving. So . . . that head of iceberg you have kicking around in your fridge? Pull the brown leaves off of it, and save it for the bunnies.

- **2 to 3 pounds of fresh tomatoes of any variety (not green)**
  or
- **1 (28-ounce) can of whole Italian-style plum tomatoes, drained of their liquid and chopped**
- **1 large loaf of country-style, crusty bread (not sourdough), such as a boule, semolina baguette or loaf, French baguette, or Italian bread**

WHAT TO DO WITH IT

- Use all the tomatoes for this dish.
- Tear or cut the bread into bite-size pieces.

HOW LONG IT WILL LAST

- This salad gets better with time. Dressed and covered, it will keep for 2 to 3 days under refrigeration.

SECONDARY

PANZANELLA

Skeptics scoff, and meat-and-potatoes fans roll their eyes: in truth, there is little that is more satisfying, or fresher in flavor, than juicy chopped tomatoes tossed with day-old crusty bread, olive oil, salt, pepper, and fragrant fresh basil—the ingredient that lends an unmistakable edge to this king of rustic Italian salads. Make this salad a day in advance; the flavors will deepen overnight. You'll never think of old bread the same way again.

2	cups torn day-old bread	1	tablespoon extra virgin olive oil
3–4	fresh tomatoes, chopped	2	tablespoons red wine vinegar
1	garlic clove, minced		Kosher salt and freshly ground pepper
¼	cup fresh basil leaves, ribboned, or ½ tablespoon dried		

Place bread in a large mixing bowl, and cover with tomatoes and garlic. Let stand for 10 minutes at room temperature.

Add basil, oil, vinegar, salt, and pepper to taste. The salad should be fairly wet. Let stand at least 30 minutes at room temperature before serving. If you have time, refrigerate overnight, and bring back to room temperature prior to serving.

Optional: *In a small bowl, using the back of a fork, mince anchovy fillet together with minced garlic clove and extra virgin olive oil. Add this blend to the salad when you add the liquid ingredients.*

Serves 4 to 6

Need "stale" bread for Panzanella or Tuscan Bread Soup (page 68)? Cut a fresh loaf into cubes and lay them on a baking sheet in a single layer. Toast, in a 300°F oven, until crisp but not brown, about 5 minutes. Cool completely, and proceed with your recipe.

ADDITIONAL SERVING RECOMMENDATIONS

- Serve as a main-course salad, with a bowl of soup and a glass of cold white wine.
- Serve as a side salad, with a light and summery main course.

HOW TO "RIBBON" FRESH BASIL (OR SPINACH, OR ANY LEAFY GREEN OR HERB)

The pros call it a "chiffonade," which, literally translated, means to cut into thin strips, or to "ribbon." However you say it, it means the same thing: thin, delicate wisps of elegant flavor that are amazingly easy and quick to prepare.

1. Take a whole, fresh basil leaf, and lay it flat.
2. Roll it up tightly lengthwise, like a cigarette.
3. Using a gentle, rocking motion, make cuts every eighth of an inch or so.

The result? A beautiful technique that can be translated to any leafy green or herb.

WHAT YOU HAVE ON HAND

- Too much fresh, frozen, or left-over corn
- Leftover canned or fresh crabmeat

WHAT TO DO WITH IT

- Shuck fresh corn into a bowl. Set aside 1½ cups of it, and freeze the rest in a heavy-duty labeled and dated freezer bag for up to 3 months.
- Set aside 1 cup of crabmeat, and use the balance within 3 days.

HOW LONG IT WILL LAST

- This salad will last, refrigerated, for 3 to 4 days.

SECONDARY

SPICY SOUTHWESTERN CORN, CRAB, AND BLACK BEAN SALAD

A delicious leftover salad that uses the BIG FOOD pantry staple black beans, this dish comes to life anytime of year, but especially in the summer, when fresh corn is available everywhere for very little money. If fresh corn is out of season, simply substitute the frozen variety.

DRESSING:

	Juice of 1 lime	½	teaspoon ground cumin
¼	cup vegetable or canola oil		Kosher salt
¾	teaspoon mild or spicy chili powder		

SALAD:

1½	cups cooked corn kernels (frozen or fresh)	1	small tomato, chopped
¾	cup canned black beans, drained and rinsed	1	medium jalapeño pepper, diced
1	cup canned backfin or lump crabmeat	1	small red onion, peeled and diced
½	red bell pepper, seeded, ribbed, and diced	¼	cup fresh cilantro, chopped, divided

FOR THE DRESSING:

Whisk together lime juice, oil, chili powder, and cumin. Add salt to taste, and set aside.

FOR THE SALAD:

In a large, nonmetallic mixing bowl, combine corn, beans, crabmeat, red pepper, tomato, jalapeño, onion, and half the cilantro.

Add the dressing, toss well, and top with the balance of the cilantro.

Serve chilled, as is or atop fresh tossed salad greens.

VARIATIONS:

• Replace the crabmeat with cold boiled shrimp; poached chicken breast or skinless, boneless leftover chicken; or fresh or canned tuna.
• Grill fresh corn before adding it to the salad.

Serves 4 to 6

The sweetness of crab complements this spicy dish well, but you can substitute boiled shrimp or leftover lobster meat in its place.

SECONDARY

CURRIED SALMON SALAD WITH GRAPES AND WALNUTS

Grapes seem to be a counterintuitive addition to savory dishes for most people, but I've discovered that they add just the right touch of tart fruitiness to rich salmon and walnuts. Filled with color, taste, and texture, this easy salad is a perfect way to use up broiled, poached, grilled, or even canned salmon. Use a mild Indian curry powder in place of Madras curry if you prefer a less spicy taste.

DRESSING:

½	cup mayonnaise		Juice of 1 large lime
1	teaspoon Madras curry powder		Kosher salt

SALAD:

2	cups flaked, previously cooked salmon (poached, grilled, broiled, or baked, without sauce)	¾	cup chopped celery
		½	cup diced red onion
1	cup seedless green grapes, halved	½	cup walnuts, unsalted

> Most mayonnaise-based dressings can also be made by substituting plain yogurt for the mayo.

FOR THE DRESSING:

In a small mixing bowl, whisk together the mayonnaise, curry powder, and lime juice; season to taste with salt and set aside.

FOR THE SALAD:

In a large mixing bowl, using your hands, gently mix salmon, grapes, celery, onion, and walnuts together; take care to keep ingredients from breaking up. Toss with dressing, and serve at room temperature as is, atop fresh baby greens, or even as a sandwich, with crisp romaine lettuce in a pita or between toasted slices of dense wheat bread.

VARIATIONS

For a twist, try adding:

• Peeled, cored, and chopped Granny Smith apple

• Raisins or currants instead of grapes

• Dried tart cherries instead of grapes

• Peeled, seeded, and diced cucumber

Serves 4 to 6

SECONDARY DISHES

• *Salmon Burgers (page 135)*

- **4 pounds package of chicken breasts**
  or
- **Leftover roasted or poached chicken breasts**
- **Industrial-size package of bacon**
- **Large package of gorgonzola or any blue cheese**
- **Hass avocados**

WHAT TO DO WITH IT

- If using fresh chicken breasts, poach 2 whole breasts (page 162) and double-wrap, label, date, and freeze the balance for up to 6 months.

- If using leftover chicken breasts, you'll need 2 whole breasts, skin removed, for this recipe.

- Remove bacon from its packaging and set aside 6 slices; double-wrap the balance in plastic wrap, place in a freezer bag, label, date, and store in the refrigerator for up to 2 weeks, or in the freezer for up to 2 months.

- Set aside ³/₄ cup of cheese, loosely double-wrap the remainder, and store in the salad crisper section of your refrigerator.

SECONDARY

CHOPPED COBB SALAD

This all-American favorite dates back to 1926, when it was created at the infamous Brown Derby restaurant in Los Angeles by owner Bob Cobb (no kidding!), who was looking for a way to use up all the leftovers that he had piling up in the refrigerator. This fact, of course, makes Cobb Salad a perfect addition to BIG FOOD. Be as creatively wild or as tame as you'd like with this flexible classic.

2	whole chicken breasts, poached and cut into cubes (if using previously cooked chicken, remove skin and cut into 3 cups of cubed pieces)
6	slices bacon, cooked until very crisp and crumbled
2	Hass avocados, peeled, pitted, and cubed
³/₄	cup crumbled gorgonzola or other blue cheese
1	medium red onion, peeled and chopped
2	firm tomatoes, chopped
1	tablespoon extra virgin olive oil
	Kosher salt and freshly ground black pepper
1	lemon, cut into wedges

This salad can be prepared and served two ways:

In a large mixing bowl, gently toss together chicken, bacon, avocados, gorgonzola, onion, and tomatoes, keeping avocados intact. Drizzle lightly with oil, season to taste with salt and pepper, and serve with the lemon wedges.

Or, on a large platter, arrange in long stripes: chicken, bacon, avocados, gorgonzola, onion, and tomatoes. Drizzle all with oil, season with salt and pepper to taste, and serve with lemon wedges.

Serves 4 to 6

THE TRUTH ABOUT AVOCADOS

Yes, they are high in fat—the good kind. Yes, they are high in nutrients—the very good kind. So why don't we eat more avocados? For many of us, they're just a little bit mysterious. And they seem to rot quickly and are often expensive. If you find yourself staring at a bag of avocados, ask yourself what you plan on doing with them. If you're primarily interested in making guacamole, buy the bag, get them home, scoop the flesh (throw out the pit!) into an airtight container, and drizzle with lime or lemon juice. This concoction will freeze for up to 6 months; you can use it as you need it, adding spoonfuls of prepared salsa to it to create a quick and simple guacamole.

If you plan to slice up your ripe avocados and use them in salads, do this as you need them within a few days of bringing them home (sliced avocado does not refrigerate or freeze well).

WHAT TO DO WITH IT

- Store avocados the way you would bananas: if they are ripe, place them in the refrigerator and use within 2 days; otherwise, leave them on the kitchen counter until ripened.

HOW LONG IT WILL LAST

- The components for this salad can be prepared in advance and stored separately for up to 3 days, except for the avocado, which should be eaten immediately after it's been peeled.

- Once assembled, consume the salad within 2 days.

GRILLED VEGETABLE SALAD WITH CHICKEN AND PINE NUTS

Light and flavorful, this "salad" is perfect for those days when you go a little crazy at the discount club or the local farmer's market. It's flexible enough to be served hot or cold, spicy or mild, and with absolutely any vegetable that you may have on hand, along with leftover chicken pulled off the bone, or fresh chicken that's been poached or grilled for the occasion. A splash of balsamic vinegar lends a hint of sweetness, and toasted pine nuts add an incomparable texture.

1	medium eggplant, cut into 1/4-inch rounds	2	garlic cloves, peeled and smashed
1/4	teaspoon kosher salt, plus more for seasoning	3	large sprigs fresh rosemary or 1 tablespoon dried
1/2	cup raw, unsalted pine nuts	1 1/2	tablespoons extra virgin olive oil
6	medium bell peppers (any color), seeded, ribbed, and cut into 1-inch squares	3	cups cooked boneless chicken (poached and chilled, or grilled, roasted, or broiled, and pulled off the bone), cubed or cut into bite-size pieces
1	large onion (red, yellow, white, Spanish, or sweet), peeled and cut into chunks	1/4	cup balsamic vinegar
1	large zucchini, cut into chunks		Freshly ground black pepper
1	large yellow summer squash, cut into chunks		

Place eggplant in a colander, and toss with 1/4 teaspoon salt. Set over a plate or in the sink to drain for 30 minutes. Place pine nuts in a dry skillet (preferably cast iron), and toss over medium heat until they are golden, about 6 minutes. Set aside to cool.

Heat grill to medium. Toss drained eggplant and peppers, onion, zucchini, squash, garlic, rosemary, and oil together in a grill bowl. Set on the grill, cover, and cook, shaking the pan once every 10 minutes, until vegetables are soft and have begun to take on color, 30 to 35 minutes.

Combine chicken with vegetables, pine nuts, and vinegar; season to taste with salt and pepper.

WHAT YOU HAVE ON HAND

- **Too many vegetables: eggplant, zucchini, summer squash, onions (red, yellow, white, Spanish, or sweet), bell peppers (red, green, yellow, orange)**
- **Leftover chicken**
  or
- **Freshly poached chicken breasts**

WHAT TO DO WITH IT

- Prepare vegetables as described; store any surplus (except for eggplant) in a dated freezer bag in the crisper.

HOW LONG IT WILL LAST

- This salad gets better with age. Keep it refrigerated in a tightly sealed freezer bag or plastic container for 3 to 5 days.

SPECIAL TOOLS YOU'LL NEED

- Grill bowl. If you do not have one, follow roasting tip.

VARIATIONS:

- Substitute cubed leftover cooked swordfish or pork for the chicken.
- While the vegetables are on the grill or in the roasting pan, add a handful of golden raisins.
- Use leftover salad for Stuffed Tomatoes.

Serves 4 to 6

If you don't have a grill bowl, it's a great tool to add to your collection; you can pick one up at any home store. As an alternative, you can oven roast the vegetables. Simply heat your oven to 400°F, chop vegetables and place in a baking dish, season with salt and pepper, toss with extra virgin olive oil, and roast until browned and softened, about 40 minutes, shaking the pan frequently.

ADDITIONAL SERVING RECOMMENDATIONS

- Serve as a main-course salad with a glass of cold Traditional Gazpacho (page 72).

SECONDARY DISHES

- *Stuffed Tomatoes (page 90)*

SECONDARY

STUFFED TOMATOES

A spectacular and highly creative leftover vehicle for those extra tomatoes you have around the kitchen every August, this quick, unconventional salad dish also offers a terrific way to use up leftover rice, bits of soft cheese, or even other salads such as tuna, chicken, or shrimp. Serve it elegantly, and no one will be the wiser.

6	medium, firm, fresh tomatoes		Extra virgin olive oil
	Kosher salt	$2/3$	cup soft cheese (for baked version)
2	cups leftover cooked white, brown, or fried rice; or Risotto (page 150) (for baked version)	2	cups leftover tuna, chicken, shrimp, or salmon salad (for chilled version)
	Freshly ground black pepper		

Slice $1/8$ inch off the stem-end of each tomato, and carefully scoop out the pulp to leave a shell approximately $1/4$-inch thick. Sprinkle the inside of each tomato lightly with salt, and invert onto a plate to drain for 30 minutes. Be judicious when salting tomatoes, which are salty on their own; err on the side of caution.

To serve hot: Preheat oven to 350°F. Stuff each tomato with leftover rice, season with salt and pepper, and drizzle with oil. Bake until tomatoes are soft but maintain their shape, about 15 minutes.

Alternatively, stuff with a combination of rice and cheese, bake at 350°F for 8 minutes. Sprinkle with extra cheese on the top, and broil for 3 minutes, until the cheese is melted and golden brown.

To serve cold: Stuff each tomato with the salad, drizzle with oil, and refrigerate for 1 to 2 hours. Serve cold.

VARIATIONS:

- Stuffed Tomatoes à la Grecque: Stuff with black olives and feta, and serve hot.
- Stuff with Grilled Vegetable Salad with Chicken and Pine Nuts (page 88), and serve cold.
- Stuff with Tuna Salad Niçoise (page 100), and serve cold.
- Stuff with Mediterranean White Bean Salad with Tuna (page 98), and serve cold.

Serves 6

WHAT TO DO WITH IT

- Set aside 1 pound of spinach for this recipe; store the rest, in the cellophane bag it came in, in your salad crisper for up to 4 days. Creamed, or cooked into a casserole, spinach freezes exceptionally well for up to 6 months.

- Set aside 1½ cups of fresh mushrooms for this recipe. Poke a large freezer bag with approximately 10 fork holes on each side. Store the balance in this ventilated bag in the salad crisper for up to a week.

- Remove bacon from its packaging and double-wrap the balance, twice, in plastic wrap. Place in a freezer bag, date, and store in the refrigerator for up to 2 weeks, or in the freezer for up to 2 months. If using frozen bacon, set aside 6 strips, and let them thaw in the refrigerator before using.

PRIMARY

WARM SPINACH SALAD WITH MUSHROOMS AND BACON

This classic and deeply civilized recipe provides a wonderful way to use up the immense bags of fresh spinach you might have in your fridge. Make this salad big or small, for brunch, lunch, or dinner. It's not necessary to cook the spinach in advance: the warmed dressing will wilt the greens. Enjoy it as is, or top with a poached or soft-boiled egg, or a warm garlic crouton, for a little more pizzazz.

VINAIGRETTE:

2	tablespoons red wine vinegar
1	teaspoon Dijon mustard
6	tablespoons extra virgin olive oil

Kosher salt and freshly ground black pepper

Optional: 1 small garlic clove, peeled and minced

SALAD:

1	tablespoon extra virgin olive oil
1	medium shallot, peeled and minced
	Freshly ground black pepper
1½	cups thinly sliced fresh mushrooms (white button, baby bella, cremini)

6	bacon strips, cooked until crisp, and then crumbled
1	pound fresh spinach, cleaned, dried, stemmed, and torn into small pieces

Optional: freshly grated Parmesan cheese

FOR THE VINAIGRETTE:

In a small bowl, whisk together vinegar and mustard. Drizzle in oil, whisking well to emulsify. Add minced garlic, if using. Season to taste with salt and pepper. Set aside.

FOR THE SALAD:

Heat oil in a small sauté pan over medium heat, until rippling but not smoking. Add shallot and cook, stirring to avoid burning, until translucent, about 5 minutes. Season with pepper.

Add mushrooms, reduce heat to medium-low, and cook until liquid is released into the pan, 7 to 8 minutes. Add bacon, and stir. Thin the mixture, if necessary, with a teaspoon of water.

In a small saucepan, heat the vinaigrette until warm.

Place spinach in a large wooden bowl. Add bacon mixture and vinaigrette, and toss together well. Serve with freshly grated Parmesan cheese, if using.

VARIATIONS
- In place of vinaigrette, top the salad with a hot poached egg, freshly cracked black pepper, and freshly grated Parmesan cheese. The hot egg will coat and wilt the spinach leaves magnificently.

Serves 4 to 6

Dress the entire salad only if you are not planning to use any leftovers. Otherwise, keeping the dressing in a separate bowl will allow you to store the leftover salad dry, then serve it again the next day.

HOW LONG IT WILL LAST

- Dressed, this salad should be served immediately.
- The dry, undressed portion can be mixed together and stored in a very large freezer bag poked with holes for up to 3 days.

WHAT YOU HAVE ON HAND

- **3 pounds boneless chicken breasts**
  or
- **3 pounds chicken breast on the bone, ribs and skin still attached**
  or
- **3 pounds chicken thighs, on or off the bone**
  or
- **Leftover cooked chicken meat, without skin**
- **BIG FOOD Mediterranean Spice Blend (page 39)**

WHAT TO DO WITH IT

- Set aside 1 pound of chicken for this recipe.
- If you plan on cooking additional chicken recipes within the next 3 days, double-wrap what you need in plastic, place it in a dated freezer bag, and refrigerate it for up to 3 days.
- Double-wrap the balance in plastic; place it in a labeled, dated freezer bag; and freeze it for up to 6 months.

HOW LONG IT WILL LAST

- Dressed, this salad will keep, refrigerated, for up to 3 days.
- Without dressing, it will keep, refrigerated, for up to 5 days.

PRIMARY/SECONDARY

WARM GRILLED CHICKEN SALAD WITH HERBS

This luscious dish offers a unique and healthy twist on everyone's favorite tried-and-true chicken-salad recipe, which generally calls for cooked chicken that's been blended with an often heavy mayonnaise-based dressing. Here, warm, char-grilled chicken (breasts, inexpensive thighs, or leftover meat) is tossed in a sweet-and-savory bath of balsamic vinegar, extra virgin olive oil, and fresh garlic, for a flavor that is mouthwateringly tasty, nutty, and clean. Remember, the better the quality vinegar and oil you use, the better the salad will be!

DRESSING:

1	cup extra virgin olive oil	1	garlic clove, peeled and minced or pressed
$\frac{1}{3}$	cup balsamic vinegar		

Optional: *pinch of sugar*

SALAD:

2	whole chicken breasts, ribs and skin attached; or 4 boneless chicken breast halves; or 1 pound of leftover chicken meat, cubed; or $1\frac{1}{2}$ pounds chicken thighs, on the bone	1	large celery stalk, chopped
		2	medium red bell peppers, seeded, ribbed, and chopped
		2	medium green bell peppers, seeded and chopped
2	tablespoons extra virgin olive oil	1	tablespoon herbes de Provence or 1 tablespoon BIG FOOD Mediterranean Spice Blend
	Pinch of kosher salt		
1	large Vidalia or other sweet onion, peeled and chopped		

The recipe makes more dressing than you'll need for the chicken, so you'll have extra. Try it on everything from simple greens to cold beef salad. Stored in a tightly sealed jar in the refrigerator, this dressing will last for 1 week. Simply shake it up when you want to use it.

FOR THE DRESSING:

Prepare the dressing by placing oil, vinegar, garlic, and sugar, if using, in a small jar with a tightly fitting lid. Shake and set aside.

FOR THE SALAD:

Heat grill to medium-high. Rub chicken all over with oil and salt. Grill over indirect heat, turning frequently, until the internal temperature reads 160°F and juices run clear.

If you are using leftover chicken meat, toss it with oil and salt, and place it in a grill basket over indirect heat, turning frequently, until it is just heated through.

When cool enough to handle, cut into small pieces, discarding any bones. (If using breasts on the bone, cut through the breastbone with kitchen shears and then, using your hands, remove breast meat in two whole pieces. If using thighs, remove the bone.)

Combine onion, celery, peppers, and herbs in a mixing bowl.

Toss the warm chicken together with the vegetables and herbs, and pass the dressing around to each guest.

VARIATIONS
- The chicken can be grilled indoors, using an electric tabletop grill, or a grill pan with ridges.
- Add peeled, seeded, and chopped tomatoes, or a 15-ounce can of whole Italian-style plum tomatoes that have been drained and chopped.

Serves 4 to 6

ADDITIONAL SERVING RECOMMENDATIONS

- Serve warm, atop mixed greens that have been drizzled with fresh lemon juice and extra virgin olive oil.
- Serve at room temperature, atop a nest of warm spaghetti that has been lightly drizzled with extra virgin olive oil.
- Serve warm, atop a Fromage Blanc Crouton (page 50).

PRIMARY

ASIAN FRESH TUNA SALAD

This light and healthy, fresh tuna salad includes many of the complex and wonderfully harmonious sweet, salty, and spicy ingredients that are typical in everyday Asian cooking. Devoid of mayonnaise or any rich binding dressing, it can be made just as easily from water-packed canned tuna as from fresh tuna bought in larger pieces; the canned version is good; the fresh, simply out of this world.

DRESSING:

¼	cup honey	1	tablespoon fresh lime juice
½	cup soy sauce	1	garlic clove, peeled and finely minced
¼	cup rice vinegar	½	teaspoon ground ginger
2	tablespoons Asian sesame oil		Pinch of red pepper flakes
2	tablespoons sherry		

SALAD:

1	pound fresh tuna or 16 ounces canned, drained	½	cup fresh or frozen broccoli florets, parboiled or defrosted
¾	cup grated carrots	½	cup chopped scallions, white and green parts
¾	cup grated cabbage		

THE TRUTH ABOUT TUNA

We've all heard them: frightening reports of high mercury levels that translate into gloom and doom for fish lovers. With tuna, safety and quality vary from product to product. For example, imported Italian canned tuna (in airtight jars, as opposed to metal containers), which is packed in extra virgin olive oil, is often of vastly better quality than its domestic sibling. Similarly, some fresh tuna ("sushi grade," for example) is of higher quality than other fresh tuna. If you're buying the fresh stuff, make it a point to ask where it comes from, and check the mercury levels and advisories at http://vm.cfsan.fda.gov/~frf/sea-mehg.html if you have any concerns. But always remember the golden rule: No matter what you choose to eat, where you buy it, how you prepare it, or if it's fresh or canned, eat it in moderation, and—all else being equal—odds are you'll be safe.

FOR THE DRESSING:

In a small bowl, whisk together honey, soy sauce, vinegar, oil, sherry, lime juice, garlic, ginger, and pepper flakes. If using fresh tuna, reserve a quarter of the dressing for the fish, and leave the remainder for the salad.

FOR THE SALAD:

If using fresh tuna, coat the fish with the reserved dressing and heat grill to medium-high, or heat broiler. Grill over indirect heat or broil for approximately 3 minutes on each side for medium-rare. Remove from heat.

Combine carrots, cabbage, broccoli, and scallions. Add dressing, and toss. If using fresh fish, cut into $\frac{1}{2}$-inch cubes and add to salad. If using canned, flake well and add to salad.

Toss well and serve.

VARIATIONS

• Try poached, broiled, or grilled salmon, halibut, swordfish, or any firm-fleshed fish in place of tuna.
• Add sliced water chestnuts and bean sprouts.

Serves 4 to 6

This salad calls for grated carrots and cabbage, both of which are available, cleaned and grated, in the produce section of most supermarkets, so you can throw together salads and slaws in a flash. Try them with or in place of mixed greens.

ADDITIONAL SERVING RECOMMENDATIONS

• Serve as an appetizer over fresh greens, sprinkled with sesame seeds.
• Serve as a main course over fresh greens set atop a nest of cold Asian-style noodles, drizzled with this salad's dressing.

WHAT YOU HAVE ON HAND

- **2 pounds fresh tuna**
  or
- **1 (36-ounce) can of water-packed canned tuna**
  or
- **Small cans of canned tuna packed in olive oil**
- **Dried white beans, preferably cannellini**
  or
- **Large cans of cooked white beans**

WHAT TO DO WITH IT

- If fresh, grill or broil the tuna as in Asian Fresh Tuna Salad, and then divide in half.
- If canned, set aside the appropriate amount for this recipe, and store the balance in an airtight container in the coldest part of your refrigerator for up to 3 days.

PRIMARY

MEDITERRANEAN WHITE BEAN SALAD WITH TUNA

This quintessentially southern French dish is ripe with the flavors of the deep blue Mediterranean, where white beans show up on nearly every table, along with fresh rosemary, garlic, tuna, lamb, and shellfish. Dried beans hold their shape better than the canned variety, but don't hesitate to use well-drained canned beans if you'd prefer.

2	cups dried white beans, preferably cannellini
7	cups water
1	small head of garlic, cloves separated and peeled
4	small sprigs fresh rosemary, or 2 tablespoons dried
2	tablespoons extra virgin olive oil, divided

1	pound fresh tuna (or 16 ounces canned, preferably packed in olive oil)
⅓	cup diced red onion
½	cup chopped tomato
	Juice of 1 large lemon, divided
	Kosher salt and freshly ground black pepper

TO PREPARE THE DRIED BEANS:

Place the beans in a sieve, and wash them well. If you are soaking them, put them in a bowl of cold water to cover, refrigerate them overnight, then drain them and proceed. If you are *not* soaking them, increase their cooking time by 30 minutes.

Place the beans in a large saucepan, and add water, garlic, and rosemary. Bring to a simmer, cover the pot, and simmer for 1½ hours (if they have not been soaked) or until they are tender. (If they have been soaked, simmer for only 1 hour.) Remove the pot from the heat, and allow the beans to stand in their cooking liquid.

If you are using canned beans, omit the water from recipe. Drain the beans well and gently heat them through with the garlic and rosemary before draining them again. Do not let them simmer for longer than 5 minutes or they will get mushy.

TO PREPARE THE SALAD:

If using fresh tuna, heat grill to medium-high, or heat broiler. Using 1 tablespoon of oil, rub each side of the fish and grill over indirect heat or broil for 3 minutes per side for medium-rare. Remove from heat, and cut into ¼-inch cubes. If using canned tuna, drain tuna well. Set aside.

Drain the cooking liquid from the beans. Add onion, tomato, remaining 1 tablespoon oil, and half of the lemon juice. Mix well. Transfer beans to a platter or individual plates, top with tuna, and drizzle with the remaining lemon juice. Season to taste with salt and pepper. Serve at room temperature.

VARIATIONS
- Add chopped vegetables to the bean salad, including fresh fennel, steamed summer squash or zucchini, cooked eggplant, or Caponata (page 108).
- Substitute swordfish for the tuna.

Serves 4 to 6

DRIED BEANS: TO SOAK OR NOT TO SOAK

Dried beans are responsible for sending more cooks into a tailspin than perhaps any other dry pantry staple. Why? Some say they need to be soaked; some say they don't. Some say they produce more natural gas than Saudi Arabia and Iraq combined; some say they don't. But the bottom line is that dried beans are nutritious, extremely inexpensive, highly versatile, and just plain delicious in a way that canned beans most often are bland and lackluster. Nevertheless, I'll admit I was afraid of the dried variety until I stumbled upon the finest method I've seen for preparing them. Paul Bertolli, longtime chef at Chez Panisse and now chef owner of Oliveto in Oakland, California, has turned me into a fearless cannellini bean maker, thanks to this simple bean recipe, which lets you soak the beans (should you be convinced that that will make a difference in their texture and/or your stomach upset), or not. The change is in the cooking time; I've increased the amount of garlic and herbs, and the flavor is utterly delicious.

HOW LONG IT WILL LAST

- Because this salad is lightly dressed and composed of simple ingredients, it will last longer than your average dressed salad. Under refrigeration, this salad, with the beans and fish combined, will last up to 3 days if you're using canned tuna, and up to 2 if you're using fresh.
- Cooked, undressed cannellini beans will freeze for up to 3 months (see page 112 for more on beans).

SECONDARY DISHES
- *Stuffed Tomatoes (page 90)*
- *White Bean Hummus (page 112)*

WHAT YOU HAVE ON HAND

- 2 pounds fresh tuna
  or
- 1 (36-ounce) can of water-packed tuna
  or
- Half of the fresh tuna set aside from the Meditteranean White Bean Salad with Tuna

WHAT TO DO WITH IT

- If using fresh tuna, cook the entire piece, and then divide it in half for use in another recipe. Double-wrap it in plastic, and store it in a freezer bag in the coldest part of your refrigerator for up to 2 days.
- If using canned tuna, set aside the appropriate amount for this recipe, and store the balance for use in another recipe to be made within 3 days. Store it in an airtight container in the coldest part of your refrigerator.

HOW LONG IT WILL LAST

- Refrigerated, this salad will last up to 3 days, without dressing.

PRIMARY/SECONDARY

TUNA SALAD NIÇOISE

According to Mediterranean food expert Martha Rose Shulman, there are four ingredients that must always be included in traditional Niçoise: tuna, lettuce, tomatoes, and anchovies. Over the years, though, the salad has evolved to also include French string beans (haricots verts), cold boiled potatoes, hard-boiled eggs, peppers, and sometimes no lettuce at all. An ideal BIG FOOD salad because of its inherent flexibility, its only limitation is your creativity.

DRESSING:

2	tablespoons red wine vinegar	Kosher salt and freshly ground black pepper
1	teaspoon Dijon mustard	
6	tablespoons extra virgin olive oil	

SALAD:

6	small new potatoes, washed and diced	1	small head Boston lettuce, washed and torn into bite-size pieces
1/2	pound French green beans (haricots verts) or tender string beans	4	medium tomatoes, chopped
1 1/2	cups cooked diced tuna, or canned	5	anchovy fillets, rinsed
1	large red onion, peeled and chopped	3	sliced hard-boiled eggs

Optional: Toasted, crusty bread, 1 small garlic clove, peeled and minced

FOR THE DRESSING:

Whisk together vinegar and mustard in a mixing bowl. Drizzle in oil, whisking well to emulsify. Season to taste with salt and pepper.

FOR THE SALAD:

Fill a large bowl with water and ice cubes. Set aside.

Fill a medium saucepan $3/4$ of the way to the top, with cold water, and add $1/2$ teaspoon kosher salt. Bring to a boil, immediately add potatoes and beans, and continue to boil for 2 to 3 minutes, until the beans have become bright green. Drain the potatoes and beans, and plunge them into the ice water for 2 minutes, to halt their cooking. Drain, and set aside.

In a large wooden salad bowl, assemble by combining potatoes, tuna, onion, lettuce, and tomatoes. Top with beans, anchovies, and eggs. Drizzle with dressing, and serve at room temperature, with a slice of toasted, crusty bread that's been rubbed with a peeled garlic clove.

Serves 4 to 6

ADDITIONAL SERVING RECOMMENDATIONS

• Serve this as a luncheon dish or as a light dinner, along with a Fromage Blanc Crouton (page 50) that's been drizzled with extra virgin olive oil.

SECONDARY DISHES

• *Pan Bagnat (page 120)*
• *Stuffed Tomatoes (page 90)*

IN THE BEGINNING

BIG FOOD ON APPETIZERS AND OTHER SMALL DISHES

"The simplest hors d'oeuvres are the best."
—Elizabeth David

I know what you're going to say.

Who eats appetizers on top of the main course these days? For the home cook, the idea of preparing appetizers to be eaten prior to dinner just seems like extra work; you know who you are and how busy your life probably is, and likely it's more than enough for you simply to get dinner on the table and everyone around it at the same time.

But for the rushed and the harried among us (and who isn't either rushed or harried these days?), appetizers are lifesavers that can, along with a small bowl of soup and a light salad, make a lovely, satisfying, but not overly filling meal. The Mediterraneans have long understood this concept, and whether you're in Greece, eating mezes, or in Spain, enjoying tapas, the idea is virtually the same: enjoying small plates of different things is gratifying, generally healthy, appetizing, and even frugal because, in the end, everything gets used up deliciously and creatively.

So call them what you will: snacks, noshes, tiny bites, hors d'oeuvres, tapas, or mezes. Lay out a few and call the whole thing a meal. But whatever you call them, BIG FOOD appetizers—which include dishes that might be eaten as a light entrée or as part of a meal—consist of American favorites like spicy cakes made from the leftover fixings for a corn and black bean salad; hummus made from leftover white beans from white bean salad; Italian-style cooked rice balls that have been mixed with cheese and lightly fried; and *Pan Bagnat*, a traditional French tuna salad sandwich that, when made between two slices of tiny cocktail bread, makes for fabulous finger food.

But most important, these appetizers offer a brilliant way to use up what you bring home in bulk: many of them freeze well, and those that don't have a long refrigerator shelf life.

- 3 cups of leftover Spicy Southwestern Corn, Crab, and Black Bean Salad, undressed, without the crabmeat (page 82)

WHAT TO DO WITH IT

- Set aside 1 cup of the salad, and mash it with a potato masher or pulverize it in a food processor.

HOW LONG IT WILL LAST

- Cooked Spicy Corn and Black Bean Cakes will keep for 3 to 4 days in the refrigerator, double-wrapped in plastic and stored in heavy-duty freezer bags.

- Cooked Spicy Corn and Black Bean Cakes will freeze for up to 6 months, double-wrapped in plastic and stored in heavy-duty freezer bags.

SECONDARY

SPICY CORN AND BLACK BEAN CAKES

Delicious components from the Spicy Southwestern Corn, Crab, and Black Bean Salad needn't languish in a bowl in the back of your refrigerator; these savory cakes are reason enough to make the salad to begin with. Perfect as a base for a poached or fried egg, perhaps topped with your favorite salsa, they make a divine brunch dish, a simple picnic snack that travels very well, or a quick dinner that freezes brilliantly for the long haul.

3	cups leftover, undressed Spicy Southwestern Corn, Crab, and Black Bean Salad, with no added crab
2	eggs, lightly beaten, or $1/2$ cup egg substitute, lightly beaten
$1/2$	cup bread crumbs or cracker crumbs
	Pinch salt
$1/4$	cup canola oil

Place 1 cup of the salad in a large mixing bowl and, using a potato masher, pulverize to a chunky paste. (Alternatively, you can do this in a food processor.) Add to the rest of the salad and blend well.

Add eggs, bread crumbs, and salt. Combine well and form into 12 patties. Refrigerate, covered, for 1 hour, or up to 4 hours, before cooking.

Heat oil in a heavy-duty nonstick sauté pan or a well-seasoned cast-iron pan over medium-high heat, until rippling but not smoking.

Add cakes to the pan, press flat with a spatula, and cook until crispy on the outside and heated through on the inside, 8 to 10 minutes. Drain on paper towels, and serve.

Yields approximately 12 cakes

ADDITIONAL SERVING RECOMMENDATIONS

- Serve at room temperature on fresh salad greens, topped with a poached or fried egg.
- Serve hot, topped with Sicilian Eggplant Salad (page 108).
- Serve hot, as a quasi-veggie burger, on a multigrain roll with sliced red onion and fresh lettuce.

HOW TO REHEAT FRIED FOODS

Have you ever tried to reheat leftover fried foods, only to find that the oil and grease have sort of—well, there's no nice way to say it—congealed during the storage process? There is a better way:

- Do not attempt to reheat fried foods in the microwave. You'll wind up with something soft, gummy, and soggy, rather than crunchy and hot on the outside and cooked and tender on the inside, which is what frying is all about.
- Heat your oven to 350°F. If you have a convection oven, all the better: heat it to 300°F, convection setting. Keep it at that temperature for 8 minutes.
- Grease a baking sheet very lightly with cooking spray or oil.
- Reduce the oven temperature to 275°F. Place the fried leftovers on a baking sheet, and reheat in the oven until heated through, about 10 minutes.

WHAT TO DO WITH IT

- Designate a freezer-proof, dated container specifically to house chicken livers.
- Every time you bring home a chicken, extract the liver from the giblet bag, and pop it in the container in the freezer. Just be sure to use the livers within 6 months; otherwise, discard.

HOW LONG IT WILL LAST

- The prepared chicken livers will last, frozen, for up to 6 months, double-wrapped in plastic and stored in a plastic container.
- The prepared chicken livers will last up to 3 days in the refrigerator, double-wrapped in plastic and sealed in a glass container.

SECONDARY

CHICKEN LIVER CROSTINI ALLA TOSCANA

The first thing I do upon bringing home large quantities (or even small quantities) of whole chickens is reach inside each bird, extract the giblet bag, and place the liver in a small container in my freezer. Often overlooked and tossed into the garbage, chicken livers are inexpensive, wonderful nuggets of concentrated flavor and protein. This traditional Tuscan appetizer is richly textured and layered with flavor; plus, it freezes brilliantly, so you can make it ahead and always have it on hand to spread on good Italian bread.

1 pound chicken livers	Freshly ground black pepper
1 tablespoon unsalted butter	Toasted slices of Italian bread for serving
1 tablespoon extra virgin olive oil	
2 anchovy fillets, finely chopped	

Optional: *1 tablespoon chicken stock, 1 tablespoon cognac, fresh parsley for garnish*

SAUTÉING IN OIL AND BUTTER

Sautéing in small amounts of extra virgin olive oil together with butter accomplishes two things:

- The oil prevents the butter from burning.
- The butter provides incomparable flavor and hastens the searing and browning of meats and vegetables.

Chicken livers are extremely high in fat and cholesterol even *without* the addition of butter, but butter helps lessen the bitter edge of the liver. Enjoy this dish in moderation—but enjoy it nonetheless.

Wash and dry chicken livers, and remove any membrane that may still be intact.

Warm butter and oil together in a heavyweight sauté pan over medium heat, until butter begins to lightly foam and sizzle. Do not let it burn.

Add chicken livers and sauté carefully (they have a tendency to burst if heated too quickly), until they are just pink inside. Remove from pan, place on a cutting board, and chop.

Place the livers in the bowl of a food processor, add anchovies, and pulverize to the consistency of a thick paste. If paste is too thick, add chicken stock and/or cognac. Add pepper to taste.

Serve at room temperature on toasted slices of Italian bread, topped with fresh chopped parsley.

Yields 1 cup of spread, serving approximately 6

If you are using previously frozen chicken livers, it is important to defrost them slowly, under refrigeration. Do not defrost at room temperature or in the microwave.

ADDITIONAL SERVING RECOMMENDATIONS

- Serve this Chicken Liver Crostini Alla Toscana on top of curly frisée salad greens, lightly dressed with extra virgin olive oil and balsamic vinegar.
- Pass crostini as hors d'oeuvres.
- For those watching their carbohydrate intake, serve as a dip with raw vegetables, or wrapped in Boston lettuce leaves instead of atop toasted bread.

PRIMARY

SICILIAN EGGPLANT SALAD (CAPONATA)

Some call this delicious, sweet and savory southern Italian dish Eggplant Relish; others call it Eggplant Salad. I call it magnificent, easy to put together, and a wonderful way to use up the vast quantities of eggplant, tomatoes, onions, and raisins that are available in bulk all year round. Make this dish in quantity, freeze some of it, and add pine nuts to the leftovers to create a traditional-style southern Italian pasta sauce.

2	tablespoons extra virgin olive oil	1/2	cup golden raisins
4	pounds eggplant, trimmed and cut into 1/2-inch cubes	1/4	cup capers, drained of their juice
2	large onions, peeled and chopped	1/4	cup balsamic vinegar
4	garlic cloves, peeled and minced	1/2	tablespoon dried basil
2	large red bell peppers, seeded, ribbed, and thinly sliced	1	tablespoon sugar
2	large green bell peppers, seeded, ribbed, and thinly sliced		Sliced Italian bread, water crackers, and/or raw vegetables for serving
4	large ripe tomatoes, chopped, or 3 cups canned Italian-style plum tomatoes, drained and chopped		

Heat oil in a large saucepan or sauté pan (preferably nonstick) over medium-high heat, until rippling but not smoking. Add eggplant, and stir well until it appears to soak up all the oil and begins to soften and turn golden brown, about 8 minutes.

Add onions, and cook slowly until they start to become translucent. Add garlic, peppers, tomatoes, raisins, capers, vinegar, basil, and sugar, blending well. Bring to a low simmer, cover, and cook for approximately 10 minutes. Taste for seasoning.

Serve hot, warm, or cold as a dip for sliced fresh Italian bread, water crackers, and/or raw vegetables.

VARIATIONS

- Add a handful of toasted pine nuts.
- Add pitted green olives.
- Add 1/2 cup tomato paste.
- Add a teaspoon of red pepper flakes.
- Add pounded anchovy fillets.
- Add fresh or dried oregano.

Serves 6

ADDITIONAL SERVING RECOMMENDATIONS

- Serve Caponata over hot tubular or flat pasta, such as spaghetti, bucatini, or pappardelle, and pass fresh Parmesan around at the table.

- Spoon Caponata onto packaged pizza dough, sprinkle with freshly grated Pecorino Romano cheese, and bake at 500°F for 8 minutes or until done.

SOGGY EGGPLANT = GREASY CAPONATA

Anyone who has ever made anything with eggplant knows that it has the consistency of a sponge: when you attempt to sauté it, all of the oil that you put in the pan miraculously disappears. Why? It gets sucked up by the eggplant. So you add more. Then *that* gets sucked up by the eggplant. So you add more. The result? A finished dish covered by an oil slick. There is a way around this: light salting.

Whether you plan to sauté your eggplant, bake it, or grill it, lightly salting this savory fruit prior to cooking, and then giving it time to drain, literally changes its cellular structure, thereby preventing it from absorbing oil. To do this, slice up the eggplant in the manner required by your recipe. Place it in a colander, and very lightly sprinkle it with kosher salt (or sea salt) on both sides. Let it stand for approximately 10 minutes. Pat the eggplant with a paper towel, and proceed with the recipe.

WHAT TO DO WITH IT

- This recipe calls for 1 pound (which is 2 cups, or 16 ounces) of ricotta. If you have less than that on hand, simply divide the recipe accordingly; for example, if you have 8 ounces of ricotta, cut the recipe in half.

- If you have more than 1 pound of cheese, measure out 2 cups for this recipe, and reserve the balance to use within 5 days, or freeze it for up to 4 months.

HOW LONG IT WILL LAST

- Baked ricotta is best served immediately but will last in a crock, tightly covered with plastic wrap, for 2 days. Reheat gently in a water bath.

PRIMARY

BAKED RICOTTA

Humongous containers of ricotta—full-fat, low-fat, nonfat—are now available every-where, often in lieu of the smaller sizes that most of us need only when we're making pasta dishes such as lasagna. This astoundingly easy dish can be infused with any variety of fresh or dried herbs and served savory or sweet. Delicious and soothing, it will become your favorite way to use what's clogging up the refrigerator after a lasagna dinner. Best of all, it's lower in fat than most cheese-based dishes; if you're watching your cholesterol intake, replace the eggs with an egg substitute.

1	pound ricotta cheese, low-fat or full-fat	$\frac{1}{2}$	teaspoon salt
2	eggs or $\frac{1}{2}$ cup egg substitute		Crackers and/or toasted bread rounds for serving
2	tablespoons chopped fresh basil or rosemary		

Optional: $\frac{1}{2}$ tablespoon grated lemon zest

Preheat oven to 400°F .

In a large bowl, combine ricotta, eggs, basil, salt, and lemon zest, if using. Blend well.

Fold the mixture into a 6-inch springform pan that has been greased with extra virgin olive oil, and place the pan in an oblong baking dish. Fill the baking dish with boiling water so that the level of the water comes up halfway to the top of the spring-form pan. Carefully place in oven and bake until lightly colored, about 30 minutes. Increase heat to broil and continue to cook until the top is brown, about 5 minutes.

Remove from baking dish, let cool for 30 minutes, and unmold. Serve with crackers or toasted bread rounds.

VARIATIONS

- For dessert: In place of the herbs and salt, add 1 cup of sugar and the seeds from one vanilla bean (or ½ teaspoon vanilla extract if pods are not available) to make Sweet Baked Ricotta; top with fresh or canned fruit, or sliced and broiled fresh figs.
- For a smoother texture, add ½ cup softened cream cheese to the ricotta, and beat lightly with an electric mixer to combine well.
- For a denser texture, increase the amount of cheese by ¼ cup, and decrease the number of eggs you are using by one.

Serves 4 to 6

THE CHEESE FREEZE

Can you freeze cheese, or can't you?

Although some purists say no, many home cooks (including me) believe that you absolutely *can* freeze certain cheeses successfully (you freeze lasagna, don't you?). Just don't defrost cheese in the microwave, and don't expect it to be the pinnacle of perfect texture, either. Bear in mind the following before you freeze your cheese:

- Cheeses with a high water or fat content usually freeze the best.
- Frozen cheeses develop a grainy texture when defrosted and are therefore suited primarily to cooking.
- *Save those rinds!* Cheese rinds from fresh Pecorino Romano, Parmesan, Asiago, or Manchego can be double-wrapped in plastic and frozen for 6 to 8 months. Add them to tomato-based soups for a delicious hit of flavor.
- Defrost frozen cheeses in the refrigerator, not at room temperature or in the microwave.
- Cheeses that freeze well include ricotta, mozzarella, Cheddar, Parmesan, Pecorino Romano, Asiago, Manchego, Camembert, and Brie.
- Freeze your cheese by double-wrapping it in plastic, then placing it in a dated, heavy-duty freezer bag. Freeze for up to 6 months.

ADDITIONAL SERVING RECOMMENDATIONS

- Serve Baked Ricotta as an accompaniment to a cold vegetable platter.
- Top with excellent-quality extra virgin olive oil.
- Serve with Oven-Roasted Tomato Soup (page 71) or Sicilian Eggplant Salad (page 108).

WHAT TO DO WITH IT

- Reserve 4 cups of beans for this recipe. Place the balance in a heavy-duty freezer bag, and freeze canned beans for up to 6 months; or store remaining dried beans in a heavy-duty freezer bag in a cool, dark location for up to 12 months.
- Dried beans keep for 12 months when stored in a cool, dark location, in an airtight container or tightly sealed freezer bag; un-opened canned beans should be stored in a cool, dark location and used within 18 months.

HOW LONG IT WILL LAST

- White Bean Hummus will keep, re-frigerated, for 4 days.

ADDITIONAL SERVING RECOMMENDATIONS

- Serve with fresh vegetables or as a base for grilled or poached fish, chicken, or shellfish.

PRIMARY

WHITE BEAN HUMMUS

Beans—dried or canned—are extremely inexpensive, very healthy, and available in large quantities in nearly every large supermarket and discount club from one end of the country to the other. Traditional hummus (opposite page) is made from garbanzo beans, those protein-packed babies that are nutty in flavor. But hummus doesn't have to begin (or end) with garbanzos: this delectable White Bean Hummus can be made with or without tahini (sesame paste), garlicky or less so, and can be used not only as a conventional dip, but as a sandwich spread as well.

4	cups canned white beans, drained and rinsed	¼	teaspoon cayenne pepper
3	tablespoons fresh lemon juice	¼	teaspoon cumin
2	tablespoons extra virgin olive oil		Salt
2–3	garlic cloves, peeled		Toasted pita triangles for serving

Optional: 1 to 2 tablespoons tahini

Place the beans, lemon juice, oil, garlic, cayenne, cumin, and tahini, if using, in the bowl of a food processor, and pulse until completely blended. Add salt to taste, and serve with toasted pita triangles.

Serves 6

Beans that can be substituted for white beans in this recipe include:
- Fava, or broad (parboil them and re-move their waxy skins prior to further cooking)
- Azuki
- Cranberry
- Flageolet
- Great northern

When storing beans in the freezer, remember to allow room for expansion in the storage vessel. Fill your freezer bags or plastic containers only up to ¾ full.

TRADITIONAL HUMMUS

Classically called Hummus Bi Tahini, this magnificent and ancient spread marries the flavors of the Middle East—garbanzo beans (also known as chickpeas), sesame, lemon, and spices—to create a nutty, sweet, tart, and brightly flavored dip that grows even more flavorful over time.

4	cups garbanzo beans, drained	3	garlic cloves, peeled
3	tablespoons tahini	2	teaspoons ground cumin
2	tablespoons extra virgin olive oil		Juice of 1 lemon
2	tablespoons water		Toasted pita triangles for serving

Optional: *1/2 teaspoon cayenne pepper, additional garlic cloves*

Place beans, tahini, oil, water, garlic, and cumin in the bowl of a food processor. Pulse until smooth. Add lemon juice and cayenne pepper, if using. Serve with toasted pita triangles.

Serves 6

Hummus that is made with tahini very often can be oily. This recipe cuts down on the amount of tahini and adds a small amount of water to create a smoother texture.

WHAT YOU HAVE ON HAND

- **Large cans of garbanzo beans**

WHAT TO DO WITH IT

- Set aside the amount called for in this recipe, and store the balance in a heavy-duty freezer bag in the freezer for up to 6 months.

HOW LONG IT WILL LAST

- Hummus will last up to 5 days in the refrigerator.
- Hummus can be frozen in plastic containers for up to 6 months. Thaw in the refrigerator; do not thaw at room temperature or in the microwave.

ADDITIONAL SERVING RECOMMENDATIONS

- Serve with fresh vegetables, as part of a meze menu.
- Serve as a base for grilled or poached fish, chicken, or shellfish.

WHAT YOU HAVE
ON HAND

WHAT YOU HAVE ON HAND

- **Leftover risotto**

WHAT TO DO WITH IT

- Set aside approximately 3 cups cooked risotto for this recipe.

HOW LONG IT WILL LAST

- Ideally, rice balls should be served fresh and hot; they can be stored in a freezer bag in the refrigerator for up to 3 days and reheated in the oven.

SECONDARY

FRIED RICE BALLS WITH MOZZARELLA

Risotto purists insist that the sticky, glutinous Italian national rice dish cannot be served as a leftover. Hogwash. Traditionally called Arancine *by the very thrifty Italian cooks who invented fried rice balls, this is possibly the most delicious way to use up leftover risotto or any short-grain rice dish. Crunchy and hot on the outside, supple and tender inside, these snacks should be served hot, as an appetizer or even (dare we say) a midnight snack.*

3	cups leftover cooked risotto	2	eggs or $\frac{1}{2}$ cup egg substitute, lightly beaten
1	pound mozzarella, cut into $\frac{1}{2}$-inch cubes	$\frac{2}{3}$	cup bread crumbs, seasoned with salt, pepper, and garlic powder to taste
	Peanut oil for frying		

Take a small amount of the leftover risotto, and form it into a ball the size of a golf ball (about a $\frac{1}{4}$ cup).

Using your hands, make a small indentation, about the size of your fingertip, in the ball, and press a cube of mozzarella into it. Repeat until all of the risotto is formed into balls.

Heat $\frac{1}{2}$ inch peanut oil in a nonstick sauté pan until temperature reaches 365°F. If you do not have a deep frying or candy thermometer, simply drop a small piece of bread into the hot oil; the bread will turn brown within 1 minute when the oil is ready.

Roll each rice ball in the egg, and then the bread crumbs. Fry in batches, a few at a time, turning to crisp all sides, until golden brown. Serve hot.

VARIATIONS

• Add any chopped leftover vegetables to the rice before forming into balls.
• Add bits of leftover ham or sausage to the rice before forming into balls.
• Substitute goat cheese, Parmesan, Asiago, Pecorino Romano, sharp white Cheddar, or queso blanco for the traditional mozzarella.

Yields approximately 12 balls

As a Chinese-takeout aficionado, I have often been faced with the dilemma of what to do with all that wonderful leftover rice that fills up my refrigerator after an evening of Mu Shu Pork. Whether it's fried, steamed, white, brown, or any of the other marvelous strains that have cropped up of late, leftover rice makes a perfect snack when combined with scallions, egg, and soy sauce, then lightly fried in peanut or canola oil. But because Chinese rice tends to be long-grain, it doesn't contain as much gluten as short-grain white, brown, or sticky rice does. If you have a fridge full of leftover long-grain rice (originally fried or steamed), combine it with an egg, flatten it into individual patties, dust it lightly with bread or cracker crumbs, and let it "set" in the refrigerator before gently frying it.

This recipe is best made with plain or vegetable risotto, but it can easily be made with Risotto with Baby Shrimp and Peas (page 150).

ADDITIONAL SERVING RECOMMENDATIONS

• Serve as an appetizer; dip in BIG FOOD Marinara Sauce (page 42).
• Serve as a side dish with BIG FOOD Herb-Roasted Chicken (page 158) or Italian-Style Pork Roast with Fennel, Garlic, and Red Pepper (page 252).

WHAT TO DO WITH IT

- Set aside 1 cup of olives for this recipe; the balance should remain refrigerated in the jar and will keep for up to 10 days.

HOW LONG IT WILL LAST

- Stored properly and refrigerated, Marinated Black Olives with Garlic and Red Pepper will keep for approximately 3 days.

PRIMARY

MARINATED BLACK OLIVES WITH GARLIC AND RED PEPPER

These utterly addictive olives can be made just as easily with green olives as with black, although the black ones always seem meatier and more flavorful to me. Stick with imported olives in a jar for this recipe; the canned ones from California are better used in Tapenade (page 118). This recipe is loosely based on the remarkable marinated black olives served at the bar at New York's Union Square Café. Save the oil, and use it for drizzling on everything from pasta to fish to bread.

1	cup dry-brined black olives	2	garlic cloves, peeled
1	cup good-quality extra virgin olive oil	1	tablespoon fennel seeds
2	tablespoons fresh rosemary or 1½ tablespoons dried	1	teaspoon red pepper flakes
		1	teaspoon grated lemon zest

Place olives in a small colander or strainer, and rinse under water to remove brine. Shake dry, and place in a glass jar with a tight-fitting lid. Add oil, rosemary, garlic, fennel, pepper flakes, and lemon zest. Seal, shake, and let stand at room temperature for 4 hours prior to serving.

Yields approximately 1¹/₂ cups

NOT JUST FOR SNACKING

On their own, these marinated black olives are an elegant and easy-to-prepare nibble to enjoy with a glass of wine. And, if you're like me, you'll find yourself always having a batch on-hand. Likewise, you'll probably also wind up with a few stray leftovers that will linger in your fridge long after your guests have departed. What to do? Marinated black olives work beautifully sprinkled chopped or whole on:

- Broiled or poached fish
- Any pasta with tomato sauce
- Roasted or poached chicken
- Fresh tomatoes drizzled with extra virgin olive oil and garlic

ADDITIONAL SERVING RECOMMENDATIONS

- Toss a handful into BIG FOOD Marinara Sauce (page 42).
- Add to chicken or fish dishes.
- Drizzle the flavor-infused oil onto bread, chicken, fish, pasta, pork, or steak.

SECONDARY DISHES

- *Pan-Braised Chicken with Lemon, Thyme, and Black Olives (page 164)*
- *Mediterranean Tuna with Black and Green Olives, Capers, and Artichoke Hearts (page 140)*

PRIMARY

TAPENADE

Briny, salty, and nothing short of lovely when spread on slices of Italian or French bread, tucked underneath the skin of a chicken that's set to be roasted, or even dolloped into a bowl of hot pasta, this traditional Provençal "dip" makes use of three inexpensive ingredients that are often found in bulk quantities: olives, lemons, and anchovies. The better the olives, the tastier this paste will be, but canned black olives from California are perfectly suitable, so long as you use better-quality anchovies to make up for the blander-tasting canned olives.

1	cup black olives, pitted (preferably Greek, or brine-cured, but canned from California are acceptable)	2	tablespoons capers, rinsed
			Juice of 1 lemon
4	anchovy fillets	1/3	cup extra virgin olive oil
			Fresh vegetables, breads, or crackers for serving

Place olives, anchovies, capers, and lemon juice in the bowl of a food processor. Pulse slowly, adding the oil in a slow and steady stream. Serve at room temperature as a dip for fresh vegetables, breads, and crackers.

Yields approximately 1 1/2 cups

HOW TO PIT AN OLIVE

Years ago, when I worked at a famous cookware store in Manhattan, I bought all sorts of fabulous tools that now go unused. One of them is an olive pitter. Sure, it claims "ease of use" and in fact, that's actually fairly true. It *is* easy to use. But it's also slow and messy, and it reminds me of that glorified hole-punch used to pierce one's ears. The best way to pit a lot of olives (if you can't buy them already pitted) is simple, and it won't make a mess of anything more than your chef's knife, your chopping board, and your hands. And there's really no chance of sending a pit flying across the room, only to be stepped on at 3:00 A.M. the next morning by your great aunt Mabel, who is poking around, searching for a midnight snack.

- Set one olive on a cutting board in front of you.
- Take your chef's knife, and hold it with the edge (not the point) facing to the right of the olive.
- Carefully drag the dull side of the knife across the olive, lengthwise, applying pressure as you go. The pit will be expelled in the process.

There are about as many ways to prepare Tapenade as there are countries that pride themselves on this dish: Italy, Spain, and Morrocco all lay claims to versions of it, and with good reason. It uses up a massive surplus of basic pantry items (oil, olives, and anchovies), stores well, is fairly healthy, and always tastes delicious. Nevertheless, some folks prefer to omit the garlic or lemon juice, some add liquor (like cognac), some add herbs (thyme or rosemary), and some would just about faint at my suggestion to go ahead and use whatever black olives you can find, so long as they are not packed in vinegar! However you prepare it, the consistency should be fairly smooth, and the taste, robust.

Experiment with this dish, make it your own, and add to it:

- Dijon mustard
- Cognac
- Brandy
- Thyme
- Summer savory
- Tuna: canned or fresh
- Green olives instead of black, or a combination of green and black

ADDITIONAL SERVING RECOMMENDATIONS

- Serve Tapenade as a condiment for grilled fish, lamb, or chicken.
- Brush Tapenade onto store-bought puff pastry, drizzle with extra virgin olive oil, sprinkle with goat cheese and thyme, and bake until golden.

SECONDARY DISHES

- *BIG FOOD Herb-Roasted Chicken (page 158) rubbed with Tapenade*

PRIMARY/SECONDARY

PAN BAGNAT ("BATHED BREAD")

One of southern France's greatest contributions to street food, Pan Bagnat is simply a glorified tuna salad sandwich on a crusty roll that has been tightly wrapped in plastic, weighted down in the refrigerator for a few hours, and then served at room temperature. A far cry from that soggy, mayo-laden tuna sandwich that your mother sent you to school with, it is stuffed with many wonderful bulk ingredients—sweet peppers, tuna, anchovies, eggs, olives—and then seasoned with olive oil, vinegar, and freshly ground black pepper. It makes an impressive luncheon dish when prepared using a large round bread, and then sliced into wedges just before serving.

1	large, crusty round loaf of bread (not sourdough)	4-5	anchovy fillets, drained of their oil
2	cups leftover Tuna Salad Niçoise or 1 cup Italian-style, canned tuna (if using leftover Niçoise, proceed to the third-to-the-last ingredient)	2	hard-boiled eggs, sliced into rounds
2	tablespoons capers	1	large tomato, sliced into rounds approximately ¼-inch thick
¼	cup black olives, pitted and chopped	1	medium red onion, peeled and sliced into thin rings
1	(8-ounce) jar of roasted sweet peppers, drained, and sliced into ¼-inch strips	3	tablespoons extra virgin olive oil
¼	pound French string beans (haricots verts), blanched	1	tablespoon red wine vinegar
			Freshly ground black pepper

Carefully slice the loaf widthwise into two equal halves and set aside. If the bread is particularly thick and "doughy," pull out about ¼ cup of the inner bread to accommodate the filling.

JOHN ASH, MFK FISHER, AND PAN BAGNAT

Culinary legend holds that the brilliant food writer MFK Fisher once invited her California colleague, chef John Ash, to her house for lunch. They prepared Pan Bagnat, which Mrs. Fisher recommended Ash wrap in plastic and then sit on for several hours while they chatted. The result: a perfectly compressed, room (if not body) temperature Pan Bagnat. Preparing it BIG FOOD style is just as easy and probably a bit more sanitary.

(If using leftover salad Niçoise, proceed to the "assembly" stage.)

In a mixing bowl, combine tuna with capers, olives, peppers, string beans, and anchovies. Using clean hands, gently blend together until well mixed.

Arrange tuna mixture in an even layer in the bottom half of the bread. Add a layer each of eggs, tomato, and onion. Drizzle with oil and vinegar and season to taste with pepper.

Cover with top half of loaf; set sandwich on top of a piece of heavy-duty plastic wrap and seal tightly. Carefully turn over and repeat. The sandwich should be completely sealed.

Place sandwich on a heavy-duty baking sheet and top with a heavy weight. Refrigerate at least 4 hours or, ideally, overnight. Bring to room temperature prior to serving.

VARIATIONS
- Use a variety of sliced meats instead of salad.
- Replace the tuna with salmon or trout.

Serves 4 to 6

Any oil-and-vinegar-based tuna salad can be used for this recipe.

ADDITIONAL SERVING RECOMMENDATIONS

- Double or triple the ingredients and make this sandwich on a party-size round roll or on a long submarine (or hoagie) roll, cut into wedges, and serve at room temperature.
- Cut into thin slices and serve as an hors d'oeuvre.
- Keep well-wrapped in plastic wrap, and send it along in Junior's school lunch box.

A WEIGHTY ISSUE

The art of making compressed sandwiches has long been practiced everywhere, from Cuba (where the famed Cuban Sandwich is literally *pressed*) to Italy (where Panini is made on a sandwich press) to, of course, the south of France, where Pan Bagnat originates. But you needn't use a formal sandwich press in order to create the perfect Pan Bagnat. Nor do you need to follow MFK Fisher's lead (see opposite page). Just make sure that the weight you use is larger than the sandwich itself. What to use?

- A heavy cast-iron skillet or larger Dutch oven, into which you set another heavyweight saucepan
- A 5-pound weight from your home gym
- Several heavy cookbooks
- A heavy saucepan into which you place a heavy bag of sugar or flour

WHAT YOU HAVE ON HAND

- **1 (2-pound) package of sausage links: Cajun, andouille, bratwurst, frankfurters, chicken sausage, boudin blanc or noir, veal, Italian hot or sweet, or vegetarian**
- **Frozen puff pastry**

WHAT TO DO WITH IT

- Break packages of sausages apart and, if frozen, thaw in refrigerator.
- Store 1 pound of sausage links in the freezer in a dated, heavy-duty freezer bag for 3 to 6 months.

HOW LONG IT WILL LAST

- Pigs in Blankets will last approximately 4 days in the refrigerator, double-plastic-wrapped and sealed in a freezer bag.
- Pigs in Blankets will last 3 to 6 months frozen in heavy-duty freezer bags.

PRIMARY

PIGS IN BLANKETS

Pigs in Blankets do strange things to adults: no matter how healthy we claim to be, or how much we attempt to assure everyone around us at cocktail parties that fresh vegetables make the best appetizers, everyone adores Pigs in Blankets, and they always seem to turn adults into children. But everyone needs to grow up a little sometimes, and here's where store-bought pastry dough and fresh sausages come in. Adapted from a recipe by superstar Emeril Lagasse, these treats can be made well in advance and frozen.

1	pound sausage links, cut into 2-inch pieces	1	package frozen puff pastry, defrosted and cut into 2 x 4-inch rectangles

Preheat oven to 350°F.

Roll each piece of sausage in a rectangle of pastry dough and place, seam-side up, on a nonstick or lightly greased baking sheet.

Bake until pastry puffs and becomes golden-brown, about 10 to 15 minutes.

Serve hot, with a variety of mustards.

ADDITIONAL SERVING RECOMMENDATIONS

- Serve as a passed hors d'oeuvre with spicy mustard.
- Serve as a snack.
- Serve for dinner or lunch, with a lightly dressed mixed green salad.

VARIATIONS

- Vegetarians will enjoy this with meatless sausage; chicken lovers can use chicken sausage of any kind; spice fanatics will adore it with chorizo or spicy Italian sausage.

Yields approximately 15 pigs

HOW TO MATCH YOUR MUSTARD TO YOUR PIGS (OR YOUR SAUCE TO YOUR DOGS)

In this recipe, you've used up all of those huge packages of sausage you brought home, and adapted your favorite childhood hors d'oeuvre to your grown-up lifestyle. If you're a vegetarian, you've used vegetarian sausage. If you don't eat pork, you've used lamb, chicken, beef, or turkey sausage. But should you use the same, boring yellow mustard for all of them? Absolutely, unequivocally, No.

Here are a few simple (and always breakable) rules for matching your mustard to your meat:

- Match spicy to sweet: If your sausage is spicy (andouille, chorizo, hot Italian), dip into a honey or fruit-flavored mustard.
- Match sweet to spicy: If your sausage is sweet (mild Italian, lamb, chicken and feta, vegetarian), dip into a spicy, more full-bodied mustard.
- Match mild to mild: If your sausage is mild (bratwurst or kielbasa), dip into a mild, more traditional mustard, such as Dijon.

BRAIN FOOD

BIG FOOD ON FISH

> *"Guests, like old fish, begin to smell after three days."*
> —Benjamin Franklin

While I suppose it is a bit out of the ordinary to open a fish chapter in a cookbook with such a quote, it makes sense in BIG FOOD. Because, as you will soon see, fish stands tail and fins above every other BIG FOOD comestible as something that does *not* keep well for longer than a few days in the refrigerator, and does not freeze well at all. (That last statement is a divisive one. I am certain that many of you reading this will disagree: *"I've frozen uncooked fish before, and it's been perfectly edible,"* you say, and perhaps that's the case for you. But generally speaking, fresh fish that's been frozen by you, at home, is certain to be mealy and lackluster.) Sure, there are plenty of fish lovers out there who take advantage of the deeply discounted prices that buying in bulk offers: they come home toting an 8-pound salmon and think they're being prudent and culinarily judicious when they cut it up into 10 fillets, wrap them well, and store them in the freezer.

Wrong.

Wrong, wrong, *wrong*.

Unfortunately, most fish that's been frozen becomes mealy, spongy, watery, and virtually inedible after it's been frozen at home. Unless it's *fresh*—in other words, not frozen on the spot by the boat that caught it or the store it was delivered to—odds are that you are buying something that already was frozen *once* and thawed en route to the market, and now you're freezing it again, which is a BIG FOOD no-no. (For more on this subject, turn to page 18.) No matter how you look at it (but especially regarding texture), freezing fish is just not a good idea.

Of course, there *are* always exceptions to a rule, and here's one: While it's best to use the fish you bring home within 48 hours, there are certain fish *dishes* that, once cooked, freeze *so* well that I've taken to making them just because I want something in my freezer that I can take out in a few months' time, defrost, and have for dinner with a little fresh sauce and a glass of wine (all I have to worry about is the sauce and uncorking my wine bottle). For example, leftover Brandade—a traditional country French dish made by blending soaked salt cod with potatoes, milk, olive oil, and garlic—can be easily transformed into New England–Style Codfish Cakes with Lemon Sauce, which can be lightly pan-fried and then frozen for up to 4 months.

In this chapter you'll also see how Salmon Burgers can easily be made from leftover tamari-spiced salmon fillet; leftover fresh tuna can be tossed with lime juice, tequila, and jalapeños and reborn as refreshing Tuna Tacos; leftover smoked salmon makes a fine addition to Penne with Vodka, Cream, and Smoked Salmon; and all of those stray frozen shrimp you have kicking around in your cold pantry can be used to cook up Spiced Shrimp Boiled in Black Beer, an amazingly fast and easy dish. So if you get a hankering for these treasures from the deep every once in a while, think *ahead* about how you plan to use them, take advantage of buying them in larger portions, and get to work: the results are delicious.

KEEPING AN EYE ON THE NEWS: EVERYTHING IN MODERATION

Anyone who reads the paper or watches the news these days gets confusing and often contradictory information regarding fish intake. On the one hand, fish is supposed to be terrific for us: even the fattiest of the lot is a "lean protein" and what fat it does contain is arguably the good sort—omega-3 and omega-6—which many medical professionals believe can lower the risk of strokes and heart attacks, as well as some cancers. On the other hand, stratospherically high mercury levels in our waters have led the Food and Drug Administration to recommend that many of us, especially pregnant women and nursing mothers, refrain from eating certain kinds of tuna, specifically albacore, more than once a week, according to an article in the *New York Times*. Other charming information that has recently come to light is the use of potentially toxic orange dyes that make farmed salmon look like the naturally raised, wild-caught variety. What to do?

• Eat fish, like all foods, in moderation.
• If at all possible, refrain from buying fish that's been plastic-wrapped for too long.
• Make sure you look at bar-code dates, and if you have even a remote inkling that it's getting a little long in the teeth, have chicken instead.
• Know where your fish comes from geographically, and keep an eye on the news in case of mercury alerts.
• Take advantage of widely available "organic" fish, which, while farmed, is dye-free and fed organic feed.
• Buy wild-caught fish whenever you see it; the price per pound may be a bit more, but what you spend will be worth it once you taste the flavor difference.
• On a warm day, fresh fish can spoil in a parked car in less than half an hour, so get the fish home and into cold storage immediately. If that's not possible, take along a small cooler filled with ice packs to keep fish cold.

BUYING AND STORING YOUR CATCH

Most refrigerators won't keep fish as cold as it needs to be for the long haul, but if you plan to cook it within 24 hours, storing it in the coldest part of your refrigerator is suitable for all but the very largest of fish (whole salmon or mammoth halibut fillets). When you go shopping for fish, also bear in mind that the fishmonger or discount club may have had it for a while, and looks can be deceiving, especially under shrink wrap. In an ideal world, you, the consumer, would be able to see the fish unwrapped and examine it closely for any signs of bruising or decay.

A key rule for fish consumption is *be flexible*. If you go out looking for tuna because you're making a tuna recipe but the salmon looks fresher, buy the salmon. If you're buying shellfish—mussels, clams, oysters, lobster—make sure they're alive and kicking when you buy them. How to do this? With mussels, clams, and oysters, gently tap on a slightly opened shell with your finger; it should close up immediately. For lobster, have the fishmonger lift it out of its tank and hold it up so that you can see its underside; if it kicks, it's alive. If it doesn't move at all, it's either in shock or dead, and shouldn't be eaten by anyone. And never, *ever* buy a shrink-wrapped lobster, no matter how good the price.

My late grandmother, Bertha Altman, had an unbeatable way of telling if whole fish was fresh: "*If it looks back at you while you're looking at it, it's fresh.*" In other words, if its eyes are clear and its scales clean, odds are you have a good one; a whole fish should look as though it's just been lifted out of the water. Another way to determine freshness is to take a sniff: fresh fish should *not* smell fishy. Instead, it should smell sweet, like the air does when you're at the beach.

But what if the fish is already wrapped, and you can't examine its eyes and peek under its hood?

• Look *closely* for signs of decay: any peculiar coloring or edges that appear to be hard, rough, or discolored mean that you should leave it.

• Whole fish stays fresher longer than cut fish. If a fishmonger tries to sell you a wrapped piece of swordfish and a larger piece is sitting, unwrapped and fresh, in the refrigerator, have him cut you a piece from the larger portion. The price per pound should be exactly the same; don't be dissuaded that it isn't, and don't accept no for an answer. Go elsewhere if need be.

• Ask where the fish came from. If you're buying Chilean sea bass, it was certainly previously frozen before it got into your hands; if you're buying North Atlantic cod and you're in Boston, odds are that it is fresh.

• Any fish that you buy stuffed, such as sole, flounder, or trout stuffed with crabmeat, should be eaten the day that it's brought home.

• Check bar-code dates, just as you do when purchasing milk and eggs.

In terms of storing fish properly, ask three different people how to do it, and odds are you'll get three different answers. My rule of thumb is an easy one to remember: unless I'm dealing with something cured (salted or smoked, like salt cod, smoked salmon, smoked trout, or smoked whitefish), I cook what I've brought home—whole fish, filleted fish, or steaks—within 24 hours. When I bring home fresh shellfish, I always eat it that night. But if something comes up, or I've brought home a large quantity of fresh fish, I do the following:

• If I've purchased fish directly from a fishmonger and it is not shrink-wrapped, I leave it in the paper and loose plastic over-wrap it's packed in. I transport it home immediately (on ice, if I've come a distance) and put it in the coldest part of my refrigerator for up to 24 hours.

• If I've purchased fish at a discount club and it *is* shrink-wrapped, I take it home and immediately remove it from its plastic. Assuming that it smells fresh, I cut it into appropriate portion sizes (for example, one side of salmon will yield approximately three or four 2-pound fillets), put them onto a large dinner plate that

THE SNIFF TEST

It's always a good idea to make friends with your supermarket fishmonger or the fish buyer at your discount club, who can tell you what's fresh, what's come in most recently, where the fish is from, and if it's been previously frozen. If you have any doubts about freshness, ask to *sniff* the goods before you plunk down your hard-earned cash. If you are buying wrapped fish, you will have a tougher time discerning its freshness by smell for obvious reasons: most fishmongers will not let you unwrap their fish to take a whiff. But what if you can't sniff the fish before you buy it? Encyclopedic food writer Mark Bittman's suggestion is a smart and gutsy one: "Try buying it, opening the package on the spot, and, if the smell is at all off, handing it right back." In other words, remember who the customer is: you.

I've already refrigerated for an hour or two, and re-wrap them *on the cold plate*. This way, the plate keeps the fish chilled from the underside, and the refrigerated air chills the top.

• When buying live lobsters, I make absolutely sure that there are holes poked into their carrying bag (if it is plastic); upon getting home, I remove them from the bag, place them in a deep lasagna pan, and keep them for no more than a few hours, unwrapped, in the coldest part of my refrigerator. *Never be tempted to put them in cold water in a pot, sink, or bathtub.* If you're buying smoked fish (which is likely wrapped), slice off the amount you need for your recipe, and keep the rest of it on the foil-coated cardboard it came on. Tightly wrap an additional two layers of plastic wrap around it to create an airtight seal, and store it in your refrigerator for up to 7 days.

BASIC FISH AND SHELLFISH COOKING TIPS

• Cook firm-fleshed fish (such as salmon, halibut, swordfish, monk-fish, cod, and whitefish) for a total of 10 minutes per inch of thickness,

bearing in mind that it will continue to cook even after it's removed from its heat source.

• If you are grilling a firm-fleshed fish, grill it over indirect heat, rotating it every few minutes to get those much-sought-after hatch marks. Remember that fattier fish will flare up even over indirect heat and will likely cook faster—at least on the exterior.

• Flaky and tender, thin fillets (such as flounder, snapper, sea bass, hake, and haddock) are best cooked quickly under or over high heat. Cook until the exterior of the fish is opaque. By the time it reaches the table, it will be done.

• If you are cooking jumbo shrimp, add them to a previously heated sauté pan or boiling stockpot. Cook just until the shrimp turn red, about $2\frac{1}{2}$ minutes, and remove them to a plate or bowl for serving. By the time they've reached the table, they will be perfectly cooked.

• Large sea scallops are best when quickly pan-seared in a bit of hot oil or butter, then popped into the oven for finishing. Make sure scallops are dry before cooking to ensure a beautiful, golden crust.

• Check out the Poke Test (page 217): it works for fish too.

• As a former Bostonian and frequent visitor to Maine, I prefer this method for cooking lobster: fill a very large pot with 3 inches of salted water, bring it to a boil, put in the lobsters, cover, and steam them for 14 minutes for the first pound, adding 2 minutes per additional pound (for example, steam a 1½-pound lobster for 15 minutes). Jasper White, a Boston chef and owner of The Summer Shack, grills his lobsters—a delicious method that imparts a salty, harborside taste to the lusty crustaceans. Unfortunately, much as I love lob-

ster, I've never had the gumption to send the little critters to meet their maker in that particular manner. That's what restaurants are for.

Gone are the days (at least in my kitchen) of drinking only white wine with fish. Although champagne and oysters are a fabulous (and nearly always lust-inducing) combination, and the often very inexpensive and highly drinkable French Muscadet is a perfect match for sole, flounder, and any mild-flavored fish, it's nice to know that when it comes to general fish consumption, your options are much broader than that. Here are a few new wine matches to keep in mind when you have fish on the brain:

• Salmon: Oregon Pinot Noir, or Burgundy
• Firm-fleshed whitefish (swordfish, cod, monkfish): Tavel or Bandol dry rosé; Antechi Vigneti di Cantalupo Il Mimo, a medium-dry rosé made from the Italian Nebbiolo grape; or inexpensive reds from the Languedoc region of France

• When steaming mussels or clams, cook them just until their shells open up; discard the ones that don't: they've *already* met their maker.

WHAT YOU HAVE ON HAND

- **A side of fresh salmon**
  or
- **1 (3-pound) salmon fillet**

WHAT TO DO WITH IT

- If you are not curing the whole side, divide the salmon into two pieces—what you will cure and what you will save. Double-wrap the remaining piece in plastic, and store it in the refrigerator for up to 2 days.

HOW LONG IT WILL LAST

- Gravlax will last for up to a week in the refrigerator, double-wrapped in plastic and kept in a ziplock freezer bag.

PRIMARY
GRAVLAX

Luscious, tender smoked salmon is nothing more than salmon fillet that has been cured with (take a guess!) smoke, which literally "cooks" and flavors the raw fish over a period of time. Gravlax, a traditional Scandinavian twist on cured salmon, lightly cures the fish with sugar, salt, herbs, and a bit of liquor (either vodka or gin). The result is a relatively inexpensive, delicious way to use those very large pieces (or even whole sides) of fresh salmon fillet that you bring home from the discount club. Start out a few days in advance of a party; your guests will be stunned.

1	(3- to 4-pound) side of salmon, boned
½	cup kosher salt
½	cup granulated sugar
2	tablespoons freshly ground black pepper
⅓	cup vodka or gin
3	large bunches of dill, chopped
	Lemon wedges

Lay salmon on top of a piece of heavy-duty plastic wrap large enough to later wrap the fish with.

Combine salt, sugar, pepper, and vodka in a mixing bowl, and blend well.

Rub flesh of the fish with the mixture, distributing it very heavily, especially over the thicker parts of the fish. Press the mixture firmly into the fish's flesh, and cover with the dill.

Wrap fish well in plastic, and then again in foil. Place in a large, deep, glass baking dish and set at least 5 pounds of weight on top.

Refrigerate at least 48 hours and up to 72 hours. Open the wrapping, and turn the salmon over every 4 hours, basting every 12 to 14 hours.

When ready to serve, remove salmon from wrapping and, using the dull side of a knife, scrape away the salt mixture and the dill, and pat dry with a paper towel.

To cut the thinnest slices possible, place the salmon skin-side down and hold the knife flat against the surface of the fish as you slice across its length. Serve ice cold with lemon wedges.

VARIATIONS
- Replace the vodka or gin with whiskey, scotch, brandy, cognac, aquavit, or hard cider.

Serves 6 to 8

SLICING GRAVLAX

At places like New York's famed Russ & Daughter's or Zabar's, the fellows behind the smoked and cured fish counter slice their smoked or cured salmon *so* thinly that you can see right through each piece. Cutting this thinly takes practice because smoked or cured salmon tends to be sticky, but when serving fresh gravlax, there simply is no better way to slice it than as thinly as possible.

1. Lay the gravlax out on a perfectly flat surface.
2. Take a very sharp, flexible slicing knife (preferably 8 inches long), and lay it flat against the fish's surface.
3. Using your other hand as a guide, gently apply pressure to the edge of the knife, and move the knife in a slicing motion from one side of the fish to the other.

GRAVLAX FOR A CROWD

If you are able to purchase a whole salmon, have your fishmonger clean and bone it for you. Double the cure ingredients, proceed with the recipe, and wrap both sides of the fish together, flesh to flesh.

ADDITIONAL SERVING RECOMMENDATIONS

- Slice Gravlax as thinly as possible, and serve it at an elegant brunch with thinly sliced black bread, crème fraîche or cream cheese, minced red onion, and capers.
- Chop up leftover Gravlax and mix into scrambled eggs, along with chopped scallions.
- Slice Gravlax as thinly as possible, and serve with bagels and cream cheese.
- Serve at midnight on New Year's Eve, with toast points and champagne or sparkling wine.
- Serve as a light lunch, with a side of Dijon mustard.

SECONDARY DISHES

- *Leftover uncooked or uncured salmon may be used to make Curried Salmon Salad with Grapes and Walnuts (page 84), Salmon Burgers (page 135), or Wine-Poached Salmon Fillet with Herbes de Provence and Horseradish Cream (page 132).*

WHAT TO DO WITH IT

- Plan to poach all the fish.
- If you've brought home a whole side of fresh salmon, lay it on a clean, dry countertop, and run your palm gently over its surface. If there are any small bones still lurking in the flesh, gingerly pull them out with the help of a pair of needle-nose pliers. Slice away the pointy tail end of the fish and the thinner head end, so that you're left with a piece of relatively even thickness. You'll poach the smaller, uneven pieces, but will reserve them for salmon burgers and/or salads.

WINE-POACHED SALMON FILLET WITH HERBES DE PROVENCE AND HORSERADISH CREAM

The first time I watched anyone poach a salmon, it was Martha Stewart, whose fish was so huge that she actually suggested cutting its head off to get it into what was clearly a very expensive, very heavy, oval copper fish poacher from France. There is a much easier (and inexpensive) way to accomplish the task, and the results are the same: a flavorful yet mild dish that can be served warm or cold with a dollop of BIG FOOD Aioli (page 35) or horseradish cream, and later reworked in salads, or as fish cakes or burgers. Poach fillets—even whole fillets—instead of the entire fish (you don't need to poach the head or the tail) using the largest lasagna pan you can find, and then serve the finished dish on a beautiful oval platter, surrounded by sliced lemons and watercress.

1	(4- to 5-pound) side of boned salmon or 4 (1-pound) fillets, skin intact
2	tablespoons herbes de Provence
½	tablespoon kosher salt
1	bottle inexpensive dry white wine or white vermouth
1	tablespoon prepared white horseradish (mild or spicy)
½	cup sour cream (fat-free, low-fat, or full-fat)
½	tablespoon fresh dill leaves

LEAVE THE SKIN ON!

For most people, salmon skin is a bit unsightly. However, it serves a purpose during the poaching, roasting, broiling, or grilling process: the skin not only keeps the fish moist but prevents it from falling apart during cooking. If you want to remove the skin prior to serving, simply peel it back and discard it.

Place the fish skin-side down in a large metal lasagna or roasting pan set over two burners on your stove top. Sprinkle with herbes de Provence and salt, and add wine to cover.

Bring the liquid to a low boil, then immediately reduce the heat to low.

Cover the pan with foil, and cook until a knife inserted into the center indicates that the interior is opaque and the fish has been cooked through, about 30 minutes. Carefully remove the fish to a platter, cover with plastic wrap, and refrigerate.

While the fish is cooling, prepare the horseradish cream: In a small bowl, mix together horseradish and sour cream. Add dill and combine, using an immersion blender. Cover and refrigerate until ready to serve.

VARIATIONS

- Poach in water.
- Poach in prepared fish or vegetable stock.
- Reserve the herb-infused poaching wine, reduce it by half in a small saucepan set over medium heat, and whisk in 2 tablespoons of butter. Serve with the fish.

Serves 6 to 8

POACHING SAFELY

Just because poaching liquid cooks at a much lower temperature than, say, a boil or a simmer, remember safety first: if you're poaching in wine, do not be tempted to move the pan into the oven. I did once, and when I opened the oven door to check on my fish, the combination of alcohol, flame, and oxygen created a fireball that licked out of the oven and threatened to ignite my eyebrows. Poach on top of the stove, always.

HOW LONG IT WILL LAST

- In deference to my stepmother, a New Englander who makes delicious poached salmon but thinks it has the half-life of plutonium, this dish will last up to 4 days in the refrigerator, tightly double-wrapped in plastic.
- The horseradish cream will last up to 4 days, tightly sealed in an airtight container in the refrigerator.

ADDITIONAL SERVING RECOMMENDATIONS

- Serve cold, with BIG FOOD Aioli (page 35), fresh lemons, and a mixed green salad.
- Serve as a cold luncheon appetizer on a bed of greens.

SECONDARY DISHES

- *Curried Salmon Salad with Grapes and Walnuts (page 84)*
- *Salmon Burgers (page 135)*

OVEN-ROASTED, TAMARI-GLAZED SALMON

WHAT YOU HAVE ON HAND

- 6 to 8 pounds of salmon

WHAT TO DO WITH IT

- Carefully slice it in half widthwise, and double-wrap the remaining portion in heavy-duty plastic wrap. Use it within 2 to 3 days.

HOW LONG IT WILL LAST

- This dish, cooked, will last up to 3 days in the refrigerator.

ADDITIONAL SERVING RECOMMENDATIONS

- Serve with rice and Roman-Style Sautéed Greens (page 195). For a spectacular presentation, make two kinds of rice—one brown, one white—and serve them side by side, topped by the fish.
- Serve atop a mound of Asian-style noodles tossed with a drizzle of soy sauce, chopped scallions, and chopped raw, unsalted peanuts.

SECONDARY DISHES

- *Asian-Style Salmon Burgers:* Using the back of a fork, mash leftover cooked salmon in a bowl, and combine it with chopped red onion, chopped celery, a dash of hot sauce, and a tablespoon of Wasabi Mayonnaise (page 35). Serve with sliced, steamed baby new potatoes, atop greens.

Glazing salmon (or steelhead trout, arctic char, or even tuna) will yield not only delicious and immediate results, but the cooked leftovers will also go the distance as Asian-Style Salmon Burgers (below) or croquettes, or as an accompaniment to wilted greens. Amazingly easy to put together and beautiful to behold, this dish makes a perfect middle-of-the-week main course or the centerpiece for a romantic dinner for two, when you have to impress but also have other things on your mind.

2	tablespoons tamari or soy sauce	1	teaspoon lime juice
1	tablespoon grated fresh ginger	1	teaspoon rice vinegar
1	tablespoon honey	1	(3- to 4-pound) salmon fillet

Preheat oven to 375°F.

Mix together tamari, ginger, honey, lime juice, and vinegar. Place salmon in an ovenproof baking dish and cover with marinade, turning to coat. Refrigerate up to 15 minutes, but no more.

Lightly coat a baking sheet with cooking spray. Place salmon skin-side down and roast until cooked through, about 10 minutes. Cut into individual fillets and serve hot.

Serves 6

Never marinate fish in any lime- or other citrus-based sauce for longer than 15 minutes. The acid from the citrus will begin to cook the fish, making your finished dish tough.

SALMON BURGERS

When is a hamburger not a hamburger? When it's made from fish (or chicken, or lamb, or turkey, or even baby rock shrimp). A new twist on an old New York classic loosely inspired by chef Michael Romano and the Union Square Café's spectacular Tuna Burger, this dish calls for leftover flaked salmon that's blended with a variety of spices and a little mustard, then pan-fried at a high temperature. With a slice of raw red onion, this burger is delicious enough to be included at your next July 4th picnic.

1½–2	pounds leftover cooked salmon fillet, flaked	1	egg, lightly beaten
2	garlic cloves, peeled and finely minced	1	tablespoon Dijon mustard
1	small onion, peeled and finely minced	1	teaspoon kosher salt
		½	teaspoon cayenne pepper
		2	tablespoons extra virgin olive oil

Optional: Bread crumbs

Mix together salmon, garlic, onion, egg, mustard, salt, and cayenne pepper. Form 4 patties approximately 3½ inches across and 1 inch thick, taking care not to compact the fish too firmly. If the mixture is too wet or not holding together, add bread crumbs as a binder.

Heat oil in a nonstick sauté pan over medium-high heat, until rippling but not smoking. Sear the patties, two at a time, until well browned on both sides, about 5 minutes per side. Serve hot.

VARIATIONS

- Substitute leftover tuna, arctic char, or steelhead trout for the salmon.
- Add a pinch of hot or mild curry to the mashed salmon.
- For an Asian flavor, add BIG FOOD Asian Spice Blend (page 40) to the fish.
- For a Mediterranean flavor, add BIG FOOD Mediterranean Spice Blend (page 39) to the fish.

Serves 4

WHAT YOU HAVE ON HAND

- 1½ to 2 pounds leftover, flaked, cooked salmon fillet

WHAT TO DO WITH IT

- Pick over the flaked salmon and remove any skin or bones.

HOW LONG IT WILL LAST

- Ideally, cooked salmon burgers should be eaten immediately. However, once cooked, they will keep for up to 3 days in the refrigerator, double-plastic-wrapped and stored in a dated, heavy-duty freezer bag, and up to 3 months in the freezer, stored the same way.

ADDITIONAL SERVING RECOMMENDATIONS

- Serve on a hamburger bun, with raw red onion and greens as a garnish, or with onion rings that have been slowly sautéed in extra virgin olive oil along with ½ teaspoon of sugar.
- Serve on top of salad greens, along with a splash of your favorite dressing.

SECONDARY

PENNE WITH VODKA, CREAM, AND SMOKED SALMON

A slightly quirky take on the classic Penne alla Vodka, this elegant, rich dish was born out of my need to use up a side of bright-red, smoked sockeye salmon that was sent to me for Christmas one year when I was right out of college. Rich, elegant, and silky, with just a hint of pepper, this dish brings together two brunch leftovers (vodka from the Bloody Marys you served, and smoked salmon) and saves the day for dinner.

1	pound penne, ziti, or other tubular pasta
1½	cups BIG FOOD Marinara Sauce or any packaged tomato sauce
⅔	cup heavy cream
1	tablespoon fresh dill, chopped
⅓	cup unflavored vodka
½	pound smoked salmon, cut into bite-size pieces
½	cup frozen peas

NO CHEESE, PLEASE

Parmesan lovers, take note: if you've ever asked for cheese to be sprinkled on that seafood pasta you ordered at a good Italian restaurant, chances are your waiter went into the kitchen and had a good laugh. Why? Like it or not, there are some pasta dishes that do not call for cheese in any form. Seafood pasta is one of those; it simply doesn't need it and is thus omitted from this dish. If you'd like to add it, feel free.

Fill a large stockpot with salted water, and bring to a boil. Cook pasta until al dente (tender, but still slightly firm to the bite).

Bring marinara sauce to a simmer in a large saucepan over medium heat. Using a soup ladle, transfer 2 tablespoons to a nonreactive bowl; add 2 tablespoons of cream to it and blend. Return it to the saucepan along with the rest of the cream, and whisk well to incorporate.

Add dill and vodka, cover, and let simmer for 10 minutes, stirring frequently. Add salmon, cover, and cook for another 5 minutes. Add peas, and cook until just heated through.

Pour sauce over the pasta, toss well, and serve hot.

Serves 4 to 6

COOKING WITH SALTY FOODS

Some ingredients, like smoked meats, chicken, and fish, along with olives and capers, are intrinsically salty and require the judicious addition of those glorious granules we've come to take for granted. In the case of this recipe, the smoked salmon tends to be extremely salty; add salt if you must, *but taste the dish first.*

SMOKED SALMON AND ASPARAGUS FRITTATA WITH CREAM CHEESE AND CHIVES

Another boon for brunch lovers, this open-faced omelet is as delectable as it is stunning and can be made in a matter of minutes. Developed the morning after a dinner party at which I served oven-roasted asparagus, this recipe can also be made with frozen asparagus. The addition of cream cheese and snipped chives (use kitchen scissors to literally snip them into 1-inch pieces) adds a punch of earthy flavor and creamy texture, although the entire dish can be reduced in cholesterol and fat by substituting egg whites for the eggs and using low-fat or fat-free cream cheese in place of the full-fat variety.

1	small shallot, peeled and minced	8	eggs, lightly beaten, or 4 eggs plus $^2/_3$ cup egg substitute, lightly beaten
$^1/_2$	pound leftover smoked salmon		
$^1/_2$	pound leftover or frozen asparagus, cut into 1-inch pieces	1	tablespoon snipped fresh chives
$^1/_2$	cup softened cream cheese	1	teaspoon white pepper

Optional: Additional chives, caviar, additional smoked salmon

WHAT YOU HAVE ON HAND

- **Smoked salmon**
- **Fresh, frozen, or leftover cooked asparagus**
- **Eggs or egg substitute**
- **Cream cheese: low-fat, fat-free, full-fat, or a combination**
- **Fresh or dried chives**

WHAT TO DO WITH IT

- Set aside $^1/_2$ pound of smoked salmon for this dish; double-plastic-wrap the balance (if you still have the backing material that it was originally packed on, seal it on that), and refrigerate for up to 3 days.
- Set aside $^1/_2$ pound leftover asparagus, or the same quantity of fresh or frozen.

HOW LONG IT WILL LAST

- This dish, double-plastic-wrapped and stored in a dated, heavy-duty freezer bag, will last up to 2 days in the refrigerator.

Preheat oven to 350°F.

Lightly coat a large, nonstick, ovenproof sauté pan with cooking spray, and set it over medium-high heat until rippling but not smoking. Add shallot and cook until softened, about 3 minutes. Add salmon and asparagus; toss and cook until everything is warmed through (the smoked salmon will turn opaque), 5 to 6 minutes. Reduce heat to medium and, using a teaspoon, dollop cream cheese into the pan.

Add eggs and, without shaking the pan, let them "set" around the other ingredients, pancake style, until the edges begin to pull away from the pan, about 6 minutes. Sprinkle in chives and pepper.

Place pan in the oven and cook until the center of the frittata sets, 8 to 10 minutes. Increase heat to broil and cook until browned, about 5 minutes.

Remove from oven, carefully place a large dinner plate facedown over the surface, and invert frittata onto the plate. Garnish with extra chives and a dollop of caviar (if using), and serve hot. Additional smoked salmon can be served as an accompaniment.

Serves 4

WHAT THEY DON'T KNOW

. . . won't hurt them. That's what my friend Alex used to say as she dropped a few champagne grapes into a flute filled with very inexpensive sparkling wine, which she presented to her guests as a fancy brunch cocktail. (They never knew.) Her heart was always in the right place, only her wallet couldn't follow. And that was okay. It's taken me years to realize that there's nothing wrong with it—as a host, you have to figure out where you can splurge and when. Serve this beautiful frittata in a lovely way, and no one will know it was made from leftover ingredients (although the fresh version is outrageously good, especially when asparagus is in season). Most discount clubs offer some sort of reasonably priced domestic caviar in addition to the expensive stuff. If you're having people over for brunch or a light dinner, go ahead and splurge a little on the inexpensive stuff, dollop it onto the frittata wedges, and give your guests and yourself a little extra TLC.

ADDITIONAL SERVING RECOMMENDATIONS

• Serve for brunch, lunch, or dinner with a salad. Bring the pan to the table, slice the frittata into wedges, and serve with toasted, German-style black bread. Top each wedge with additional smoked salmon and, if you really want to splurge, a dollop of caviar.

WHAT TO DO WITH IT

- If not making the entire tuna, wrap the remainder in plastic and store it in a dated, heavy-duty freezer bag for up to 24 hours. (My suggestion: Make all of it.)
- Store leftover olives in an airtight container in the refrigerator for up to 10 days, or prepare Tapenade (page 118).

HOW LONG IT WILL LAST

- Leftovers should be used within 24 hours.

PRIMARY/SECONDARY

MEDITERRANEAN TUNA WITH BLACK AND GREEN OLIVES, CAPERS, AND ARTICHOKE HEARTS

Tuna, by its very nature, is a difficult fish to cook. This fact was brought home to me by New York chef Anne Rosezweig, when I watched her prepare peppered tuna loin. She did not move from the pan for a second until the dish was completed and plated: the cooking of tuna requires undivided attention. One minute too long and it's dry as a bone; err on the quick side, and you've got sushi (more on this, opposite page). A quick-cooking, highly piquant braise that's perfect for a Mediterranean-style Christmas Eve (especially if your celebration involves eating and then getting everyone to church on time), this one-pot dish ensures that the enormous piece of fresh tuna you brought home from the discount club will be cooked to perfection.

2	tablespoons extra virgin olive oil	$1/2$	cup green olives, pitted
2	garlic cloves, peeled and minced	$1/2$	cup black olives, pitted
1	shallot, peeled and minced	2	tablespoons capers, rinsed
$1/2$	tablespoon BIG FOOD Mediterranean Spice Blend	$3/4$	cup frozen artichoke hearts, thawed, coarsely chopped, and drizzled with 1 tablespoon fresh lemon juice
2	pounds whole tuna steak or loin		
$1/2$	cup inexpensive dry white wine		
1	(16-ounce) can Italian-style plum tomatoes, drained		

Heat oil in a medium nonreactive saucepan or Dutch oven with a lid over medium heat, until rippling but not smoking.

Add garlic and shallot, and cook until softened. Add spice mix, and blend until the mixture becomes aromatic. Reduce heat to medium-low.

Add tuna, turning it carefully to coat with garlic mixture. Add wine, tomatoes, olives, capers, and artichoke hearts. Cover and let simmer gently for 25 minutes.

Increase heat to medium, remove cover, and cook 5 minutes more. Serve hot.

VARIATIONS
- Make this dish with swordfish, cod, monkfish, peeled and cleaned jumbo shrimp, or snapper.

Serves 4 to 6

THE TRUTH ABOUT CHARLIE THE TUNA

Poor tuna—that deeply abused, overused, overprocessed sea creature that has been so humiliated over the years: first they canned him, then they put glasses on him and called him Charlie, and now, in four-star restaurants from New York to Mongolia, he's being served nearly raw—or rather, *black and blue*, as rare tuna is called in the restaurant industry—unless he's mishandled and is therefore dry and overcooked. That's the problem with tuna: there's no middle ground. It's canned, it's raw, it's carbonized, or it's swimming in mercury. But the bottom line is always the same: whether canned or fresh, when it's good, it's very, very good. What to look for when you're shopping for tuna, canned or fresh:

Bright-red, shrink-wrapped tuna. This tuna is usually caught in the South or Eastern Pacific and generally quick-frozen and packaged on the boat that caught it. Looks are deceiving with this particular kind of tuna because it may look fresher than it actually is—and because it's shrink-wrapped, you can't do the sniff test. I rarely buy this variety for that reason. Generally, the finest grade goes to Japan, where it's consumed raw as sushi or sashimi.

Yellowfin tuna, or ahi. This is generally what you'll find at a discount club or good supermarket. Its flesh ranges in color from bright, Day-Glo red to light red to light brown. Yellowfin is graded with a rating of 1 through 3: 1, of sushi quality and usually available only to restaurants; 2, suitable for retail supermarkets and discount clubs; and 3 . . . you shouldn't go near. Again, if you can't smell it, trust your eyes, and steer clear of signs of bruising, decay, and dryness.

Canned tuna. Today, thankfully, we have more choices in this market than we used to. My personal choice is always Italian or European-style tuna, which has been packed in extra virgin olive oil (hint: save the oil and use it on pasta later). Buy glass-jarred tuna if you can find it, and make sure, if you can, that the tuna hasn't come from an area riddled with mercury.

ADDITIONAL SERVING RECOMMENDATIONS

- Serve accompanied by garlic toasts spread with Brandade (page 144).

SECONDARY DISHES

- *Tuna Tacos with Lime and Cilantro:* Cube leftover tuna and toss with the juice of 1 lime, 1 tablespoon of tequila, and 1 small minced jalapeño. Let sit for 10 minutes, stirring occasionally. Remove from marinade, and wrap in warm flour tortillas. Serve with shredded lettuce and diced red onion.

- *Tuna with Couscous and Vegetables:* Dice and toss leftover tuna with leftover olives, garlic, artichokes, and tomatoes. Serve atop a mound of instant couscous; drizzle with fresh lemon juice, and top with fresh chopped mint. (This can also be made with canned tuna.)

PAN-FRIED SPICY CRAB CAKES WITH RED PEPPER MAYONNAISE

WHAT YOU HAVE ON HAND

- 2 (2-pound) cans 100 percent lump or backfin crabmeat
- Mayonnaise

WHAT TO DO WITH IT

- Make this dish in bulk and freeze the remaining crab cakes for up to 4 months.
- Make this recipe and store the remaining unopened crab in its can, in the refrigerator, for up to 2 weeks.

HOW LONG IT WILL LAST

- Crab cakes are ideally served immediately. Stored in airtight containers in the refrigerator, they will last, cooked, up to 3 days; "free frozen," double-plastic-wrapped, and frozen in dated, heavy-duty freezer bags, they will last up to 4 months.
- The mayo will keep up to 2 weeks, refrigerated in an airtight container.

I used to serve crab as a fancy treat during the holidays. But today, excellent quality, lower-priced crabmeat—lump and backfin—can be purchased year-round and nation-wide in nearly every good supermarket, fish shop, or discount club. These cakes, which were adapted from a traditional version originally published in Gourmet Magazine, *freeze beautifully, so make them in bulk and put them away for those hungry drop-in guests who show up expecting a little more than a cup of tea.*

CRAB CAKES:

1	cup milk, whole or low-fat
³/₄	cup bread crumbs
1	pound lump or backfin crabmeat
2	large eggs, lightly beaten
¹/₂	cup heavy cream
1	small celery stalk, finely minced
1	shallot, peeled and finely minced
1	garlic clove, peeled and finely minced
1	teaspoon Worcestershire sauce
¹/₂	teaspoon hot sauce
1	tablespoon canola oil
1	tablespoon unsalted butter

MAYONNAISE:

¹/₂	cup prepared mayonnaise, low-, non-, or full-fat
	Juice of 1 lemon
1	(6-ounce) jar roasted sweet red peppers packed in olive oil or water, drained and chopped
¹/₄	teaspoon hot sauce

THE ART OF FREE FREEZING

Freezing burgers, fish cakes, crab cakes, meatballs, and even fresh berries can be hazardous if you put everything together in one freezer bag and then shove it into the bowels of your cold storage, because the bag's contents wind up sticking together. How to avoid this? "Free" freeze any of the above on long, narrow cookie sheets covered with a layer of plastic wrap; once frozen, they then go into freezer bags for the long haul, thus eliminating the necessity of defrosting an entire batch of meatballs when you need only a few.

FOR THE CRAB CAKES:

Place milk and bread crumbs in a small bowl, and let stand for 10 minutes. Strain, and discard the milk.

Using clean hands, blend together crabmeat and soaked bread crumbs in a medium bowl. Add eggs, cream, celery, shallot, garlic, Worcestershire sauce, and hot sauce, and combine well. If mixture is too wet, add an extra tablespoon of dry bread crumbs.

Heat oil and butter in a large, nonstick sauté pan set over medium-high heat, until rippling but not smoking and any foam from the butter just begins to subside.

Using a large soup spoon, scoop up approximately 2 heaping tablespoons of the crab mixture and drop it into the pan, flattening it if desired. Cook until golden brown, about 3 to 4 minutes per side. Set on a warm plate, cover with aluminum foil, and repeat until all of the mixture is used.

FOR THE MAYONNAISE:

Place mayonnaise, lemon juice, peppers, and hot sauce in a blender and mix together (you can also do this with an immersion blender). Taste for seasoning, and serve immediately with the crab cakes.

VARIATIONS
- Make smaller cakes, and serve them as hors d'oeuvres.
- Substitute the following for the crab: leftover jumbo shrimp, finely chopped; leftover salmon, flaked; leftover tuna, flaked; leftover red snapper, flaked; baby rock shrimp, minced; lobster meat.

Serves 4 to 6

ADDITIONAL SERVING RECOMMENDATIONS

- Serve as an elegant appetizer on a bed of fresh greens. Put the mayo in a squirt bottle and design a zigzig pattern over the cakes.
- Serve as a midweek dinner, with steamed rice or Smashed New Potatoes (page 249) and Roman-Style Sautéed Greens (page 195).
- Serve on a toasted sourdough roll with lettuce, tomato, and a slice of raw red onion. Dollop with Red Pepper Mayonnaise or tartar sauce.

BRANDADE

WHAT YOU HAVE ON HAND

- **1 to 2 pounds of dried salt cod**
- **Baking potatoes**
- **Milk**
- **Garlic**
- **Extra virgin olive oil**

WHAT TO DO WITH IT

- Fill a large rectangular baking dish or bowl with water, and soak the fish for 24 to 36 hours, until it is plump and soft (if necessary, break the cod into pieces). Change the water every 12 hours.
- Set aside 2 medium baking potatoes for this dish; store the balance in a cool, dark location away from onions or fruit.

HOW LONG IT WILL LAST

- Brandade, stored in the refrigerator in an airtight container, will last for up to 3 days. Turn leftovers into New England–Style Codfish Cakes with Lemon Sauce (page 146).

If you are lucky enough (as I am) to live in a part of the world where there is a large French, Canadian, Portuguese, or Italian population, you will certainly come across immense, unsightly, stiff, and extremely inexpensive boards of dried salt cod around Christmastime. Considered by many to be peasant food, salt cod soaked in water or milk and blended with garlic, potatoes, and more milk becomes tender, flavorful, and luscious. This French Provençale dish is the centerpiece of my Christmas Eve meal: served warm on toasts at midnight, it's a delicious and comforting way to welcome in the holiday. The best part? The leftovers can be turned into spectacular New England–style codfish cakes that can freeze for up to 4 months. Leave it to the Yankees.

1	pound dried salt cod, soaked 24–36 hours	4	garlic cloves, peeled
1	tablespoon herbes de Provence	4	tablespoons extra virgin olive oil, plus extra for drizzling
2	medium baking potatoes, peeled and cubed		Kosher salt and freshly ground black pepper
1	cup milk, divided		

Optional: *Freshly chopped flat-leaf parsley and toasted rounds of French or Italian bread, for serving*

Place cod in a rectangular, ovenproof baking dish or deep sauté pan, sprinkle with herbes de Provence, and fill with water to cover. Bring to a boil, immediately reduce heat to lowest setting, cover with aluminum foil, and cook for 40 minutes. Remove fish from heat and place on a platter. Gently pick it over, removing any bones or skin. Crumble and flake the fish, and place in a mixing bowl.

Place potatoes in a saucepan and fill with water to cover. Bring to a low boil and cook until soft, approximately 30 minutes. Drain potatoes, return to the pan, add half of the milk, and mash with a hand-held potato masher. Set aside.

Preheat oven to 350°F.

Pulse fish, potatoes, remaining milk, garlic, and oil in a food processor until creamy. If mixture is too thick and pasty, add additional milk by the tablespoon. Season to taste with salt and pepper.

Transfer mixture to an ovenproof baking dish, drizzle with additional oil, and bake until the top just begins to take on some color, about 10 minutes.

Sprinkle with parsley, if using, and serve warm, with rounds of toasted French or Italian bread drizzled with extra virgin olive oil, if desired.

VARIATIONS
• Omit the potatoes and add more milk.
• Poach the cod in fish stock or wine instead of water.

Serves 6 to 8

SECONDARY DISHES

• *New England–Style Codfish Cakes with Lemon Sauce (page 146)*

• *After soaking the fish, use it as a substitution for tuna in Mediterranean Tuna with Black and Green Olives, Capers, and Artichoke Hearts (page 140).*

SECONDARY

NEW ENGLAND–STYLE CODFISH CAKES WITH LEMON SAUCE

Meet the parsimonious codfish cake, that staple of Yankee frugality that, according to her biographer, found its way onto the childhood table of Julia Child when her New England mother, stuck in sunny Pasadena, California, needed a reminder of home. Often bland and often canned, the codfish cake is elevated to black-tie status in this recipe, which was developed a few days after Christmas one year when I was faced with a container filled with leftover Brandade. The result was a success: delectable and packed with flavor; and with a nod to Yankee ingenuity, they freeze up to 4 months.

³⁄₄	pound (1½ cups) leftover Brandade	½	teaspoon kosher salt
2	eggs, beaten	½	teaspoon white pepper
1	cup bread crumbs	2	tablespoons canola oil
			Lemon Sauce

Place the Brandade in a large mixing bowl. Add eggs and combine well. If the mixture is extremely wet, mix in 2 to 3 tablespoons of the bread crumbs.

In a separate bowl and using a fork, combine the remaining bread crumbs, salt, and pepper.

Heat oil in a large, nonstick sauté pan over medium-high heat, until rippling but not smoking.

Take a handful of the Brandade mixture, form it into a patty, and dredge it in the bread-crumb mixture. Shake off excess crumbs, and immediately place the patty in the pan.

Pan-fry the cakes, a few at a time, until they are golden brown on all sides, approximately 6 minutes per side. Drain on paper towels, keep warm, and serve immediately with Lemon Sauce.

VARIATIONS

• Prepare the same dish with leftover salmon salad, tuna salad, or smoked whitefish.
• Add 1 tablespoon of drained and rinsed capers to the sauce, 5 minutes prior to serving.

Yields approximately 8 cakes

ADDITIONAL SERVING RECOMMENDATIONS

• For breakfast: topped with a poached egg and a rasher of bacon
• For lunch: on a bed of mixed greens
• For dinner: with a side of rice and vegetables of your choosing

WHAT TO DO WITH IT

- Peel the skin back on one side of the fish and remove all of the meat; turn the fish over and repeat. Discard skin and bones.
- Set aside 1½ cups sour cream, and store the balance in the refrigerator in its original container for up to 10 days.
- Set aside 3 to 4 tablespoons mayonnaise for this recipe, and store the balance in the refrigerator in its original container for up to 2 weeks.
- Set aside 1 medium onion; store the balance in a mesh bag in a cool, dark location away from potatoes or fruit.

HOW LONG IT WILL LAST

- Houston Street Whitefish Salad will last, stored in an airtight container, in your refrigerator for up to 5 days.

PRIMARY

HOUSTON STREET WHITEFISH SALAD

On the Lower East Side of Manhattan lies a thoroughfare called Houston Street; head west, and it's filled with the shops and galleries of Soho. Head east, and you will find yourself in the middle of old immigrant New York—and of Russ & Daughter's. In business since 1914, this shop counted among its customers everyone from Isaac Bashevis Singer to my grandfather, Henry Altman, and the rest of the writers and editors of the Jewish Daily Forward. Russ & Daughter's is a must-see for people from far and wide, especially those of us craving Jewish soul food. If the closest you can come to it is a huge smoked whitefish purchased at a discount club, don't worry: this recipe isn't theirs, but it'll help with the craving until you can get to the Big Apple.

1½	cups sour cream	1	(4- to 5-pound) smoked whitefish, skin, bones, and head discarded
3–4	tablespoons prepared mayonnaise		
	Juice of half a lemon	4	celery stalks, finely minced
1	medium onion, peeled and finely minced	1	tablespoon fresh dill
		1	teaspoon white pepper

FISH

Mix sour cream and mayonnaise together in a small mixing bowl. Add lemon juice and onion, blend well, place in an airtight container, and refrigerate for 1 hour.

Flake and mash the fish in a large mixing bowl, taking care to remove any small bones. Add the sour cream mixture and celery; combine well. Taste for seasoning, then add dill and pepper. Blend well. Serve cold.

VARIATIONS
- Substitute any of the following for the smoked whitefish: smoked salmon, poached salmon, leftover salt cod.
- Omit the sour cream and make an all-mayonnaise dressing.
- Add a pinch of cayenne pepper.

Serves 6

ADDITIONAL SERVING RECOMMENDATIONS
- For the quintessential Jewish brunch dish, reserve the skin, head, and tail of the fish. Form the salad into the shape of the original fish, cover with the skin, and serve as if it were fresh from the lakes of Minnesota.
- Serve it on hot, toasted bagels.
- Serve it dolloped onto fresh greens.

SECONDARY DISHES
- *Stuffed Tomatoes (page 90)*

RISOTTO WITH BABY SHRIMP AND PEAS

Enormous bags of frozen shrimp are among the most terrific buys to be had when you're shopping in bulk. I always keep a few bags of various sizes in my freezer, for quick dinners of Spicy Shrimp Boiled in Black Beer (page 152), or to toss with some pasta and BIG FOOD Marinara Sauce (page 42). But rice is also a great thing to buy in bulk, especially the short-grained, glutinous arborio rice that's used to make risotto. This lovely delicacy takes about 40 minutes to put together, start to finish, and uses other typical BIG FOOD items—onions, vegetable stock, baby shrimp, and frozen peas. The result is tender and delicious, and the leftovers can be made into addictive Fried Rice Balls (page 114) . . . if you have any left, that is.

2	tablespoons unsalted butter	$\frac{1}{2}$	pound uncooked, defrosted baby shrimp or rock shrimp
1	medium onion, peeled and finely minced	1	cup frozen peas, defrosted
2	cups arborio rice		
4–5	cups packaged vegetable (or seafood) stock		

Optional: *1 tablespoon chopped flat-leaf parsley, freshly grated Parmesan cheese*

> Substitute dry white wine for half of the stock called for in this dish.

WHAT YOU HAVE ON HAND

- **Short-grain, arborio rice**
- **Baby shrimp (or salad shrimp or rock shrimp)**
- **Frozen peas**
- **Packaged vegetable stock**
- **Onions**

WHAT TO DO WITH IT

- Set aside 2 cups of arborio rice, and store the balance in an air-tight container in your pantry. If it's tightly sealed, it should last indefinitely.

- Set aside $\frac{1}{2}$ pound of baby shrimp; defrost slowly by placing in a colander under cool running water. Freeze the balance in a dated, heavy-duty freezer bag for up to 6 months.

- Set aside 1 cup of frozen peas, and defrost slowly by placing in a colander under cool running water. Freeze the balance in a dated, heavy-duty freezer bag for up to 4 months.

- Set aside 1 medium onion, and store the balance in a mesh bag in a cool, dark location away from potatoes or fruit.

- Set aside 4 cups of packaged vegetable stock; store the balance in the refrigerator for up to 10 days, or freeze in a dated, heavy-duty freezer bag for up to 6 months.

Melt butter in a medium, straight-sided sauté pan or a medium saucepan, over medium-low heat. Add onion and cook until just softened, taking care not to let it brown.

Add rice and stir well, making sure that each grain is coated with butter.

Increase heat to medium. When the rice begins to turn opaque and sounds like it is crackling, add $\frac{1}{2}$ cup of the stock. Stir constantly, until stock is absorbed by the rice, and add another $\frac{1}{2}$ cup. Repeat until you have only $\frac{1}{2}$ cup of the stock left. *This is a slow process, so be patient. Risotto should never be made in a rush.*

Add shrimp and peas, and stir gently but well. Pour in the remaining stock, and stir until incorporated.

Serve immediately, garnished with parsley and grated cheese, if using.

VARIATIONS

- Add a few threads of saffron to the stock.
- Omit the shrimp, use chicken stock, and add bits of diced prosciutto.
- Omit the shrimp, replace the vegetable stock with beef stock and red wine, and add bits of fresh mushroom. Garnish with sage leaves.

Serves 4 to 6

THE TRICK TO COOKING RISOTTO

Don't be afraid! The only thing you have to remember when you cook risotto is that you must keep stirring and adding liquid (usually about 4 cups of water, stock, or wine to 1½ cups of rice) to it, until the rice is cooked through and stops absorbing any additional liquid. Always test a grain or two on the end of a spoon: the finished product should be just a tiny bit toothsome yet creamy, the inside supple and melt-in-your-mouth good. Defrost any additional ingredients prior to adding them, so that you don't add any unnecessary liquid to the dish.

HOW LONG IT WILL LAST

- Leftovers will keep up to 3 days in an airtight container in the refrigerator.

SECONDARY DISHES

- *Fried Rice Balls (page 114)*

PRIMARY

SPICED SHRIMP BOILED IN BLACK BEER

Exactly what it claims to be, this simple one-pot dish preferably requires the following: a pound of unpeeled jumbo or large shrimp; spices; a few bottles of dark beer; a porch; a summer afternoon; and a picnic table. Spread out the newspaper, boil 'em up, and call it the fastest summertime dinner in the East (or the West).

1–2	pounds jumbo or large frozen, unpeeled, uncooked shrimp	2	tablespoons Old Bay Seasoning
2	large bottles dark beer	1	lemon, cut into wedges

Optional: BIG FOOD Cocktail Sauce

Place shrimp in a colander under cool running water to defrost. Drain and set aside.

Bring beer to a boil in a large stockpot over medium heat. Add seasoning and continue to boil for 5 minutes more.

Add shrimp and cook until pink, about 5 minutes. Remove with a slotted spoon and serve hot, in as rustic a manner as possible, with nothing but a squirt of lemon and a dollop of BIG FOOD Cocktail Sauce, if using.

Serves 4 to 6

SECONDARY DISHES

- *Salmon Burger substitution (page 135)*
- *Pan-Fried Spicy Crab Cakes with Red Pepper Mayonnaise substitution (page 142)*

THE KEY TO TENDER SHRIMP

It may not be the neatest or the fastest way to prepare shrimp, but if you want your shrimp to be tender and juicy (rather than hard, rubbery, and unappetizing), cook them shell-on. But then, you ask, how do you remove that nasty little "digestive" tract that runs along the back of the little creatures? Simple:

- If you are buying bags of frozen shrimp in bulk, make sure that they are labeled "Cleaned, Unpeeled." This means that the digestive tract was removed prior to the freezing process.
- If you are buying shrimp from a fish counter or fish monger, make sure to ask for shell-on shrimp that have been cleaned.
- If your fresh, unpeeled shrimp haven't been pre-cleaned, forget about using those little red plastic "de-veining" implements. Instead, under cold running water, place the edge of a very sharp paring knife along the back side of the shrimp, carefully slicing through the shell. Remove the digestive tract, and you're good to go.

INTO THE HEN-HOUSE

BIG FOOD ON POULTRY

> "I always give my bird a generous butter massage before I put it in the oven. Why? Because I think the chicken likes it."
> —Julia Child

According to my mother, I was not a fussy child: I ate anything, so long as it was chicken.

Everyone's favorite bird had a place on my family's table with such terrific regularity that my parents joked that if I ate any more of it, I'd grow wings. I still love the stuff and very often find myself serving it to my *own* family at least a few nights a week. It's delicious, mild, easy to cook, comforting, and flexible enough to be turned into astonishingly great leftovers, and it stores well both in the refrigerator and the freezer. The big bonus to all of this practicality, of course, is that most kids love poultry in nearly any form, making it a boon to those of us who have cranky and/or finicky little ones to feed either school lunches made at home or quick dinners after soccer practice.

Today, whole chickens are widely available in a vast array of sizes, which correlate directly to their age

TALKING TURKEY

When talking about poultry, it is necessary to clarify exactly what we mean: in culinary terms, poultry includes chicken at various ages and sizes, and "game birds" like turkey and duck. For the sake of BIG FOOD, and because most folks rarely buy duck in bulk, the poultry section of this book will focus primarily on chicken and turkey.

(and often their tenderness). For example, those petite birds packaged under the label "Rock Cornish Game Hens," are in fact a young hybrid hen conjured up by the Tyson Foods folks back in 1965. Generally packaged together in threes, fours, or even sixes, these game hens can be bought in bulk, frozen, and quickly defrosted to make a wonderfully flavorful, fast-roasting individual bird (and an elegant plate). Slightly smaller than the Rock Cornish hens are what are called *poussin*, or *squab*; diminutive, sweet, and utterly delectable, they require little more than a squirt of lemon, a drizzle of extra virgin olive oil, and a turn of the pepper shaker;

sliced right up the backbone and then spread flat (butterflied), they cook very quickly and will therefore turn to rubber instantaneously if not watched carefully. Following the poussin in size order are the well-known *broiler,* the *fryer,* the very popular *roaster* (which generally weighs in at over 3 pounds, and as much as 6 pounds), the *capon* (a castrated male chicken), the *pullet* (an older hen and, should one be available to you, possibly the finest choice for a soup but less so for a roaster), and the *stewing fowl,* which should never, ever be mistaken for a roaster (but is suitable for long-cooking stews and braises). Its meat is too old, tough, and gamy to be eaten as you would a fryer or a roaster.

Most discount clubs and large supermarkets now carry poultry in nearly every conceivable configuration. Large, inexpensive packages of wings or legs are available to those who prefer dark meat. Chicken sausage can replace traditional pork sausage anywhere it's needed, from tomato sauce to homemade pizza or *Zuppa di Cannellini con Scarola* (page 66) to Pigs in Blankets (page 122), to the brilliantly freezable Chicken Sausage and Peppers (page 170).

Inexpensive whole roasters can be easily cut up (opposite page) for parts or roasted in their entirety, the leftovers of either used everywhere from Paella (page 192) to that great American favorite Chicken Potpie (page 174). And skinless, boneless chicken breasts are available today in immense packages that range from 3 pounds to 10: break them apart into individual serving packages, refrigerate what you need, and freeze what you don't. Or buy less expensive whole breasts on the bone, and skin and bone them yourself.

STORING CHICKEN SAFELY

Much attention has been paid to the safe preparation and storage of chicken products, and with good reason: stored incorrectly and handled carelessly, chicken can harbor enough bacteria to make entire armies deathly ill. In all seriousness, it is of *extreme importance* (especially when purchasing chicken in large quantities) that we get into the habit of taking the following preparation and storage precautions when handling everyone's favorite bird.

• When working with raw chicken, always use a solid plastic cutting board. Scrub the board with hot, soapy water immediately after each use and prior to using it for anything else. When in doubt, immediately run your plastic cutting boards through a dishwasher cycle.

• Any knives or other utensils that come into contact with raw chicken must be washed thoroughly with hot, soapy water immediately after each use.

CHICKEN STORAGE CHART

MEAT CUT	REFRIGERATE	FREEZE
Whole Chicken	Up to 2 days	Up to 8 months
Breasts	Up to 2 days	Up to 8 months
Parts (dark meat)	Up to 2 days	6–8 months
Ground Chicken	Up to 2 days	3–4 months

• Frozen chicken should be defrosted in the refrigerator, in its original airtight packaging, in a bowl of very cold water (change the water every 45 minutes, to ensure that it stays cold), or in the microwave. *Never, ever defrost chicken on your kitchen counter.*

• Discard any marinade used to coat a chicken during storage. Never be tempted to baste a cooking chicken with its cold marinade.

• There is no such thing as "rare" chicken. Chicken is considered done when its juices run clear and, more important, when an instant-read thermometer inserted into the breast reads 160°F. Ground chicken is done at 165°F.

• If a recipe calls for the bird to be "patted dry" prior to cooking, make sure you use paper towels (which you will then throw away). Never use a dish towel!

HOW TO CUT UP A WHOLE CHICKEN

As most cost-conscious shoppers know, buying cut-up chicken (boneless, skinless, boneless and skinless, breasts, wings, legs, and so on) is always more expensive than buying it whole and cutting it up yourself. When it comes to shopping at discount clubs, you have a vast array of choices—everything from shrink-wrapped four-packs of 3-pound birds to enough wings to keep the Air Force in the air for a very long time. What's best to cook with when you're making soups? Honestly, it doesn't really matter. It's your choice. Some say light meat, which is flavorful but less fatty; some say dark meat, which is extremely flavorful and much higher in fat. Making soup from whole chickens is a terrific way to ensure a plethora of tender, inexpensive chicken that you can later use in a multitude of ways. That said, making soup from *precut* chicken parts is a terrific way to get the most flavor for your buck, particularly if you prefer to use dark meat and inexpensive, bony pieces, like thighs, wings, and legs, all of which you can buy packaged. Likewise, while barbecuing or grilling assorted, precut chicken parts is an easy way to give everyone what they want, it can also be an expensive proposition. Therefore, I prefer buying my bulk chickens whole and then cutting them up myself. The result is nearly identical to buying parts, only better, because if I buy three chickens, I can freeze two whole ones and cut up the third, or freeze what I've cut up, and always have those parts on hand for soups and stews.

Cutting up your own chickens is in no way as difficult as it sounds: chances are, you're not a professional butcher, and frankly, neither am I. But over the years, I've managed to get this down to a simple science: cut your chicken in half lengthwise, and then each piece in half widthwise. If you're making a stew, such as Paella, you can even cut those pieces in half again. All you need are a pair of sharp kitchen shears and a very sharp chef's knife.

1. Using sharp kitchen shears, cut the chicken in half along the breast-bone.
2. Turn it over, snip along both sides of the backbone, and remove it. (You can freeze it to use later for the BIG FOOD Basic Chicken Stock (page 58) recipe.)
3. You're now left with two chicken halves. Take one half, lay it skin-side up, and, using a sharp chef's knife, cut it in half width-wise, between the leg and the wing. If you run into difficulty, simply place the knife where you want it, and give it a good pound with your other hand.
4. Repeat on the second half.
5. If desired, cut the remaining pieces in half again.

WHAT YOU HAVE ON HAND

- A three-pack of 3- to 4-pound roasters
- BIG FOOD Mediterranean Spice Blend (page 39)
- BIG FOOD Basic Chicken Stock (page 58)

WHAT TO DO WITH IT

- Set one of the birds aside for this recipe.
- Open the giblet bag and transfer the chicken liver to a small container in your freezer.
- If you are not going to use the other birds immediately, remove them from their outer wrapping (*not* their individual wrapping), place each one in its own heavy-duty, dated freezer bag, and store in the freezer for up to 8 months.

HOW LONG IT WILL LAST

- Double-wrapped in plastic, store this dish up to 4 days in the refrigerator or for 4 months in the freezer.
- Removed from the bone, the chicken meat will last for up to 4 days, stored in a dated freezer bag in the refrigerator.

Grating lemon zest *directly* onto a roasting chicken when it's nearly done adds surprising impact.

PRIMARY

BIG FOOD HERB-ROASTED CHICKEN

Talk to 10 different people, and chances are, you'll get 10 different methods for making the big daddy of all comfort foods, roast chicken. I've made it in every conceivable manner, and, as always, I've decided that simplest is best. Season this bird liberally inside and out, shove half a lemon into its cavity, and you're good to go; baste it a few times, but the less done to it, the better. The result is a juicy, tender, aromatic bird that will provide wondrously succulent leftovers for use in a variety of other dishes.

1	(3½- to 4-pound) chicken, giblet bag removed	2	medium carrots, halved width-wise
2	teaspoons kosher salt, divided	1	large onion, peeled and quartered
2	lemons, halved	1	cup dry white wine, or 1 cup BIG FOOD Basic Chicken Stock or packaged stock
1	tablespoon extra virgin olive oil		
1½	tablespoons BIG FOOD Mediterranean Spice Blend, divided		
	Zest of 1 lemon		

Preheat oven to 450°F.

Trim excess fat flaps from the ends of the chicken and discard. Pat dry inside and out, and thoroughly rub 1 teaspoon of the salt into the cavity of the bird.

Gently squeeze one of the lemon halves into the cavity, and then insert it into the cavity.

Rub skin with oil, and turn bird breast-side down. Rub underside with ½ tablespoon of the spice rub, and turn bird breast-side up.

Rub top with the zest and the remaining 1 tablespoon spice rub.

Place bird on a rack set in a medium roasting pan, and scatter carrots and onion around it. Pour wine over vegetables and baste once, then place in oven.

Roast 15 minutes, then reduce heat to 350°F. Roast for 1 hour, basting every 10 to 15 minutes.

Squeeze remaining lemons directly over the breast, and continue to roast bird until skin is nicely browned, leg juices run clear, and internal temperature, taken from breast, reaches 160°F, and from the thickest part of the thigh, 170°F, about 1½ hours total.

Place bird on a platter, sprinkle with remaining 1 teaspoon salt, and let rest 10 minutes before carving.

If you are inclined to make pan gravy:

- Remove vegetables from roasting pan and discard.
- Place the pan over two stove-top burners, over medium-high heat, and add 1 cup of chicken stock or white wine.
- Bring to a boil, scraping up bits on the bottom of the pan with a wooden spoon.
- Continue to cook until the quantity of gravy is reduced by half.
- Season with salt and pepper to taste.

VARIATIONS

- If you're feeling particularly healthy (or cholesterol is of no concern), rub the chicken with unsalted butter instead of olive oil, but set the initial cooking temperature to 400°F rather than 450°F.
- Gently separate the skin from the flesh of the bird and massage the meat with Tapenade (page 118) prior to roasting.
- Prepare the bird as in the original recipe, but instead of or in addition to lemon, stuff the bird with a large handful of fresh rosemary, tarragon, or thyme.
- While the chicken is roasting, scatter a combination of pitted green and black olives over it.

Serves 4 to 6

WHY SHOULD A CHICKEN REST PRIOR TO BEING CARVED?

After taking the time to lovingly and carefully roast a bird that has your family or your guests salivating with great anticipation, the worst possible (and mean) thing you can do to it (or meat or turkey, for that matter) is to carve it immediately. Why?

When you pull a freshly roasted chicken from the oven, it is still cooking, even though it is no longer exposed to its heat source. Its juices are still flowing, and if you slice into it immediately, those lovely juices will continue to flow . . . right out of the bird and onto your cutting board (and probably the floor). Giving the bird a few minutes to rest allows the juices to settle within the meat itself. The result is a succulent and tender chicken, as opposed to, say, something with the consistency of balsa.

ADDITIONAL SERVING RECOMMENDATIONS

- Present the whole chicken on a lovely china platter, and serve it tableside.
- Cool the finished, roasted bird in the refrigerator, carve into quarters (page 157), and pack for a picnic.
- Serve with a mix of pan-roasted root vegetables and herbed new potatoes.
- Split a smaller chicken down the breastbone and the backbone, and serve one of the halves to each of two hungry diners.
- Serve as an old-fashioned Sunday dinner, with the Perfect Baked Potato (page 221).

SECONDARY DISHES

- *Fettucine with Lemon Chicken, Parmesan, and Wine (page 184)*
- *Pappardelle with Chicken Ragu (page 186)*
- *Asian Chicken-Stuffed Lettuce Rolls (page 168)*
- *Grilled Vegetable Salad with Chicken and Pine Nuts (page 88)*
- *Warm Grilled Chicken Salad with Herbs (page 94)*
- *Chicken Croquettes with Lemon Sauce (page 176)*
- *Quesadilla of Chicken, Chilies, Tequila, and Lime (page 182)*
- *Paella (page 192)*
- *Chicken Liver Crostini alla Toscana (page 106)*

WHAT YOU HAVE ON HAND

- **4 to 6 pounds of cut-up chicken parts (thighs, legs, breasts, wings) or**
- **1 roasted chicken (whole or parts)**
- **Apricot preserves**
- **Dijon mustard**

WHAT TO DO WITH IT

- Set aside half of the mixed chicken parts (approximately 2 to 3 pounds) for this dish, double-wrap the balance, and freeze in a dated, heavy-duty freezer bag for 8 months.

HOW LONG IT WILL LAST

- This dish will last, refrigerated in a heavy-duty freezer bag or double-plastic-wrapped, for up to 4 days.
- Double-plastic-wrap any leftovers; place in a labeled, dated, heavy-duty freezer bag; and freeze this dish, with its sauce, for up to 3 months.

PRIMARY/SECONDARY

APRICOT-GLAZED ROASTED CHICKEN

Make this delectable dish when you want to do something quick, simple, inexpensive, and very elegant; the apricot glaze (made from store-bought apricot preserves and Dijon mustard) can be prepared a day in advance and refrigerated, and cut-up chicken parts speed the cooking process. To make it even faster, brush this glaze on a roasted chicken that has been cut apart, and simply reheat. A keeper, should you have any chicken parts on hand, or extra whole birds that you want to cook quickly.

4	tablespoons apricot preserves
2	tablespoons Dijon mustard
2	tablespoons dry white wine or water
1	tablespoon honey
$\frac{1}{2}$	tablespoon soy sauce
$\frac{1}{4}$	teaspoon red pepper flakes

3	pounds fresh or roasted chicken parts, on bone and with skin intact, or 1 fresh or roasted whole chicken, cut up (see page 157 for instructions on how to cut up chicken)
$1\frac{1}{2}$	tablespoons extra virgin olive oil
	Kosher salt and freshly ground black pepper

Preheat oven to 400°F.

Place preserves, mustard, wine, honey, soy sauce, and pepper flakes in a small saucepan over medium heat. Cook, stirring frequently, until thinned and heated through. Taste for seasoning, adding more pepper flakes to increase spiciness or soy sauce to increase saltiness. Cover and remove from heat.

Make this dish with store-roasted chicken or chicken parts for a quick dinner.

If using uncooked chicken:

Rub chicken with oil, and season lightly with salt and pepper.

Place chicken parts skin-side up in a broiler pan or ovenproof baking dish, and roast for 10 minutes. Turn pieces over, and continue to cook for another 5 minutes. Baste liberally with the apricot glaze, turn over, and repeat. Reduce heat to 375° F.

Continue to cook, basting repeatedly with both the remainder of the glaze and the pan juices, until a thermometer inserted into the meat reads 160°F and juices run clear, 35 to 40 minutes more. Serve hot or at room temperature.

If using a roasted chicken:

Preheat oven to 350°F.

Baste chicken liberally with apricot glaze, place in a broiler pan or ovenproof baking dish, and bake, basting frequently, until chicken is completely reheated (but not recooked) and glaze has thickened, 10 to 15 minutes. Serve hot or at room temperature.

VARIATIONS

• Add 1 tablespoon of orange juice to the sauce for a tangier flavor.
• Sprinkle the finished dish with slivered almonds that have been toasted at 200°F until lightly golden.

Serves 4

ADDITIONAL SERVING RECOMMENDATIONS

• Prepare this recipe in bulk, and serve buffet-style at a barbecue.
• Serve with sliced apricots, both dried and fresh.
• Prepare this recipe on the grill for added flavor.

SECONDARY DISHES

• Pull leftover chicken off the bone, and toss with wild rice, pine nuts, and chopped apricots. Serve cold.
• Oven-Barbecued Pulled Chicken with Spicy Apricot Sauce (page 180)

PRIMARY

WINE-AND-HERB-POACHED CHICKEN BREASTS

There is no easier way to prepare a multitude of chicken breasts for future use than to poach them: it's fast, delicious, and light, and the result can be served over fresh greens for a hearty yet light salad. Poaching also yields the most flexible chicken leftovers: they can be turned into everything from a Quesadilla of Chicken, Chilies, Tequila, and Lime (page 182), to Warm Grilled Chicken Salad with Herbs (page 94), to Asian Chicken-Stuffed Lettuce Rolls (page 168), to everyone's childhood favorite, the humble yet magnificent Chicken Croquette (page 176).

4	cups white wine or dry vermouth	3–4	pounds skinless (or skinless, boneless) chicken breasts
4	cups water		
2	tablespoons BIG FOOD Mediterranean Spice Blend or Herbes de Provence	1	sheet aluminum foil, large enough to cover your largest roasting pan
1	tablespoon whole black peppercorns		
	Pinch of kosher salt		

Set your largest roasting pan over two burners on stove top; carefully fill with equal parts wine and water, to three-quarters full, adding additional liquid if necessary.

Add spice blend, peppercorns, and salt, and bring to an active, rolling simmer.

Using tongs or a slotted spoon, place breasts into liquid. Reduce heat to low, and cover pan with foil.

Poach until chicken is cooked through, testing to see that meat is firm (but not hard) to the touch, 20 to 30 minutes. Transfer to a platter and let cool.

This recipe is designed for bulk cooking; if you wish to make a smaller portion, reduce the amount of chicken by half, but keep the poaching liquid proportionally the same.

VARIATIONS

- Poach only in water, wine, or stock.
- Add the juice of a lemon to the poaching liquid during the first 5 minutes of poaching.
- Add sliced onions to the poaching liquid prior to bringing it to a simmer.

Serves 6

CAN I EAT THE WHITE THING?

And what *is* the white thing, anyway?

Chances are, if you've ever made anything with skinless, boneless chicken breasts, you've encountered something that I've come to call The White Thing. First—what is it? The White Thing is nothing more than cartilage that at one time secured the meat to the bone (aren't you glad you're not a vegetarian?). It is inedible and should absolutely be snipped out with a good pair of kitchen shears. No, you can't eat The White Thing, and neither should your guests or your children.

ADDITIONAL SERVING RECOMMENDATIONS

- Serve cold, sliced on the bias, over any mixed greens or Roman-Style Sautéed Greens (page 195).
- Slice into thin pieces and serve in Asian Chicken Soup with Greens (page 60).

SECONDARY DISHES

- *Warm Grilled Chicken Salad with Herbs (page 94)*
- *Grilled Vegetable Salad with Chicken and Pine Nuts (page 88)*
- *Paella (page 192)*
- *Quesadilla of Chicken, Chilies, Tequila, and Lime (page 182)*
- *Fettucine with Lemon Chicken, Parmesan, and Wine (page 184)*
- *Asian Chicken-Stuffed Lettuce Rolls (page 168)*
- *Chicken Croquettes (page 176)*
- *Chicken Potpie (page 174)*

PAN-BRAISED CHICKEN WITH LEMON, THYME, AND BLACK OLIVES

Nearly every Mediterranean nation lays claim to a version of this delicious one-pot dish. A slow braise that combines the flavors and textures of chicken, lemon, olives, garlic, wine, and herbs, this recipe calls for the addition of two whole lemons, cut into eighths and tossed into the pan with the olives (which, in turn, provide most of the salt in this dish). When the meal is served, the lemons can be sliced and squeezed into the sauce.

3	tablespoons extra virgin olive oil	$2/3$	cup leftover BIG FOOD Basic Chicken Stock or packaged stock
1	(3- to 4-pound) chicken, cut into 8 pieces, giblets reserved (if available)	1	cup dry white wine or white vermouth
2	garlic cloves, peeled and finely minced		Juice of 1 large lemon
8	sprigs fresh thyme or 1 table-spoon dried, divided	2	lemons, cut into eighths
3	garlic cloves, peeled and smashed	$3/4$	cup pitted green olives
	Freshly ground black pepper	$1/2$	cup pitted black olives
			Kosher salt

Preheat oven to 350°F.

In a large (preferably 12-inch), ovenproof, straight-sided sauté pan with lid, heat oil until rippling but not smoking. Add chicken pieces, skin-side down, taking care not to crowd the pan (do this in batches, if necessary). Brown skin-side well, remove to a platter, and carefully wipe all but approximately 1½ tablespoons oil from the pan.

Add minced garlic, and sauté until softened, about 4 minutes. Lay 4 sprigs thyme, or sprinkle ½ tablespoon of dried thyme, over minced garlic. Return chicken pieces to the pan, skin-side up, arranging them on top of the thyme.

Add smashed garlic and giblets (if you have them), scattering them around the chicken, and season lightly with pepper.

WHAT YOU HAVE ON HAND

- 3 (3- to 4-pound) shrink-wrapped, whole chickens or 6 to 8 pounds of chicken parts
- Large containers of black or green olives
- Fresh thyme
- BIG FOOD Basic Chicken Stock (page 58)

WHAT TO DO WITH IT

- Set aside 1 (3- to 4-pound) whole chicken for this dish. Keep the other chickens wrapped in their original wrapping, place in a dated freezer bag, and freeze for 6 to 8 months.
- If using chicken parts, set aside 3 to 4 pounds for this dish. Use the balance within 3 days or double-plastic-wrap, place in a dated freezer bag, and freeze for up to 6 to 8 months.

HOW LONG IT WILL LAST

- This dish will last in the refrigerator for up to 3 days, double-plastic-wrapped and sealed in a heavy-duty dated freezer bag.
- This dish will freeze for up to 4 to 6 months, sealed in a labeled, dated, heavy-duty freezer bag.

Add stock, wine, and lemon juice, and bring to a low boil. Reduce to a simmer, add lemon wedges, and scatter remaining 4 thyme sprigs or ½ tablespoon dried thyme over the chicken.

Add olives, cover, and place in oven for 45 minutes, basting frequently with the pan sauce.

Remove cover, increase heat to 425°F, and continue to cook for an additional 15 minutes. Remove from oven and let rest for 5 to 8 minutes. Drizzle chicken with pan sauce, adding salt and pepper if necessary, and serve hot in shallow soup bowls, with a slice of crusty garlic toast.

VARIATIONS

• Replace lemons with Meyer lemons, if available. (Meyer lemons are thought to be a cross between the lemon and the mandarin orange, and are sweeter than the regular variety.)

Serves 4 to 6

ADDITIONAL SERVING RECOMMENDATIONS

• Serve this dish hot, over rice.

SECONDARY DISHES

• *Pappardelle with Chicken Ragu (page 186)*

WHAT TO DO WITH IT

- Set aside 1 whole chicken for this dish. Keep the other chickens wrapped in their original wrapping, place in a dated freezer bag, and freeze for up to 8 months.

- If using chicken parts, set aside 3 to 4 pounds for this dish. Use the balance within 3 days, or double-plastic-wrap, place in a dated freezer bag, and freeze for up to 8 months.

- Honey, kept in a very tightly sealed container in a cool, dark location (not the refrigerator), will keep indefinitely.

HOW LONG IT WILL LAST

- This dish will last in the refrigerator for up to 4 days, double-plastic-wrapped and sealed in a dated, heavy-duty freezer bag.

- This dish will freeze for up to 4 to 6 months, sealed in a labeled, dated, heavy-duty freezer bag.

PRIMARY

CHICKEN BRAISED WITH FIGS, HONEY, AND RED WINE

When I created this recipe for the LA Times Syndicate, I had no inkling that it would become a family favorite and be such a spectacular BIG FOOD recipe, because it uses up so many larder staples (wine, chicken stock, honey, herbs, and garlic). A traditional southern Italian blend of flavors, the dish is a flavorful taste-and-texture combination of salty, sweet, and savory that's rustic enough to be served to a hungry crowd after a soccer game, and elegant enough for a dinner party. Best of all, it gets better after it's sat a day in the fridge.

1½	tablespoons extra virgin olive oil		Kosher salt and freshly ground black pepper
½	cup pancetta or thick-sliced honey-baked ham, cut into ¼-inch dice	⅔	cup BIG FOOD Basic Chicken Stock or packaged stock
1	(3- to 4-pound) chicken, cut into 4 to 6 pieces, giblets reserved		Juice of 1 lemon
2	garlic cloves, peeled and minced	1	cup dry red wine
3–4	sprigs fresh rosemary or 1 tablespoon dried	¼	cup honey
2	garlic cloves, peeled, whole	3–4	fresh figs, quartered lengthwise

Preheat oven to 350°F.

Heat oil in large, ovenproof, straight-sided sauté pan with lid over medium heat, until rippling but not smoking. Add pancetta and cook slowly until brown. Remove from pan and reserve.

Add chicken pieces, skin-side down, taking care not to crowd pan, and cook until well browned. (Do this in batches, if necessary.) Remove to platter and carefully remove all but approximately 1½ tablespoons oil from pan.

Add minced garlic and sauté slowly until softened, about 5 minutes. Lay rosemary over garlic and return chicken pieces to pan, skin-side up when possible, arranging them on top of the rosemary.

Add whole garlic cloves and giblets, scattering them around chicken. Season lightly with salt and pepper.

Add stock, lemon juice, and wine. Bring to low boil. Reduce to simmer and, using a turkey baster or spoon, transfer approximately ¼ cup of the sauce to a small bowl. Add honey to sauce in bowl, blend well, and pour back over chicken. Cover, place in oven, and bake, basting frequently, for 45 minutes.

Remove cover, increase heat to 425°F, and continue cooking until sauce has thickened and chicken is just starting to brown, 15 to 20 minutes (watch carefully; this can happen quickly). Carefully fold in reserved pancetta and figs. Bake until figs have softened a bit, 3 to 5 minutes. Remove from oven and let rest 5 to 8 minutes. Season to taste with salt, pepper, and more lemon juice, if needed. Serve in shallow bowls with a slice of toasted crusty bread to sop up the sauce.

VARIATIONS
• Omit the lemon, and add pitted black and green olives.

Serves 4 to 6

If you are planning to go the whole hog and buy fresh figs for this dish, do remember that they're expensive, so for maximum economy, cut up the chicken yourself (page 157).

- Leftover chicken
- Soy sauce
- Scallions
- Boston lettuce
- Limes
- Unsalted, roasted peanuts

WHAT TO DO WITH IT

- Remove the skin from the chicken, and pull the meat off the bone. Cut it into long, 1/4-inch-wide pieces, and set it aside for this recipe.

HOW LONG IT WILL LAST

- The dressing/dipping sauce for this recipe will last up to 1 week in a tightly sealed, refrigerated container.
- The chicken can be stored in the refrigerator in a dated, heavy-duty freezer bag for up to 3 days.
- The lettuce rolls must be eaten immediately, so let your guests assemble their own!

SECONDARY

ASIAN CHICKEN-STUFFED LETTUCE ROLLS

A great way to use up leftover meat or poultry is to flavor it with a specific essence—Asian, Mexican, Italian, for example—and then wrap it. Italians make meat-filled crespelle, or a lasagna with chopped chicken, veal, pork, or beef; Mexicans might turn their leftovers into a burrito or Mexican Tortilla Pie (page 198), which can be frozen like a lasagna. When it's too hot for anything heavy but you still want a lot of flavor, this recipe saves the day. It's easy to prepare (marinate the chopped chicken the night before and pick up a head of Boston lettuce on the way home from work), fun to put together (especially for kids), and you can spice it up as hot or as mild as you like.

VINAIGRETTE:

4	tablespoons soy sauce		1	tablespoon toasted sesame oil
2	tablespoons rice vinegar or white vinegar		1	garlic clove, peeled and smashed
2	scallions, thinly sliced (white part only)		1/2	tablespoon grated fresh ginger or 1 teaspoon dried
	Juice of 1 lime		1	teaspoon granulated sugar
			1/4	teaspoon cayenne pepper

CHICKEN:

3	cups cooked, sliced, skinless, boneless chicken			Juice of 1 lime
1	tablespoon soy sauce		2	heads Boston lettuce, leaves removed, washed, dried, and laid flat
1/2	tablespoon toasted sesame oil			

Optional: 2 tablespoons chopped fresh cilantro; 1/2 cup chopped roasted, unsalted peanuts

FOR THE VINAIGRETTE:

Combine soy sauce, vinegar, scallions, lime juice, oil, garlic, ginger, sugar, and cayenne in a glass container with a tight seal. Shake well.

FOR THE CHICKEN:

Place chicken in a large bowl and toss with soy sauce, oil, and lime juice. If you want to serve the chicken warm, heat it in the microwave for 60 seconds prior to serving. Mix in cilantro and peanuts, if using.

TO ASSEMBLE THE DISH:

Let each diner take a few lettuce leaves and some chicken. Drizzle the chicken with the vinaigrette, roll it up in the lettuce leaves, and enjoy.

VARIATIONS
- Add additional cilantro.
- Add cold bean sprouts to the chicken mixture.
- Add julienne carrots and snow peas to the chicken mixture.
- Roll up the mixture in rice paper wrappers instead of the lettuce.

Serves 4 to 6

ADDITIONAL SERVING RECOMMENDATIONS
- Serve the chicken warm, the lettuce leaves cold, and the dressing at room temperature.
- Serve this dish family-style. Pass around pretty, Asian-style oval platters of the chicken and lettuce leaves, and provide individual bowls of dipping sauce.

SECONDARY DISHES
- *Asian Chicken Soup with Greens (page 60)*
- *Use the vinaigrette in Asian Slaw: buy packaged julienne carrots, red cabbage, and white cabbage, and toss with the vinaigrette.*

HOW TO PEEL A GARLIC CLOVE

Every once in a while, one needs a garlic press—that funky-looking implement that is so impossible to clean that more than one company is now packaging the tool along with a little plastic cleaner, which you will invariably lose (the way I did). There's got to be a better way to peel the papery jackets off of those tender nuggets of flavor and nutty warmth.

- Take a clove of garlic and set it in front of you on a chopping board.
- Using the flat of your chef's knife, press firmly onto clove. The peel will slip right off.
- If your recipe calls for a "smashed" clove, follow the instructions above, but remove the peel and repeat with greater pressure.

CHICKEN SAUSAGE AND PEPPERS

- 5- to 6-pound packages of Italian-style chicken sausage
- Large packages of fresh peppers: bell peppers, sweet or hot Italian peppers, or a combination
- Canned Italian-style tomatoes

WHAT TO DO WITH IT

- Reserve 2 pounds of sausages (approximately 6 to 8 links, depending on their size) for this recipe. Double-wrap the remaining sausages and freeze in a labeled, dated, heavy-duty freezer bag for up to 8 months.

HOW LONG IT WILL LAST

- Chicken Sausage and Peppers will last, stored in an airtight container in the refrigerator, for up to 4 days.
- Freeze Chicken Sausage and Peppers in an airtight, freezer-proof container or heavy-duty, dated freezer bag for up to 6 months.

On a rainy Sunday in a tiny apartment near Rome, I was shaken out of my doldrums by the mouthwatering smell of peppers frying in olive oil. Sweet, nutty, and utterly delectable, this Proustian rush of aroma sent me hurtling back to my days growing up among Italian families, who would prepare this simple and gorgeous dish at the spur of the moment. Comfort food at its finest, this recipe calls for the healthier chicken sausage that is now available in bulk nearly everywhere, but feel free to use traditional Italian pork sausage if your cholesterol is up for the ride (or down for the count).

2	pounds Italian-style chicken sausage, sweet, spicy, or both	2	large orange bell peppers, seeded, ribbed, and sliced into 1/2-inch strips
3	tablespoons extra virgin olive oil	3	garlic cloves, peeled and minced
1	large sweet onion (such as Vidalia), peeled and thinly sliced	1/4	teaspoon red pepper flakes
2	large red bell peppers, seeded, ribbed, and sliced into 1/2-inch strips	1	cup canned crushed Italian-style tomatoes
2	large green bell peppers, seeded, ribbed, and sliced into 1/2-inch strips	1/2	cup dry red wine
			Kosher salt

OPTIONAL: *Sliced button mushrooms, pitted black olives, splash of balsamic vinegar*

Line a large platter with paper towels and place beside stove top. Prick sausages all over with a fork.

Heat 2 tablespoons of oil in a large sauté pan over medium-high heat, until rippling but not smoking. Add sausages, working in batches, if necessary, and sear until brown on all sides, about 10 minutes.

Remove sausages to towel-lined platter, and allow to cool. Carefully wipe inside of pan with a dry paper towel and return it to heat, reducing heat to medium.

Heat the remaining 1 tablespoon of oil, add onion, and cook until translucent but not at all browned, 6 to 8 minutes. Add peppers, garlic, and red pepper flakes; blend well, cooking until peppers are completely wilted, about 8 minutes.

While vegetables are cooking, slice sausages into 2-inch pieces, on the bias, and return to pan. Add tomatoes and wine. Cover and simmer for approximately 20 minutes. Season with salt to taste, and serve hot.

VARIATIONS

- Go 100 percent vegetarian or vegan by using meatless sausage.
- Use traditional Italian pork sausages.
- Use turkey sausage.
- Use Polish sausage (kielbasa), German sausage (bratwurst), or French sausage (boudin blanc).
- Use flavored American sausages (chicken with feta and spinach, or duck).
- Use traditional Moroccan lamb sausage (mergeuz), omit the tomatoes, and add a pinch of cumin.
- Grill the sausages rather than sautéing them first, and proceed directly to cooking the vegetables.

Serves 6

Make this recipe for a crowd by doubling (or tripling) all proportions and preparing it in a roasting pan.

ADDITIONAL SERVING RECOMMENDATIONS

- Serve on an Italian-style roll (a hoagie or a hero, depending on where you live).
- Serve atop hearty pasta, such as shells or penne.
- Wrap in soft *lavash* (Middle Eastern flatbread) or stuff into a pita.

SECONDARY DISHES

- *Torta Rustica (page 208)*

FREEZING PEPPERS

Owing to their high water content, peppers freeze very well (which is a good thing, considering the immense bags available in warehouse clubs and large supermarkets). Frozen whole or sliced into rings or squares, they keep for an average of 3 to 4 months stored in a heavy-duty freezer bag.

If you come home lugging your weight in these low-cal, full-flavor, sweet gems and you have no immediate plans to use all of them, simply do the following:

- Slice the top off the pepper and remove the pod and seeds. (Alternately, slice the pepper into rings or squares.)
- Invert the whole pepper onto a cookie sheet lined with a piece of parchment paper. (Or place slices or squares onto the sheet, not touching each other.)
- Place the entire cookie sheet in the freezer, until pepper is complete frozen; remove, place in heavy-duty freezer bag, and return to the freezer for 3 to 4 months.

To defrost, remove bag from freezer and let stand at room temperature for 45 minutes.

WHAT TO DO WITH IT

- If using whole chicken breasts, see page 157 for instructions on how to bone and skin.
- If preparing all the chicken, proceed directly to the recipe. If preparing a portion of the chicken, set aside the amount you intend to cook; separate the remaining breasts, double-wrap them individually, and freeze them in a labeled, dated, heavy-duty freezer bag, two to a bag, for up to 8 months.

HOW LONG IT WILL LAST

- Double-plastic-wrapped and stored in an airtight container or dated freezer bag, Chicken Saltimbocca will last up to 3 days in the refrigerator or up to 3 months in the freezer.

PRIMARY

CHICKEN SALTIMBOCCA

Translating literally to "jumps in the mouth," saltimbocca is a simple and highly flavorful little dish that takes seconds to prepare, making it perfect for a quick dinner, and it's even better when you've brought home your weight in boneless chicken (or turkey) breasts. I like to make it the traditional way, with as few accoutrements as possible: a touch of sage, a thin slice of prosciutto, a little wine, and a drop of lemon.

2	pounds skinless, boneless chicken breasts, halved width-wise	$\frac{1}{2}$	cup dry white wine or dry vermouth
$\frac{1}{2}$	pound prosciutto, thinly sliced	$\frac{1}{4}$	cup chicken stock (leftover BIG FOOD Basic Chicken Stock or packaged)
1	whole sage leaf per breast half (about 10 leaves)		Juice of 1 lemon
1	tablespoon extra virgin olive oil	1	teaspoon grated lemon zest
1	tablespoon unsalted butter		Freshly ground black pepper

Lay breast halves flat on a clean, plastic cutting board, cut-side facing up. Cover each with 1 slice of prosciutto, tucking in any stray edges so that prosciutto is even with breast. Place 1 sage leaf atop and in the center of prosciutto, roll breast up tightly, and secure with 1 toothpick. Repeat until all the chicken breasts have been rolled.

Heat oil with butter until rippling and foaming but not smoking. Do not let butter brown (or it will go rancid). Working in batches, add rolled breasts, seam-side down, to pan. Do not shake the pan.

Cook 3 minutes, then turn and brown remaining sides, about 3 minutes per side. Remove to a platter and repeat with remaining breasts. Refrain from shaking the pan while browning. Remove the remaining breasts to a platter and set aside.

Add wine, stock, lemon juice and zest, and pepper to the pan. Increase heat to high, and bring to a boil for 3 minutes.

Return rolls to the pan and coat with sauce. Reduce to a low simmer, cover, and cook until chicken is cooked through, about 8 minutes. Season to taste with pepper. Remove toothpicks and serve hot.

VARIATIONS
- Make this dish with turkey cutlets or the traditional thin veal cutlets.
- Place a thin slice of Fontina cheese between the chicken and prosciutto.

Serves 6

DON'T BEAT YOUR BREASTS!

Unless you purchase your chicken breasts already thinly sliced, odds are that they will be thick (approximately ¾-inch thick) when you unpack them. What to do? Slice them width-wise if they're very thick.

To slice thick boneless chicken breasts, you will need:

- A very sharp, nonserrated slicing knife
- A plastic cutting board

1. If breasts are boneless but whole, slice them down the middle.
2. Slice away the "tenderloin," and freeze it for later use in any of the BIG FOOD recipes requiring boneless chicken.
3. One side of the breast will have a nearly invisible membranous coating, making it look smooth and shiny. The other side will be rougher and look striated.
4. Turn it shiny-side up, with its "point" facing you, and its widest part facing the top of the cutting board.
5. Carefully hold the breast in place with the palm of your hand (not your fingers), and gingerly slice width-wise through the center.

WHICH BONELESS MEATS CAN BE POUNDED WHEN NECESSARY:

- Pork loin slices or chops
- Lamb cutlets or chops
- Veal cutlets or chops
- . . . but not chicken.

WHEN YOU SHOULD POUND PORK, LAMB, OR VEAL, OR SLICE CHICKEN:

- When you're rolling the meat around something
- When you're deep-frying the meat
- When you want it to cook as quickly as possible

WHEN SHOULD YOU NOT POUND PORK, LAMB, OR VEAL, OR SLICE CHICKEN:

- When what you're cooking will take some time over direct or indirect heat (on the grill, in a braise, as a roast, in the oven, in a soup, in a stew, or in a poacher)

SPECIAL TOOLS YOU'LL NEED

- Flat or round, uncolored wooden toothpicks for securing meat

ADDITIONAL SERVING RECOMMENDATIONS

- Serve hot on top of long, skinny pasta tossed with extra virgin olive oil, garlic, and a sprinkling of fresh sage.
- Serve hot on steamed rice or risotto (page 150).
- Serve cold sliced into rounds on top of Roman-Style Sautéed Greens (page 195).

WHAT YOU HAVE ON HAND

- **Leftover skinless, boneless chicken meat, light or dark**
- **Store-bought puff pastry or frozen savory pie crusts**
- **Large bags of frozen or fresh carrots, peas, onions, potatoes**
- **BIG FOOD Basic Chicken Stock (page 58), packaged chicken stock, or strained leftover Traditional Jewish-Style Chicken Soup (page 56)**

WHAT TO DO WITH IT

- Chop the chicken into bite-size pieces.
- Defrost frozen vegetables; cut fresh vegetables into bite-size pieces.
- Roll out pastry according to package instructions.

This flexible recipe makes one large, family-size Chicken Potpie in a 3-quart oblong baking dish, or 12 small ones. Either way, make sure you are using oven-to-freezer, microwavable bakeware. All ingredients can be doubled or tripled, if you want to make extra.

SECONDARY

CHICKEN POTPIE

Those of us who frequently make a big pot of chicken soup or roast an oversize bird often face the conundrum of what to do with all that leftover meat. (By now, you should certainly have an inkling.) But if you've grown weary of chicken salads or chicken pastas, and you also have a good amount of leftover vegetables—fresh or frozen—then this recipe is for you. It calls for store-bought puff pastry, and freezes for the (very) long haul. What could be easier? Make these in individual-size freezer-to-oven baking dishes, and serve them as comforting, spur-of-the-moment meals to everyone from the hungriest child to the crankiest grown-up.

4	tablespoons unsalted butter
6	tablespoons unbleached, all purpose flour
3	cups leftover BIG FOOD Basic Chicken Stock, packaged chicken stock, or well-strained Traditional Jewish-Style Chicken Soup
2	tablespoons mixed, chopped fresh herbs (parsley, sage, rosemary, thyme), or 1 tablespoon dried
	Kosher salt and freshly ground black pepper
3	cups cooked skinless, boneless chicken meat, cut into bite-size pieces
2	medium potatoes, peeled and cut into bite-size chunks
1	medium onion, peeled and sliced, or 1 cup whole pearl onions
1	cup carrots, peeled and cut into bite-size chunks
1	cup peas
1	cup sliced mushrooms
1	(1-pound) box frozen puff pastry, defrosted according to package instructions, or 2 packaged savory pie crusts, softened and rolled together to create one large crust

Preheat oven to 425°F.

Melt butter in a large saucepan over medium heat. When it begins to foam, sprinkle in flour, stirring constantly with a wooden spoon (do not let mixture darken), until all of the flour has been added and mixture is smooth, about 3 minutes. Add stock in a slow and steady stream, whisking constantly. Continue to cook until sauce has the consistency of thick gravy. Add herbs and season with salt and pepper to taste; reduce heat to lowest setting to keep gravy warm until ready to use.

In a large bowl, combine chicken with potatoes, onion, carrots, peas, and mushrooms. Set aside.

Place puff pastry or pie dough on a lightly floured surface and, using the casserole you plan to bake in, trace a perfectly sized crust. If using pastry, invert casserole onto pastry and trace around it with a sharp knife. If using standard pie dough, follow the same procedure, but give yourself a little extra room—approximately half an inch—so that the dough overlaps onto the sides of the casserole dish. Set the pastry or dough aside.

Place chicken-and-vegetable mixture and gravy into casserole (evenly dividing ingredients if you are using individual dishes). Top with pastry or dough, pinching around edges to seal in ingredients.

Place on a rimmed baking sheet, and bake until the dough is golden brown and has risen, approximately 45 minutes. Serve hot.

VARIATIONS
- Substitute turkey for the chicken.
- Go vegetarian, using vegetables and vegetable stock.

Serves 6 to 8

USING STORE-BOUGHT PUFF PASTRY OR PIE CRUSTS

One can assume (correctly) that homemade puff pastry is the best kind; unfortunately, it is a masterly and often frustratingly difficult task to undertake in a rush. But by all means, if you have the time and a little peace of mind, it is well worth your while to make the stuff. Look for recipes by the American Zen master of French cookery herself, Julia Child, and the equally spectacular cookbook author, Jean Anderson. Send the kids and the husband to a long double feature, roll up your sleeves, and have at it. Your life may never be the same.

But if you have neither the time nor the inclination, fear not: good-quality packaged puff pastry is available everywhere, as are prepared pie crusts. If you choose to go the pie-crust route, make absolutely sure you're buying the savory (as opposed to the sweetened) kind.

HOW LONG IT WILL LAST

- Chicken Potpie will keep in the refrigerator for up to 3 days, double-wrapped in plastic.
- Chicken Potpie will freeze, double-wrapped in plastic and sealed in a labeled, dated freezer bag, for up to 8 months.

CHICKEN CROQUETTES WITH LEMON SAUCE

In spite of their association with diners and truck stops, Chicken Croquettes are a highly respected food in my home. They freeze for months at a time; marry a light, crunchy exterior to a hot, tender filling; and can be served at the fanciest of ladies' luncheons as an appetizer (or as a quick dinner, with a small salad and a nice glass of wine).

CROQUETTES:

3	packed cups very finely minced or ground cooked skinless, bone-less chicken	1½	cups bread crumbs or crushed saltines, divided
1	medium onion, peeled and finely minced	1	teaspoon kosher salt, divided
			Canola oil for frying
3	eggs, lightly beaten together, plus 1 egg, lightly beaten in a separate, shallow bowl	¼	teaspoon cayenne pepper

LEMON SAUCE:

1½	tablespoons unsalted butter	2	cups leftover BIG FOOD Basic Chicken Stock or packaged stock
1½	tablespoons unbleached, all purpose flour		Juice of 2 lemons

Optional: *1 tablespoon capers, soaked in water and drained*

WHAT YOU HAVE ON HAND

- **Leftover cooked skinless, bone-less chicken**
- **Bread crumbs or saltines**
- **BIG FOOD Basic Chicken Stock (page 58) or packaged stock**

WHAT TO DO WITH IT

- Set aside 2 to 3 cups of leftover cooked chicken for this recipe; double-wrap the balance in plastic, and refrigerate for up to 3 days.
- Set aside 1½ cups of bread or cracker crumbs for this recipe, and store the balance in an airtight container in a cool, dark location for up to 2 weeks.

HOW LONG IT WILL LAST

- Chicken Croquettes will keep, double-plastic-wrapped and sealed in an airtight container, for up to 4 days in the refrigerator.
- Chicken Croquettes will keep, double-plastic-wrapped and sealed in a labeled, dated freezer bag, for up to 8 months in the freezer.

ON GRINDING CHICKEN AND OTHER MEATS

Ideally, cooked chicken (and anything else you might ever want to grind) should be ground in a tool meant specifically for that purpose. My old-fashioned grinder was bought for $5 at a tag sale, clamps to the side of the table, and produces perfectly ground (fill in the blank) every time I use it. However, it does take some time and patience—especially to clean. What's a cook to do? Purists will hate me for saying this, but I give you permission: go ahead and use your food processor, with its standard blade. Works like a charm.

FOR THE CROQUETTES:

Combine chicken and onion in a large bowl. Add 3 beaten eggs and blend well.

Add ½ cup of the bread crumbs and ½ teaspoon of the salt, and blend well; the mixture should be neither too wet nor too dry.

Form croquettes by taking a handful of chicken mixture (approximately 1 large soupspoon's worth) and rolling it between your palms to form a 2-inch-thick log. Set it on a plate, and repeat until all of the mixture has been used.

Heat 1 inch of oil in a deep, straight-sided sauté pan, to 375°F. (Test this with a special candy or deep fry thermometer—*not* a meat thermometer—or sprinkle a few bread crumbs into the oil. If they go brown immediately, the oil is the right temperature.)

While oil heats, place remaining bread crumbs in a wide soup bowl, and season with cayenne pepper and the remaining ½ teaspoon salt.

When oil is ready, take one croquette at a time, roll it in the remaining beaten egg and then in bread crumbs, shake off the excess, and carefully place it in the frying pan, using long tongs. Fry a few at a time, taking care not to crowd the pan (or the croquettes will steam rather than fry), until golden brown. Keep finished croquettes warm on an ovenproof plate, covered with aluminum foil. Serve warm with Lemon Sauce.

FOR THE LEMON SAUCE:

Melt the butter in a small saucepan over medium heat. Whisk in flour, until a thick paste is formed.

Add chicken stock in a slow and steady stream, whisking constantly, until thick and smooth, 3 to 4 minutes. Whisk in lemon juice and capers, if using. Serve immediately, alongside or atop croquettes.

VARIATIONS
- Substitute canned tuna or salmon for the chicken.
- Substitute leftover turkey for the chicken.
- Substitute leftover Brandade (page 144) for the chicken.

Yields 12 to 14 croquettes

ADDITIONAL SERVING RECOMMENDATIONS

- Serve croquettes:
  - Hot on a bed of Roman-Style Sautéed Greens (page 195), drizzled with Lemon Sauce.
  - At room temperature on a mixed green salad dressed with Vinaigrette (page 92) or your favorite packaged dressing.
- Serve Lemon Sauce with:
  - Croquettes of any variety (see "Variations").
  - Broiled fish of any variety.
  - Wine-and-Herb-Poached Chicken Breasts (page 162).

WHAT TO DO WITH IT

- Set aside 4 pounds of skinless, boneless chicken for this recipe; double-plastic-wrap the balance, and store in a labeled, dated, heavy-duty freezer bag in the freezer for up to 8 months.
- Set aside the appropriate amount of onions for this recipe, and store the balance in a mesh bag in a cool, dark location, away from potatoes.

HOW LONG IT WILL LAST

- Balik Fish will last up to 3 days sealed in an airtight container in the refrigerator.
- Balik Fish will freeze for up to 6 months, double-plastic-wrapped and sealed in labeled, dated, heavy-duty freezer bags.

ADDITIONAL SERVING RECOMMENDATIONS

- Serve cold as an appetizer, on a bed of greens and with a dollop of horseradish.

PRIMARY/SECONDARY

PAPA'S BALIK FISH

"When is a fish not a fish? When it's a chicken," said my uncle Marvin Gordon about these tender chicken dumplings known, for reasons unfathomable, as Balik Fish, also possibly pronounced Bilig Fish (or, in low German/Yiddish, "Cheap Fish"). This dish was introduced to me by my late father, Cy Altman, who learned how to make them from his mother when she was already into her nineties.

4	packed cups finely minced or ground skinless, boneless chicken	3	carrots, peeled and cut into 2-inch pieces
1	medium onion, peeled and finely minced	2	celery stalks, cut into 2-inch pieces
3	eggs, lightly beaten	1	large onion, peeled and thinly sliced
½	cup bread crumbs	1	tablespoon chopped fresh parsley, dill, or chervil
½	teaspoon sugar		Lemon sauce, page 176
½	teaspoon kosher salt		
1	garlic clove, peeled and finely minced		

Combine chicken, onion, eggs, bread crumbs, sugar, salt, and garlic. Using clean hands, blend mixture together thoroughly. If mixture is very wet, continue to add bread crumbs by the tablespoon; the mixture should easily form into logs but not stick to your hands.

Form Balik Fish by taking a handful of chicken mixture (approximately 1 large soupspoon's worth) and rolling it between your palms to form a 2-inch-thick log. Set it on a plate, and repeat until all of the mixture has been used. Cover with plastic wrap and refrigerate for 1 hour.

Place carrots, celery, onion, and herbs in a large, wide saucepan, fill halfway with cold water, cover, and bring to a simmer, until liquid is infused, about 30 minutes.

Carefully lower logs into the liquid, replace cover, and cook until Balik Fish are cooked through, about 1 hour. Serve hot as a main course, drizzled with Lemon Sauce (page 176).

This is a perfect gefilte fish substitute for those who are allergic to fish.

VARIATIONS

- Replace the chicken with ground fresh whitefish, halibut, or pike, and you have gefilte fish.
- Add chicken broth or wine to the poaching liquid.

Serves 6 to 8

FOOL'S CHICKEN

Stevie Romanoff, home cook extraordinaire, blessed me years ago with this recipe, which came by way of her mother-in-law, Judy Boggess (who gave it its memorable moniker for a reason understood after the dish's assembly is completed). A nod to simplicity and slow cooking, Fool's Chicken is a boon to those of us who like to stock up on things like sliced deli meat (or, in this case, packaged dried beef) and large tubs of sour cream, and always have some of each lurking in the fridge. Make this filling meal when the temperature takes a big dip; start it early in the day, put it in the oven, and forget all about it until dinnertime.

2	(2½-ounce) packages of dried beef (preferably Buddig brand)	½	cup dry white wine
6	skinless, boneless chicken breasts	½	tablespoon freshly ground black pepper
1	(16-ounce) container sour cream (full-fat, low-fat, or fat-free)	1	teaspoon kosher salt
1	(15-ounce) can Campbell's Golden Mushroom soup	1	teaspoon garlic powder
		½	teaspoon nutmeg
			Hot rice or egg noodles

Preheat oven to 300°F.

Lightly coat the bottom of a deep casserole with cooking spray. Tear the slices of dried beef into bite-size pieces, and lay them evenly on the bottom of the casserole.

Roll chicken breasts into cylinders and place each one on its end, on top of the dried beef.

In a mixing bowl, whisk together sour cream, soup, wine, pepper, salt, garlic powder, and nutmeg.

Pour mixture over chicken and cook for 3 hours. Serve hot, over rice or lightly peppered egg noodles.

VARIATIONS

- For a leaner version of this dish, use fat-free or low-fat sour cream, and/or extra-lean sliced ham instead of beef.
- Wrap each chicken breast with one strip of bacon.
- Add sliced mushrooms to the sauce.

Serves 4 to 6

WHAT YOU HAVE ON HAND

- **Large packages of skinless, boneless chicken breasts**
- **Dried beef (look for the Buddig Beef brand)**
- **Sour cream**
- **Bacon**

WHAT TO DO WITH IT

- Set aside 6 skinless, boneless chicken breasts; double-plastic-wrap the balance, and store in a dated, heavy-duty freezer bag in the refrigerator for up to 3 days. Wrapped the same way, they will keep in the freezer for up to 8 months.
- Use 2 whole packages of dried beef for this dish.

HOW LONG IT WILL LAST

- This dish will last, stored in an airtight container in the refrigerator, for up to 4 days.

SECONDARY DISHES

- *Slice leftover chicken into pieces, add half a cup of sliced, lightly sautéed mushrooms, and reheat slowly in the Fool's Chicken sauce combined with a tablespoon of hot Hungarian paprika.*

WHAT YOU HAVE ON HAND

- Leftover chicken, on or off the bone, preferably without skin
- BIG FOOD Barbecue Sauce (page 37)
- Hamburger rolls

WHAT TO DO WITH IT

- Depending on how much leftover chicken you have and how much *cue* you want to make, pull the leftover chicken off the bone (or if it's cooked and boneless, simply tear it into strips with your clean hands); discard the skin. Store any remaining leftover chicken in a dated, heavy-duty freezer bag in the refrigerator for up to 3 days from the time the original dish was cooked.
- Set aside the number of hamburger rolls you desire for the appropriate number of hungry mouths you are feeding. Store the balance in a labeled, dated, heavy-duty freezer bag in the freezer for up to 6 months.

HOW LONG IT WILL LAST

- Oven-Barbecued Pulled Chicken will last in the refrigerator for up to 4 days, stored in a heavy-duty, dated freezer bag.
- Oven-Barbecued Pulled Chicken will last in the freezer for up to 6 months, stored in a labeled, heavy-duty, dated freezer bag.

SECONDARY

OVEN-BARBECUED PULLED CHICKEN WITH SPICY APRICOT SAUCE

There comes a time in every barbecue-lover's life when he or she must turn away from the grill and head into the kitchen. The weather may be bad, you may live in an apartment, or you simply may not have enough time to do the dry rub/barbecue sauce/smoke thing. This recipe, which has repeatedly fooled many of my barbecue-loving friends, is a simple, delicious, and healthy alternative. All you need is your oven, a few cups of leftover chicken, BIG FOOD Barbecue Sauce, a few dollops of apricot preserves, and you're good to go. Make this dish as mild or spicy as you like, and serve it as plain or as gussied up as the occasion calls for. The secret, as they say, is in the sauce.

2–3 cups cooked chicken (light or dark, drumsticks, thighs, breasts, or wings), skin removed

2 cups BIG FOOD Barbecue Sauce or packaged sauce

4 tablespoons apricot preserves

Optional: Chicken stock

Preheat oven to 300°F.

Using your (clean) hands, pull chicken meat from bones. If the chicken is boneless, simply pull it apart lengthwise, tearing away long thin strips of meat. Place in a nonreactive mixing bowl. In a separate bowl, combine barbecue sauce with preserves; stir together to blend well.

Heat $1/2$ cup of apricot barbecue sauce in a small saucepan over medium heat until it's just warm. Spoon over chicken, and toss well to combine.

Lightly spray a large roasting or sauté pan with cooking spray, and place chicken in it. Drizzle 1 cup of the remaining apricot barbecue sauce directly over chicken, blend well, cover with aluminum foil, and bake, basting every 15 minutes, for 1 hour. (If the blend seems too dry, add a few tablespoons of chicken stock combined with barbecue sauce.)

Serve hot, topped with the remaining apricot barbecue sauce.

VARIATIONS

• Make this dish with fresh, uncooked chicken: Follow the Apricot-Glazed Roasted Chicken on page 160, but instead of basting with the apricot and mustard glaze, baste the bird with barbecue sauce. Cool the cooked chicken, pull meat from the bones, and continue with the rest of the recipe.

Serves 6

ADVICE ON FREEZING BREAD AND ROLLS

It used to be my staunch position that bread is the staff of life and therefore should not be frozen. While I still believe that it is the staff of life and should be enjoyed with some level of sacredness, even if it's wrapped around a bologna sandwich (remember, most of us take a form of bread for religious reasons, whether it is matzo or challah or the Host), bread dough these days is often filled with all sorts of weird things that make it last—unfrozen or unrefrigerated—forever. Suddenly, what used to have to be stored carefully or eaten quickly now lasts a preternaturally long time. Nevertheless, I have become a serious bread-freezing person because it works so well; it also enables you to buy the freshest, most delicious stuff you can find, and keep it without having to gorge yourself on it all in one sitting.

Really good bread and rolls of all sorts are now available in bulk pretty much everywhere, from your local supermarket to your favorite discount club. Look for interesting versions, like sourdough rolls and multigrain *ciabattas* and Latvian black breads and white pullman loaves. Set aside what you immediately need while it's still fresh, remove the remainder from its store packaging, double-plastic-wrap, and freeze in a labeled, heavy-duty, dated freezer bag for up to 3 months. To thaw the bread, simply remove it from the freezer, and let it sit on the counter for a few hours *in its plastic wrap*. Bread that has been frozen and thawed should not, however, be re-frozen.

ADDITIONAL SERVING RECOMMENDATIONS

• Serve as you would your traditional favorite Southern barbecue—with sides of Mature Mac and Cheese (page 270), Roman-Style Sautéed Greens (page 195), coleslaw, and biscuits. Spoon extra sauce directly over the biscuits.

• Serve Carolina style: Spoon the chicken mixture over a hamburger bun, top with coleslaw and barbecue sauce, and enjoy (with lots of napkins).

WHAT YOU HAVE ON HAND

- **Leftover skinless, boneless chicken meat**
- **Large tortillas: flour, corn, flavored**
- **Cheese: Cheddar, Fontina, Monterey Jack, Brie**
- **Chilies: preferably jalapeño (pickled or fresh)**

WHAT TO DO WITH IT

- Set aside 1 cup of shredded leftover cooked chicken for this recipe; refrigerate the balance for up to 3 days in a dated, heavy-duty freezer bag.
- Set aside 2 tortillas for this recipe, and freeze the balance for up to 4 months in a labeled, dated, heavy-duty freezer bag.
- Set aside the quantity of cheese needed for this recipe, and refrigerate or freeze the balance according to the cheese storage information on page 111.

HOW LONG IT WILL LAST

- This quesadilla, cooked, will last up to 3 days in the refrigerator, double-plastic-wrapped and stored in a dated, heavy-duty freezer bag.

SECONDARY

QUESADILLA OF CHICKEN, CHILIES, TEQUILA, AND LIME

First of all, no, you will not get drunk from the tequila. Second, you can feel free to use as few or as many chilies as you care to. Third, if you detest cilantro (at least 50 percent of the general adult population seems to), replace it with fresh basil. The beauty of this recipe is in its flexibility. You can sandwich leftover chicken meat between just about any kind of tortilla (flavored or unflavored, corn or flour, although I like corn). Plus, you can use nearly any cheese (low-fat, nonfat, or all-fat; Monterey Jack, Brie, or Cheddar), and enjoy it as a main course or an appetizer to Mexican Chicken Soup (page 62), dolloped with sour cream or your favorite salsa, and guacamole (page 196). A terrific leftover in and of itself, once baked you can store quesadillas in the refrigerator for several days and enjoy them all over again as a hot or cold snack.

½	cup tequila	2	large soft tortillas (flour, corn, or flavored)
¼	cup fresh lime juice		
¾	cup packed cilantro leaves, minced	1	cup grated cheese (Cheddar, Monterey Jack, Brie, Fontina, or Gouda)
1	pickled jalapeño, minced		
1	tablespoon sugar		
1	cup leftover cooked, shredded, skinless chicken meat		

Optional: *More jalapeños, salsa, more than one type of cheese*

In a mixing bowl, whisk together tequila, lime juice, jalapeño, and sugar. Pour into a large, heavy-duty freezer bag.

Add chicken, zip bag tightly closed, and gently toss so that all of the chicken is coated with marinade. Refrigerate for 15 minutes or up to 1 hour.

Remove chicken from bag and discard marinade.

Preheat oven to 350°F.

Lightly coat two large nonstick, ovenproof sauté pans with cooking spray. Heat pans over medium-high heat. Lay one tortilla in each pan, and toast until bottom begins to brown, about 3 minutes. Quickly transfer one of the tortillas to a plate and cover loosely with foil to keep warm.

Reduce heat to medium. Sprinkle half of the cheese over the tortilla in the pan, and top with chicken. Sprinkle the remaining cheese on top of the chicken, and place the second tortilla, browned-side up, directly on top of it, then weight it down for 5 minutes with another pan.

Place pan in oven, and bake until cheese melts and filling is hot, 12 to 15 minutes. Serve hot.

VARIATIONS

- Replace the tequila marinade with your favorite salsa, and continue with the recipe.
- Substitute turkey or beef for the chicken.
- Omit the marinade entirely, and use leftover Oven-Barbecued Pulled Chicken (page 180).
- Omit the marinade entirely, and substitute scrambled or fried eggs or egg substitute for the chicken for a breakfast quesadilla.

Serves 4

ADDITIONAL SERVING RECOMMENDATIONS

- Serve like a pizza, divided into quarters and topped with guacamole, salsa, sour cream, chopped red onion, and/or minced pickled jalapeños.
- Slice into bite-size portions, and serve as an appetizer.

SECONDARY DISHES

- *Use leftover flour or corn tortillas in the classic Mexican comfort food: chilaquiles. Fry the leftover tortillas, and top with chili sauce and eggs.*

- **Leftover skinless, boneless chicken**
- **Lemons**
- **Parmesan cheese**
- **Bread crumbs**
- **BIG FOOD Basic Chicken Stock (page 58) or packaged stock**

WHAT TO DO WITH IT

- Set aside 2 cups leftover chicken for this recipe; refrigerate the balance for up to 3 days in a dated, heavy-duty freezer bag.

- Set aside 3 lemons for this recipe; store the balance in plastic bags in your salad crisper, and they'll keep for approximately 6 weeks. Stored in a bowl at room temperature (where they are also lovely to look at—they make a great centerpiece), they will keep for approximately 10 days.

- Freshly grate 1½ cups of Parmesan cheese and set it aside for this recipe; the balance should be double-wrapped in waxed paper and stored in your refrigerator for up to 3 weeks.

SECONDARY

FETTUCINE WITH LEMON CHICKEN, PARMESAN, AND WINE

This recipe, which was devised out of a refrigerator empty but for some leftover chicken, a fresh hunk of Parmesan, and a bit of dry white wine, is a simple luxury that can be amended further with the addition of pitted black olives, the odd anchovy, and even leftover Roman-Style Sautéed Greens (page 195).

1	tablespoon kosher salt
1	pound dried fettucine
2	tablespoons extra virgin olive oil
2	garlic cloves, peeled and minced
2	cups sliced skinless, boneless, leftover chicken
⅓	cup leftover BIG FOOD Basic Chicken Stock or packaged stock
⅓	cup dry white wine
	Juice of 3 large lemons, divided
3	sprigs fresh thyme or 1 tablespoon dried
	Freshly ground black pepper
	Zest of 1 lemon
1½	cups freshly grated Parmesan cheese, and more for topping

Optional: ½ cup bread crumbs

USING ZEST FOR MORE FLAVOR

Cooking with the zest of a lemon (or a lime, an orange, or even a grapefruit) is a fabulous way to impart an extra punch of flavor to a dish without squeezing additional fruit. But zesting itself can be a confusing technique. Thankfully, it has become far more popular recently, due in large part to the emergence of a simple zesting tool that we cooks have borrowed from the woodworker's shop: the Microplane.

To zest a lemon:

- Lay the Microplane down over a small bowl and, assuming you are right-handed, hold it steady with your left hand.
- Hold a lemon in your right hand and grate it back and forth against the Microplane, rotating it frequently (once you get down to the whitish pith, it's time to rotate).
- Or, simply hold the Microplane as you would a cheese grater, and "zest" the lemon directly over your dish.

Fill a large stockpot with water, add salt, and bring to a boil. Cook fettucine until al dente (tender, but still slightly firm to the bite).

While pasta is cooking, heat oil in a large sauté pan set over medium heat, until rippling but not smoking. Add garlic and sauté until very lightly browned, about 5 minutes.

Add chicken and stir well. Add stock, wine, and a third of the lemon juice. Reduce to a simmer, cover, and cook until flavors combine, about 8 minutes.

Add thyme and pepper to taste, and toss well.

When pasta is ready, scoop out 1 cup of the cooking water and reserve. Drain pasta, toss with the chicken, and, using tongs, carefully blend so that the chicken is distributed throughout.

Add the remaining lemon juice and the zest. Toss, cover, reduce heat to low, and simmer for 5 minutes. If pasta appears dry, add pasta water to it by the spoonful until you have a thin sauce.

Increase heat to medium, and sprinkle in all but ¼ cup of the cheese, stirring several times while adding cheese to blend well. Place into warm bowls, dust with the remaining ¼ cup of cheese, and serve hot, passing a grater and an extra chunk of Parmesan around the table.

VARIATIONS

- Tip the pasta into a buttered casserole dish, top with bread crumbs and Parmesan, and bake at 350°F, until the top is golden brown.

Serves 6

RESERVING PASTA WATER

Very often, we see recipes that call for the cook to reserve a small amount of pasta water prior to dumping the rest out. Why?

Pasta water is filled with sloughed-off glutens—that sticky stuff that makes rice hold together and pasta stick together in water that's been unsalted (which is partially why we salt it). Adding small amounts of pasta water to sauce provides body, whether it's a red sauce, a white sauce, or just extra virgin olive oil and garlic.

HOW LONG IT WILL LAST

- This dish will last, sealed in an air-tight plastic container or double-plastic-wrapped, for up to 4 days in the refrigerator.

SECONDARY

PAPPARDELLE WITH CHICKEN RAGU

One of my favorite ways to use up leftover chicken (or lamb, turkey, duck, and especially rabbit—a rare occurrence) is to toss it with red wine, tomato sauce, and the meaty juices that have accumulated with the leftover meat. Stewed slowly and blended with garlic, onions, carrots, celery, and herbs, the result is a quasi-traditional, delicious ragu—that very hearty Italian sauce that is a meal in a bowl.

2	tablespoons extra virgin olive oil		2	cups dry red wine
1	medium onion, peeled and finely minced		1	teaspoon dried oregano
2	carrots, peeled and roughly chopped		1	teaspoon dried basil
2	celery stalks, chopped		1	teaspoon kosher salt
2	garlic cloves, peeled and minced		½	cup leftover BIG FOOD Basic Chicken Stock, or packaged stock
3	cups thinly sliced or torn skinless, boneless, leftover chicken		1	pound pappardelle or similarly wide-cut, ribbony noodles
1	(28-ounce) can crushed Italian-style tomatoes			Parmesan cheese for serving

Optional: *Pinch of red pepper flakes*

Heat oil in a large saucepan or Dutch oven over medium heat until rippling but not smoking. Add onion, carrots, and celery. Cook until translucent, about 8 minutes. Do *not* let vegetables brown.

Add garlic and cook for 1 minute. Add chicken, mix well, and cook until warmed through.

Add tomatoes and wine, bring to a boil, and cook for 5 minutes. Add oregano, basil, salt, and red pepper flakes, if using. Reduce to a low simmer, cover, and cook for 45 minutes, stirring frequently. (If mixture becomes too thick, add spoonfuls of red wine to maintain a gravylike consistency.)

Add stock and increase to a low boil for 5 minutes. Stir well, reduce to a simmer, cover, and cook for 30 more minutes.

While sauce is cooking, fill a large stockpot with salted water and bring to a boil. Cook pasta until al dente (tender, but still slightly firm to the bite). Scoop out and reserve 1 cup of pasta water. Drain pasta and keep warm.

Add 2 tablespoons pasta water to sauce, increase heat, and cook until sauce is gravylike, about 8 minutes. Toss pasta with sauce, adding more pasta water if necessary to moisten sauce. Serve hot, with freshly grated Parmesan cheese.

VARIATIONS
- Substitute turkey, lamb, or roast duck for the chicken.
- Substitute fettucine or tagliatelle for the pappardelle.

Serves 6

COOKING WITH WINE

Mentioning the words "cooking with wine" is often enough to send some people into a sheer frenzy. On the one hand, it conjures up images of Dan Aykroyd's famous impersonation of Julia Child . . . the one where he has a little too much cooking sherry and "slices the dickens" out of his finger. On the other hand, it can be utterly confusing: What wine should be used? Where should it be purchased? How should it be stored?

The answer is simple: Never cook with a wine that you wouldn't happily sit down and drink. This does not mean that you should pour a 1983 Chateauneuf du Pape all over your chicken. It means that if a recipe calls for a dry red wine, it's perfectly fine to walk into your nearest wine shop and say to the proprietor, "I am making a dish that calls for a dry red wine, and I would like to spend no more than $10 on it." If that salesman is a good one, he'll know exactly where to lead you. Cooking with wine does *not* mean using those supposed "cooking wines" sold in supermarkets; leave them where they sit: on the shelves.

We usually don't have a lot of leftover wine in my home, but whatever we save generally gets corked and stored in the refrigerator. Therefore, if I have half a bottle that's a few days old staring back at me from inside my fridge, it counts as a leftover, and I know that I must cook something with it.

ADDITIONAL SERVING RECOMMENDATIONS
- Serve in deep, wide bowls with a slice of toasted crusty bread and a side dish of Roman-Style Sautéed Greens (page 195).

WHAT YOU HAVE ON HAND

- Leftover chicken
- Dried or fresh Mediterranean herbs: BIG FOOD Mediterranean Spice Blend (page 39); fresh oregano, basil, and fennel seed; or herbes de Provence
- Small hamburger buns

WHAT TO DO WITH IT

- Set aside 2 cups of leftover chicken for this dish, and store the balance in a dated, heavy-duty freezer bag.

HOW LONG IT WILL LAST

- Sliders made from leftover chicken will last up to 3 days, refrigerated.
- Sliders made from leftover chicken will last up to 3 months, frozen.
- Sliders made from uncooked chicken will last up to 4 days, refrigerated.
- Sliders made from uncooked chicken will last up to 6 months, frozen.

SECONDARY

CHICKEN SLIDERS WITH MEDITERRANEAN HERBS

Making burgers of any sort (chicken, turkey, beef, lamb, salmon, or veggie) is the perfect way to do something great with leftovers, especially when you're feeding little mouths. Children love burgers of all kinds because they can be made small (like sliders) and manageable for tiny hands and mouths, which can easily assemble and disassemble them. These Chicken Sliders are made with leftover chicken that's been ground or pulverized in a food processor and combined with herbs and spices; the trick here to prevent the already cooked meat from turning into little herb-flavored hockey pucks is to "cook" them very quickly at a very high temperature. Or make a batch from a large container of store-ground chicken; freeze them uncooked on a cookie sheet; place a few together in a dated, heavy-duty freezer bag; and store in the freezer for up to 6 months. Either way, dinner is done before you can say Dagwood.

2–3	cups ground leftover skinless, boneless chicken; or 2–3 cups uncooked ground chicken	1½	teaspoons kosher salt
1	medium onion, peeled and finely minced	¼	teaspoon freshly ground black pepper
1	tablespoon BIG FOOD Mediterranean Spice Blend or ¼ tablespoon each dried oregano, basil, parsley, and fennel seed		Toasted hamburger buns or English muffins

Optional: Bread crumbs, Fromage Fort (page 34) for topping

Place chicken (cooked or uncooked) in a large bowl. Add onion, spice mix, salt, and pepper. If mixture feels too wet, add 1 tablespoon bread crumbs.

Form 12 patties, approximately 3 inches wide and 1 inch thick, and place on a platter. (If you are making sliders ahead of time, separate patties in layers between sheets of waxed paper and wrap in plastic, and refrigerate them for up to 2 hours). Sliders can also be frozen at this point.

If baking sliders:

Preheat oven to 400°F.

Lightly coat a heavy-duty baking sheet with cooking spray, and place sliders on sheet approximately one-half inch apart. Cover with aluminum foil.

Reduce oven to 350°F. Heat precooked sliders until warmed through, 8 to 10 minutes. If using uncooked sliders, cook until a thermometer inserted into the center reads 160°F (approximately 8 to 10 minutes). If topping with Fromage Fort, add it to sliders during the last 5 minutes of cooking.

If pan-frying sliders:

Lightly coat a large sauté pan with nonstick spray, and heat over medium-high heat.

Cook precooked sliders, turning once, until both sides are crisp and golden, and sliders are warmed throughout, about 8 minutes. If using uncooked sliders, cook until a thermometer inserted into the center reads 160°F (approximately 8 to 10 minutes). If topping with Fromage Fort, add it to the sliders during the last 5 minutes of cooking.

Serve on warm, toasted hamburger buns or English muffins.

VARIATIONS

- Replace the Mediterranean spices with 1 teaspoon of cumin and ½ teaspoon of coriander for a Middle Eastern flavor.
- Substitute ground lamb, turkey, or beef for the chicken.

Yields approximately 12 sliders

HAVE A SLIDER PARTY

Sliders (and burgers in general) are terrific for quick meals and kids' parties, where the last thing you want to think about is what to cook. If you're freezing them for the long haul (longer than a few months or days), make them from ground, uncooked chicken meat; freeze them, uncooked, on a baking sheet; and store two or three to a heavy-duty freezer bag. When the time comes, defrost them in your refrigerator, pop them in the oven, and let each small (or big!) person assemble his or her own burger with a choice of sides.

ADDITIONAL SERVING RECOMMENDATIONS

- Serve Chicken Sliders (or regular-size chicken burgers) without the bun, warm, on a bed of greens.
- Serve Chicken Sliders with the bun, accompanied by sliced onion, relish, pickles, and/or BIG FOOD Aioli (page 35).
- Serve stuffed into warm pita bread, with a touch of White Bean Hummus (page 112) or Traditional Hummus (page 113) and salad greens.

SECONDARY DISHES

- *Leftover uncooked Chicken Sliders can be mixed together and rolled into small meatballs. Bake on a baking sheet at 350°F until cooked through, about 30 to 40 minutes; cool, and freeze in a labeled, dated, heavy-duty freezer bag for up to 6 months.*
- *Leftover cooked Chicken Sliders can be crumbled together; mixed with carrots, peas, and white sauce (page 75); topped with mashed potatoes; and turned into Shepherd's Pie (page 202).*

WHAT YOU HAVE ON HAND

- 6 to 8 pounds uncooked chicken parts (preferably thighs)
- Bell peppers: red, green, yellow, orange
- Fresh mushrooms
- Bacon or pancetta (Italian bacon)
- Onions
- Canned Italian-style tomatoes, crushed or whole

WHAT TO DO WITH IT

- Set aside 3 to 4 pounds of chicken for this recipe; freeze the balance in a labeled, dated, heavy-duty freezer bag for up to 8 months. Or, refrigerate the balance in a dated, heavy-duty freezer bag for up to 3 days.
- Set aside ¼ pound bacon or pancetta for this recipe; double-plastic-wrap the balance and freeze in a dated, heavy-duty freezer bag for up to 6 months, or refrigerate for up to 14 days.

HOW LONG IT WILL LAST

- Hunter's Chicken will last, sealed in an airtight plastic container in the refrigerator, for up to 4 days.
- Hunter's Chicken will last, stored in a labeled, dated, heavy-duty freezer bag in the freezer, for up to 6 months.

PRIMARY

HUNTER'S CHICKEN

Rich, aromatic, filling, and deeply satisfying, this old-fashioned chicken stew can be made with either leftover chicken parts or fresh, uncooked chicken parts. I like to use inexpensive chicken thighs, which are the most flavorful, tender, and succulent part of the bird, and can often be used whenever and wherever dry white meat chicken is called for.

¼	cup extra virgin olive oil
3–4	pounds chicken parts, preferably thighs (or 1 whole chicken, cut up)
¼	pound bacon or pancetta, cut into ¼-inch dice
1	large onion, peeled and roughly chopped
4	garlic cloves, peeled and minced
1	large green pepper, seeded, ribbed, and cut into squares
1	large red pepper, seeded, ribbed, and cut into squares
1	large yellow pepper, seeded, ribbed, and cut into squares
¾	cup sliced mushrooms
1	(28-ounce) can Italian-style tomatoes, crushed or whole
1	cup dry red wine or dry Marsala
½	tablespoon dried rosemary
	Kosher salt and freshly ground black pepper

THE NECESSITY OF COOKING WITH SMOKED MEATS

Adding small quantities of bacon, ham, pancetta (unsmoked, cured Italian bacon), or prosciutto is a great way to add a strong punch of hearty flavor to stews, soups, and braises. But if religious observance or health concerns preclude you from cooking with pork, simply use thickly cut turkey ham or bacon, which can be found at any supermarket deli counter.

Heat oil in a large, heavy-duty saucepan or Dutch oven over medium-high heat, until rippling but not smoking. Place chicken in pan, skin-side down, taking care not to crowd it (do this in batches, if necessary), and cook until well browned, about 8 minutes. Remove from pan and set aside.

Using tongs and a paper towel, carefully wipe excess fat out of the pan.

Add bacon and cook until it begins to lightly crisp, about 6 minutes. Add onion and garlic. Cook until translucent, 6 to 8 minutes.

Add peppers and cook, stirring frequently, until softened. Return chicken to the pan, blending well with vegetables. Cover, reduce heat to medium-low, and cook for 15 minutes.

Add mushrooms and tomatoes, breaking whole tomatoes with the back of a fork. Add wine and, using a wooden spoon, scrape up any meaty bits that have stuck to the bottom of the pot. Cover and simmer for 20 minutes. Add rosemary and season with salt and pepper to taste. Continue to cook until chicken and vegetables are tender and aromatic, and sauce has thickened, 15 to 20 minutes more.

Serve hot in large, warm bowls, with a slice of crusty bread.

Serves 4 to 6

ADDITIONAL SERVING RECOMMENDATIONS
- Serve over steamed rice.
- Serve over plain pasta.

SECONDARY DISHES
- *Pappardelle with Chicken Ragu (page 186)*

WHAT TO DO WITH IT

- Set aside 3 cups of leftover roasted chicken; store the balance in the refrigerator in a dated, heavy-duty freezer bag for up to 3 days.
- Set aside five sausages for this recipe; double-plastic-wrap the balance, and store in a labeled, dated, heavy-duty freezer bag for up to 6 months.
- Set aside one onion for this dish, and store the balance in a mesh bag in a cool, dark location, away from potatoes and fruit.
- Set aside two medium peppers for this dish, and freeze the balance as on page 171.

HOW LONG IT WILL LAST

- Paella will last, refrigerated and stored in an airtight container, for up to 4 days.

SECONDARY

PAELLA

Paella—often referred to as the national dish of Spain—includes not only leftover roast chicken but a variety of other ingredients that can be purchased in bulk. Most traditional recipes call for short-grain rice such as Italian arborio, which is admittedly delicious but sometimes unwieldy. I've made it with basic, American, long-grain rice, and the results are lovely, as they are in this recipe, which was adapted from the late, great food writer and editor Michael Field.

4	tablespoons extra virgin olive oil, divided	1½	cups leftover BIG FOOD Basic Chicken Stock or packaged stock, divided
5	large sausages (chicken, pork, vegetarian, sweet or hot Italian), about 4 ounces each	1	teaspoon saffron, dissolved in the above stock
1	medium onion, peeled and finely chopped	1	cup canned whole Italian-style tomatoes, drained and chopped
2	garlic cloves, peeled and finely minced	3	cups leftover chicken, cut into chunks, skin discarded
1	large green pepper, seeded, ribbed, and cut into 2-inch strips	12	large shrimp, shelled and defrosted, if frozen
1	large red pepper, seeded, ribbed, and cut into 2-inch strips	1	cup frozen artichoke hearts, defrosted and halved
1	cup long-grain or arborio rice (not minute or instant)	1	cup frozen peas

Preheat oven to 350°F.

Heat 1 tablespoon oil in a large, heavy-duty, ovenproof sauté pan over medium heat, until rippling but not smoking. Add sausages and cook until well browned, 6 to 8 minutes. Remove with tongs to drain on paper towels. When cool, cut on the bias into 1-inch pieces.

Carefully wipe the pan of excess fat, and add the remaining 3 tablespoons oil. Heat until rippling but not smoking, add onion and garlic, and cook until translucent, about 6 minutes. Add peppers, stir, and continue to cook until softened, about 10 minutes.

Add rice and blend thoroughly, coating all of the grains with oil.

Add 1 cup of the stock (with the dissolved saffron) and the tomatoes. Bring to a boil, then transfer pan to oven. Cook 15 to 20 minutes, until rice is cooked through.

Remove pan from oven and place on stove top over high heat, adding additional stock if rice appears dry. Bring to a boil.

Add, and carefully bury beneath the rice, the reserved sausage, along with chicken, shrimp, artichokes, and peas. Cover and cook for about 10 minutes, until everything is heated through. Serve hot.

VARIATIONS

• During the last step of the recipe, add other fresh shellfish (clams, mussels, lobster tails) or cubed, leftover ham.

Serves 6

Paella is actually the name of the wide, flat pan that is traditionally used to make this dish. You, however, can feel free to use the biggest sauté pan you own.

STOCKING UP ON FROZEN GOODS

Many moons ago, everyone and their brother thought that frozen foods were the way to go if you were in a rush (and even if you weren't). Frozen fish, frozen meat, frozen this, frozen that . . . the world's ingredients were always available. Nowadays, most of us are concerned with freshness and chemicals, and rightly so: why buy something frozen when you can have the same thing fresh, all year round? I agree, wholeheartedly.

However, some frozen foods today are *so* good and *so* high in quality that it seems ridiculous not to have them stowed away for that moment in the dead of winter when you are just dying for the brightness of lovely baby peas. What to keep in your freezer?

• Baby peas: Add them to soups, stews, rice and pasta dishes.
• Frozen spinach: Drain, chop, and make a quick creamed spinach by blending it with a little white sauce (page 75), grated Parmesan, and nutmeg.
• Artichoke hearts: Defrost them, slice, and toss with Tuna Salad Niçoise (page 100), or marinate them overnight in Vinaigrette (page 92) and serve as hors d'oeuvres.
• Shrimp: Buy frozen shrimp uncooked. Defrost, peel, sauté with extra virgin olive oil and garlic, and toss with linguine; slice them lengthwise, marinate in Asian Vinaigrette (page 96), sauté quickly, and serve with steamed rice. Shrimp is the only frozen swimmer that I keep in my larder. Why? Shrimp are simple to cook, packed with protein, and freeze well if they're raw.

ADDITIONAL SERVING RECOMMENDATIONS

• The perfect rustic dinner party dish, Paella can be served out of the pan it is made in; allow guests to help themselves.

SECONDARY DISHES

• *Blend leftovers together with a good quantity of stock and wine, and enjoy as a stew.*

WHAT YOU HAVE ON HAND

- Leftover cooked skinless, bone-less chicken
- Sausage: chicken, Cajun, an-douille, Italian sweet or hot, pork, kielbasa, bratwurst, vegetarian
- Canned, crushed Italian-style tomatoes
- Onion
- Bell peppers
- BIG FOOD Basic Chicken Stock (page 58) or packaged stock

WHAT TO DO WITH IT

- Set aside 3 cups of leftover chicken; store the balance in the refrigerator in a dated, heavy-duty freezer bag for up to 3 days.
- Set aside five sausages for this recipe; double-plastic-wrap the balance, and store in a labeled, dated, heavy-duty freezer bag for up to 6 months.
- Set aside one large onion for this dish, and store the balance in a mesh bag in a cool, dark location, away from potatoes and fruit.
- Set aside three medium peppers for this dish, and freeze the balance as on page 171.

SECONDARY

CHICKEN GUMBO WITH ROMAN-STYLE SAUTÉED GREENS

Straight from the melting pot that is the Louisiana Bayou comes gumbo, a hearty stew that reflects the region's Indian, African, French, and Spanish influences. The BIG FOOD beauty of gumbo is that you can stow it away in your freezer for those nights when you want to defrost just a little bit of spice in your life.

1½	pounds sausage, preferably smoked and spicy (such as andouille)
1½	tablespoons unsalted butter
1	tablespoon vegetable oil, divided
3	medium celery stalks, chopped
1	large onion, peeled and chopped
2	garlic cloves, peeled and chopped
1½	tablespoons unbleached, all purpose flour
2	red bell peppers, seeded, ribbed, and cut into bite-size pieces
2	green bell peppers, seeded, ribbed, and cut into bite-size pieces

1	cup leftover BIG FOOD Basic Chicken Stock or packaged stock
2–3	cups chopped leftover chicken, skin discarded
1	(28-ounce) can crushed Italian-style tomatoes
1	teaspoon Worcestershire sauce
1	teaspoon dried thyme
½	teaspoon cayenne pepper
	Kosher salt and freshly ground black pepper
	Tabasco sauce
	Hot rice

Prick sausages twice with a fork and set in a medium saucepan. Cover with water, and simmer until cooked through, 8 to 10 minutes. Slice into 2-inch pieces and set aside.

In a large, heavyweight saucepan or Dutch oven, melt butter over medium heat until it just begins to foam. Add ½ tablespoon of oil, celery, onion, and garlic. Cook, stirring frequently so that vegetables do not brown, until softened, about 8 minutes. Remove from pan and reserve.

Add the remaining ½ tablespoon oil, sprinkle in flour, and whisk well, cooking until mixture is a dark tan color, about 5 minutes.

Immediately add reserved vegetables to the pot, along with peppers and stock. Blend well, bring to a simmer, cover, and cook until peppers are softened, 6 to 8 minutes, taking care to avoid burning. (If it seems dry, add a tablespoon of additional stock or water.)

Add chicken, reserved sausages, tomatoes and their liquid, Worcestershire sauce, thyme, and cayenne pepper. Bring gumbo to a boil for 5 minutes, cover, reduce to a simmer, and cook until the sauce has thickened, 20 to 30 minutes. Add salt, pepper, additional Worcestershire, and Tabasco to taste. Serve hot, over rice, accompanied by Roman-Style Sautéed Greens (see below).

Serves 4 to 6

ROMAN-STYLE SAUTÉED GREENS

Simple, delicious, and easy, this ubiquitous side dish finds its way onto my table nearly every night, in one form or another, whether I'm eating pork, fish, steak, or chicken.

3	large bunches broccoli rabe, mustard greens, kale, or chard	$1/4$	teaspoon red pepper flakes
2	tablespoons extra virgin olive oil		Kosher salt and freshly ground black pepper
3	garlic cloves, peeled and minced, divided		Juice of 1 lemon
$3/4$	cup leftover BIG FOOD Basic Chicken Stock (page 58) or packaged stock		

Chop woody stems from greens and discard. Slice leaves into bite-size pieces.

Heat oil in a very large sauté pan over medium-high heat, until rippling but not smoking. Add half of the garlic, and cook until it just begins to take on color, about 2–3 minutes.

Add greens and, using long-handled tongs, turn leaves over repeatedly until well-coated with oil. Add stock, remaining garlic, and pepper flakes. Blend well, reduce to a low simmer, cover, and cook until greens are tender, about 20 minutes.

Season to taste with salt and pepper, and drizzle with fresh lemon juice just prior to serving.

Serves 4 to 6

HOW LONG IT
WILL LAST

HOW LONG IT WILL LAST

- Chicken Gumbo will last up to 4 days in the refrigerator, stored in an airtight container.
- Chicken Gumbo will last up to 6 months in the freezer, stored in a labeled, dated, heavy-duty freezer bag.

ADDITIONAL SERVING RECOMMENDATIONS

- Serve in bowls, with a slice of fresh, crusty bread.

WHAT YOU HAVE ON HAND

- Leftover cooked skinless, boneless chicken
- Your favorite store-bought salsa
- Large bag of onions
- Bell peppers

WHAT TO DO WITH IT

- Remove skin and bones from the chicken, and discard. Cut chicken into strips and set aside.
- Set aside 3 onions for this dish, and store the balance in a cool dark place, away from potatoes and fruit.

HOW LONG IT WILL LAST

- Fajitas are meant to be assembled and eaten immediately; if you have any leftovers, store the makings separately for a quick "assemble and heat" the next day.

SECONDARY

CHICKEN FAJITAS

Warm, comforting, and simple to prepare, chicken fajitas are a terrific vehicle for using up leftover boneless chicken meat in a healthy and flavorful way. Each diner can make fajitas as spicy or mild as he or she likes, and as overstuffed or as dainty as is preferred. Children love to prepare their own meals with their own two hands. Face it, Mom, it's fun: give Junior a plate of chicken, a few soft tortillas, some vegetables, and maybe a little cheese or guacamole, and all will be right with the world.

3	cups thinly sliced leftover skinless, boneless chicken
2	tablespoons salsa, plus extra for serving
2	tablespoons canola oil
3	onions, peeled and sliced into rounds
3	bell peppers, seeded, ribbed, and sliced into ½-inch strips
	Kosher salt and freshly ground black pepper
8	large, soft tortillas (flour, corn, or whole wheat)

Preheat oven to 300°F.

Combine chicken and salsa in a mixing bowl. Blend well and set aside.

Heat oil in a large sauté pan over medium heat, until rippling but not smoking. Add onions, and sauté until lightly browned and softened, 8 to 10 minutes. Transfer to an ovenproof bowl, cover with foil, and place in oven.

STYMIED BY GUACAMOLE?

Don't be. If you crave guacamole the way I do, but you don't want to spend your time chopping onions or cilantro, do what I do: make it easy on yourself. Cut ripe Hass avocados in half, and remove the pit by gently tapping it with the blade of a sharp chef's knife, which will enter the surface of the pit. Make a 45-degree twist with the knife, and out pops the pit. Scoop out the flesh of the guacamole and place in a bowl. Mash, add 1 to 2 tablespoons of your favorite salsa, and that's that. If you prefer a more traditional, elemental guacamole, repeat the first step, and add the juice of 1 lime, 1 tablespoon of fresh chopped cilantro, a pinch of salt, perhaps a chopped jalapeño—and you're done.

Place peppers in sauté pan, season to taste with salt and pepper, and cook until softened, about 10 minutes. Mix peppers together with onions, replace foil, and return to oven.

In a separate, nonstick pan over medium-low heat, warm tortillas, one at a time, until they are soft and begin to puff. Set them one by one on an ovenproof plate, cover loosely with foil, and place in oven.

Place chicken in same pan and sauté until heated through.

Remove vegetables and tortillas from oven, and assemble the fajitas: Take 1 tortilla and fill it with chicken and vegetables. Top with additional salsa and serve hot.

VARIATIONS

Optional ingredients can include:
• Guacamole (see opposite page)
• Shredded Monterey Jack cheese
• Chopped, pickled jalapeños
• Chopped tomatoes
• Chopped, pitted black olives

Serves 4 to 6

ADDITIONAL SERVING RECOMMENDATIONS

• Allow each diner to assemble their own fajitas: prepare large plates of chicken, onions, peppers, and additional optional ingredients (see "Variations").

SECONDARY DISHES

• *Use leftover vegetables in Torta Rustica (page 208).*

LEFTOVER MUST-HAVES

Every year, magazines far and wide tell us what fall's must-have wardrobe pieces are; I think of leftovers in exactly the same way. Fill your pantry with the appropriate accessories, and you'll be ready to deal with whatever lurks in the depths of your fridge. In this case, one of the bedrocks of good leftovers preparation is the soft tortilla. Whether you choose flour, corn, or whole wheat, traditional soft tortillas can turn leftover chicken, meat, and even seafood into a fajita or a fast quesadilla in a matter of minutes. They freeze very well and are always worth having on hand in bulk.

- Leftover cooked chicken
- Salsa
- Cheese: grated or whole Monterey Jack, Asiago, Cheddar
- Onions
- Bell peppers

WHAT TO DO WITH IT

- Remove any skin and bones from leftover chicken, and discard. Cut chicken into strips and set aside.

- Set aside 3 onions for this dish, and store the balance in a cool, dark place, away from potatoes and fruit.

- Use as much or as little cheese in this dish as preferred.

HOW LONG IT WILL LAST

- Double-plastic-wrapped and re-frigerated, Mexican Tortilla Pie will last for approximately 4 days.

- Double-plastic-wrapped and then sealed in a dated, heavy-duty freezer bag, this dish will last 2 to 3 months.

SECONDARY

MEXICAN TORTILLA PIE

Layers of soft corn tortillas envelop chicken, vegetables, cheese, and salsa in this ter-rific leftover vehicle that is based (very loosely) on lasagna. Be as creative or as con-servative as you'd like with this dish: made in bulk, it can feed a small, hungry army. Conversely, it can be made in individual-size baking dishes and then frozen for a quick, spicy meal at the end of a long day.

2	tablespoons canola oil	2	cups thinly sliced leftover skinless, boneless chicken
3	large onions, peeled and sliced	2	cups grated or shredded cheeses, including Monterey Jack, Cheddar, or queso blanco
4	medium bell peppers, seeded, ribbed, and sliced into $\frac{1}{2}$-inch strips	4	(10-inch) corn tortillas
2	cups prepared salsa		

A WORD ON USING STORE-BOUGHT SALSA

These days, salsas come in all sorts of shapes, sizes, varieties, and flavors. For the purpose of this dish—which calls for a lot of salsa—I would suggest one of milder flavor, since the last thing you want to do is mask the lovely corn essence that comes from the tortillas as they cook. Feel free to mix your salsas: combine a black-bean salsa with a milder *pico de gallo*, or drizzle one layer with green-tomatillo salsa and the next with mango salsa. Your options are endless.

Preheat oven to 350°F.

Heat oil in a large sauté pan over medium heat, until rippling but not smoking. Add onions and peppers, and cook until softened, about 10 minutes. Set aside.

Using a 9- to 10-inch round casserole dish, begin the layering process:

Ladle a few tablespoons of the salsa onto the bottom of the dish, and top with a quarter of the chicken, vegetables, and cheese. Top with 1 tortilla and repeat. The top layer should be salsa, drizzled with a layer of cheese that will melt in the oven.

Bake until hot throughout and golden brown on top, 50 to 60 minutes. Slice and serve hot.

VARIATIONS

- Replace the chicken with turkey or beef.
- Replace the chicken with ground chicken, turkey, or beef.
- Vegetarians can replace the chicken with cubed, oven-roasted firm tofu, or increase the quantity of vegetables used.

Serves 4 to 6

Make this dish in individual oven-to-freezer casserole dishes.

ADDITIONAL SERVING RECOMMENDATIONS

- Slice into wedges and serve hot, with a mixed green salad or a dollop of guacamole (page 196).

WHAT TO DO WITH IT

- Chop the turkey as fine as you can get it without grinding it, and set it aside. If you have any left over, refrigerate it in a dated, heavy-duty freezer bag for up to 4 days from its original roasting time.
- Set aside 3 onions for this dish, and store the balance in a cool, dark location, away from any fruits (or potatoes, see below).
- Set aside 2 large potatoes for this dish, and store the balance in a cool, dark location away from (you guessed it) onions.

HOW LONG IT WILL LAST

- Sealed in a dated, heavy-duty freezer bag, this dish will last for an additional 3 days from the bird's original roasting date.

SECONDARY
TURKEY HASH

Like most people, I think that the Thanksgiving turkey we all gorge ourselves on is merely an excuse to have extraordinary leftovers, and there is nothing better for a mid-fall lunch than all-American hash. Whether you make it with leftover corned beef or even smoked trout, hash is a homey diner staple gone haute couture: recipes abound, but there's only one real keeper, and it involves sautéing bacon, potatoes, onions, and any number of "protein" additions . . . and then topping the whole thing with a poached egg. Enjoy this version when the rest of America is making turkey sandwiches at the end of November.

2	tablespoons canola, peanut, or extra virgin olive oil		6	bacon strips, cooked crisp and crumbled
2	large potatoes, skin on and diced		2–3	cups minced leftover skinless turkey
3	medium onions, peeled and minced			Freshly ground black pepper
2	green bell peppers, seeded, ribbed, and diced			

OPTIONAL: *Poached egg (opposite page)*

Heat oil in a large sauté pan over medium heat, until rippling but not smoking.

Add potatoes and cook, frequently pressing with the back of a wooden spoon or a spatula, until they begin to brown, 8 to 10 minutes.

Add onions, and cook until translucent and just beginning to take on some color, about 7 minutes. Add peppers and bacon, and continue to cook until the water released by the peppers has evaporated and vegetables are softened, about 10 minutes.

Add turkey, press the mixture into the pan again as above, and cook until hash is well-browned and hot throughout, about 10 minutes.

Add pepper to taste and serve hot, topped with a poached egg.

The word *hash* comes from the French verb *hacher*, "to chop."

VARIATIONS

- Replace turkey with leftover corned beef, chicken, beef, fresh or smoked salmon, fresh or smoked trout, red snapper, or cod (dried or fresh).
- Add a dash of hot sauce.
- Add a pinch of thyme.
- Add garlic to the sauté (in small or large quantities).
- Replace potatoes with sweet potatoes.

Serves 4 to 6

THE PERFECT POACHED EGG

Forget about those little metal egg-shaped contraptions that you lower into a pot of simmering water. For this fool-proof recipe, which is adapted from Julia Child's Mastering the Art of French Cooking, *all you need is the back end of a wooden spoon.*

| 2 | tablespoons white vinegar |
| 4 | large eggs |

Fill saucepan three-quarters of the way to the top with water, and bring to a simmer. Add vinegar.

Crack eggs, one into each custard cup, taking care not to break the yolks. Holding the custard cups very close to the surface of the water, carefully slip each egg into the simmering water, one at a time. Using the dowel end of the wooden spoon, gently and quickly "fold" the whites over their respective yolks.

Cover the saucepan, remove it from the heat, and do not peek for 4 minutes. Using a slotted spoon, remove each egg, and serve immediately on turkey hash, toast, or on a fresh frisée salad.

Serves 2

ADDITIONAL SERVING RECOMMENDATIONS

- Serve it for breakfast. Serve it for lunch. Serve it for dinner. But no matter how you serve it, add a poached egg and a turn of the pepper mill, and enjoy it with a glass of wine (except at breakfast).

SPECIAL TOOLS YOU'LL NEED

- *Medium saucepan with tight-fitting lid*
- *Wooden spoon*
- *4 Small glass custard dishes*
- *Slotted spoon*
- *Timer*

SECONDARY
TURKEY SHEPHERD'S PIE

If you've eaten turkey, our true-blue American holiday game bird with a texture not un-like balsa, it was probably concealed under a heaping load of sweet potato pie, cranberry sauce, stuffing, mashed potatoes, peas and carrots, gravy, gravy, and more gravy. What to do with the leftovers? Years ago, the Washington Post's longtime food editor, Phyllis Richman, offered me her holiday-leftovers plan: "When God gives you turkey, vegetables, gravy, and mashed potatoes, you're meant to do one thing with them: make shepherd's pie in individual ramekins or soufflé dishes, and then freeze them. They make great late-night meals, and they keep for months." Thus, a BIG FOOD secondary dish was born.

3	cups cubed leftover turkey, preferably skinless
2-3	cups leftover mixed vegetables: carrots, peas, green beans, broccoli, cubed turnips
2	cups leftover gravy
2	medium onions, peeled and roughly chopped
1	celery stalk, roughly chopped
2	cups leftover mashed potatoes, heated slightly and softened with 1/4 cup milk

This flexible recipe can be increased or decreased based upon how much you have left after the big meal; you might have enough to prepare several small, individual soufflé dishes which then can be frozen, or you might have enough to make one large, family-size Shepherd's Pie in an oblong baking dish or a pie plate. Either way, make sure that you are using oven-to-freezer, microwavable bakeware.

If mashed potatoes weren't on your menu and therefore cannot be used as the heavenly blanket under which your leftovers will happily rest, simply substitute store-bought frozen puff pastry, make small potpies instead, and freeze them all the same.

Preheat oven to 350°F.

Lightly grease soufflé pans, baking dish, or pie plate with softened butter or cooking spray.

Combine turkey, mixed vegetables, gravy, onions, and celery in a mixing bowl, and gently mix well. Ladle proportional amounts into your baking dish(es), so that the mixture is half an inch from the top of the dish.

Top with a half-inch layer of mashed potatoes, spreading carefully to fully cover the mixture. Flatten potatoes evenly, using the underside of a fork.

Place baking dish(es) on a baking sheet, and bake until potatoes begin to take on color and the dish is hot throughout, about 20 minutes.

Increase heat to broil, and broil pie(s) until the top is browned and beginning to crisp, 3 to 5 minutes. Serve hot.

If you are inclined to freeze for a later date:

Let cool completely before freezing. To reheat frozen pies, loosely cover with aluminum foil and heat in oven at 350°F for 35 to 40 minutes. Remove foil and continue to cook until heated through, about 20 minutes more.

VARIATIONS
- Use fresh or leftover ground beef, pork, chicken, or lamb in place of turkey.
- Use puff pastry in place of mashed potatoes.

Serves 6

ADDITIONAL SERVING RECOMMENDATIONS

- Serve anytime: if making individual portions, serve directly out of their ramekins with a lightly dressed salad, followed by seasonal fresh fruit.

PRIMARY

ITALIAN-STYLE TURKEY MEATBALLS

The lusty ladies of the BIG FOOD world because they're so embarrassingly cheap and easy, these meatballs (known in Italian as polpette*) can be made any number of ways, with any number of meats and/or poultry, thereby making them supremely economical. If you're a BIG FOOD shopper, you probably have at least some ground meat lurking in your freezer or fridge. What to do? Make meatballs. Have only a small amount? Make a few big meatballs. Prepared from ground meat or poultry purchased in bulk, meatballs can be baked and then added to pastas or soups, or enjoyed on their own with a little sauce; conversely, they can be cooked in the sauce itself: easy, economical, and outrageously delicious.*

½	cup milk	1	egg, lightly beaten
½	teaspoon nutmeg	2	tablespoons tomato paste
½	cup bread crumbs seasoned with 1 tablespoon BIG FOOD Mediterranean Spice Blend	2	pounds ground turkey
		¼	cup grated Parmesan
2	medium onions, peeled and finely minced or grated	¼	cup grated Locatelli Romano
		½	tablespoon kosher salt
3	garlic cloves, peeled and finely chopped	½	tablespoon freshly ground black pepper

TO BAKE, TO FRY, OR TO STEW?

I have most often seen traditional Italian meatballs cooked in the sauce they will be served in. They may be browned quickly in a frying pan, but then they are popped into the sauce for finishing. Conversely, they may be dry-baked on a baking sheet and *then* added to soup or sauce. Because this version is made from turkey—a lean meat—I recommend baking them quickly under a sheet of foil, then adding to stew or soups (such as Tortellini en Brodo, page 59) for finishing. If you choose to make these morsels from a more traditional combination of beef and pork, it is perfectly acceptable—even preferable—to let them entirely cook in the sauce they're going to be served with.

Preheat oven to 350°F.

Pour milk into a small bowl and add nutmeg. Add bread crumbs, and let rest for 10 minutes. Using a fine mesh strainer, strain bread crumbs and discard milk.

In a large mixing bowl, combine onions, garlic, egg, tomato paste, turkey, cheeses, soaked bread crumbs, salt, and pepper. Using your (clean) hands, blend very well to combine thoroughly.

Lightly coat a large nonstick baking sheet with cooking spray. Form mixture into balls no bigger than 1½ inches in diameter and set them on the baking sheet, 1 inch apart.

Cover with aluminum foil and bake for 10 minutes. If serving meatballs with sauce, remove from oven and finish cooking in BIG FOOD Marinara Sauce or your favorite packaged sauce for an additional 15 minutes, until meatballs are cooked through. If you're not serving them with sauce, bake for 25 to 30 minutes more.

VARIATIONS
Instead of turkey, use:
• Ground pork
• Ground beef
• Ground lamb
• Ground chicken

Yields 14 to 18 meatballs

ADDITIONAL SERVING RECOMMENDATIONS

• Serve these meatballs with spaghetti or a similar pasta, and a ladleful of BIG FOOD Marinara Sauce (page 42).

• Serve meatballs in hoagie or hero rolls, sprinkled with freshly grated Parmesan cheese and baked.

• Serve them in Pasta e Fagiole (page 70) or in Tortellini en Brodo (page 59).

WHAT YOU HAVE ON HAND

- Leftover cooked skinless, boneless chicken
- BIG FOOD Basic Chicken Stock (page 58), or packaged stock
- Canned white beans
- Canned posole
- Onions

WHAT TO DO WITH IT

- Cube the cooked chicken if possible, and set aside 2 cups for this recipe. Store the remainder in the refrigerator in a dated, heavy-duty freezer bag for up to 3 days.
- If you have a surplus of canned beans, drain what's left in the can, and store in airtight containers in the refrigerator for up to 4 days.

HOW LONG IT WILL LAST

- Refrigerate this dish in an airtight container for up to 4 days.
- Freeze this dish in labeled, dated, heavy-duty freezer bags for up to 3 months.

SECONDARY

CHICKEN CHILI STEW WITH WHITE BEANS AND POSOLE

Love traditional chili but looking for a change of pace that's lighter in both fat and calories, but equally as flavorful? This dish fits the bill. Born out of necessity (I was single, it was dinnertime, and all I had was leftover chicken, a few cans of white beans, a can of posole, and some spicy peppers), it is delicious served either hot or at room temperature. Enjoy this modern chili with a hot corn tortilla and a squirt of fresh lime juice.

2	tablespoons extra virgin olive oil or canola oil	1	(16-ounce) can posole, drained
1	medium onion, peeled and chopped coarsely	1/4	cup fresh cilantro, chopped
2	garlic cloves, peeled and minced	2	teaspoons fresh oregano, minced, or 1 teaspoon dried
2	cups leftover skinless, boneless chicken, cubed or chopped	1	teaspoon ground cumin
3/4	cup leftover BIG FOOD Basic Chicken Stock or packaged stock	2	pickled jalapeños, chopped (or more, if desired)
1	(16-ounce) can white beans		Juice of 2 limes, divided

Heat oil in a large saucepan or Dutch oven over medium heat, until rippling but not smoking. Add onion and cook until translucent, about 10 minutes. Add garlic and cook 5 minutes more.

Add chicken and stock, bring to a low simmer, cover, and cook for 10 minutes. Add beans (and their liquid), posole, cilantro, oregano, cumin, and jalapeños. Continue to cook, covered, for 10 minutes more.

Remove cover, add half of the lime juice and simmer until liquid is reduced by half, about 20 minutes. Toss with the remaining lime juice just prior to serving.

VARIATIONS

- Substitute cubed beef for chicken, and replace the chicken stock with beef or vegetable stock. Add black beans instead of white, along with a small can of tomato paste mixed with water.
- Substitute leftover turkey for chicken.
- Add 1 cup of chopped tomatoes in step one.

Serves 4 to 6

THE SCOOP ON POSOLE

We see it on the same shelves as canned beans, mysterious in its countenance. And unless we are of Mexican lineage or have a particular yen for that kind of food, we scratch our heads in (as the King of Siam would say) wonderment. What exactly is posole, and what is it used for?

Posole, for starters, is both an ingredient and a spicy Mexican corn stew, traditionally served on Christmas Eve. However (and for our sakes), posole is also a hard "field" corn that has been soaked in a solution of powdered lime and water until soft; the liquid is allowed to evaporate, and the kernels are dried. Often packaged as "hominy" (which in fact is a bit different), canned posole is a spectacular addition to soups, stews (like Brazilian Feijoada, page 250), and chili of every variety (especially vegetarian ones). Robustly fragrant, canned posole is nothing short of delicious, nutritious, and very easy to use.

A LITTLE LIME MEANS LESS SALT

You've noticed: there is no salt called for or even suggested in this recipe. Why? Sodium-intake-watchers everywhere will be thrilled to know that the flavor of lime mimics salt so well that using even a pinch will be overkill (so to speak). Other salt replacements include:

• Vinegar

• Lemon juice

ADDITIONAL SERVING RECOMMENDATIONS

• Serve hot, in deep crocks, with a slice of fresh lime and a warm corn tortilla.

• Top with diced red onions, minced pickled or fresh jalapeños, and/or a drizzle of your favorite hot sauce.

WHAT YOU HAVE ON HAND

- **Fresh or leftover chicken sausage**
- **Eggs and/or egg substitute**
- **Fresh or leftover sautéed vegetables: onions, peppers, kale, spinach, sliced mushrooms**

WHAT TO DO WITH IT

- If you are starting with fresh sausage, set aside 6 links for this recipe; double-plastic-wrap the balance, and store in a dated, heavy-duty freezer bag in the refrigerator for up to 4 days, or freeze for up to 8 months.

HOW LONG IT WILL LAST

- This dish will last, double-plastic-wrapped and refrigerated, in a dated, heavy-duty freezer bag for up to 3 days.

PRIMARY/SECONDARY

TORTA RUSTICA

When is an omelet not an omelet? When it's Torta Rustica, the simplest way to use left-over cooked (or uncooked) chicken sausage, sautéed vegetables, and roasted potatoes. (It can be made from entirely fresh ingredients as well.) Luscious, rich, and packed with a mélange of flavor, Torta Rustica can be served hot or cold, made with hot or spicy sausage, and topped with a golden crust of grated cheese (or not). A boon for picnickers or for adventurous children who take their lunches to school, it also travels very well.

6	chicken sausages, mild or spicy	1	pound baby new potatoes, quartered
2	tablespoons extra virgin olive oil, plus additional for drizzling	1	tablespoon chopped fresh rosemary, or $\frac{1}{2}$ tablespoon dried
2	medium onions, peeled and chopped		Kosher salt and freshly ground black pepper
4	bell peppers (red, green, or yellow, or mixed) seeded, ribbed, and cut into 1-inch strips	8	eggs, or 4 eggs plus $\frac{2}{3}$ cup egg substitute, beaten well
2	garlic cloves, peeled and minced		

Optional: Freshly grated Parmesan cheese

If using fresh, previously uncooked sausage: Poke each link twice with a fork, and simmer in approximately 2 inches of water in a deep saucepan, until cooked through. Remove and let cool. Slice on the bias, into 2-inch pieces, and set aside.

If using leftover sausage: Slice links on the bias, as above, and set aside.

Preheat oven to 350°F.

Heat oil in a large oven-proof nonstick sauté pan over medium heat, until rippling but not smoking. Add onions and sauté, stirring frequently, until translucent, about 10 minutes, taking care not to brown them.

Add peppers and garlic, and cook until softened, about 8 minutes.

Add potatoes, cover, and cook until fork-tender, 10 to 12 minutes.

Add reserved sausage and rosemary, and mix well. Add salt and pepper to taste.

Reduce the heat to medium low, and pour in eggs. Do not shake or touch the pan; let eggs bathe vegetables and sausage and "set," like a pancake.

Sprinkle with grated cheese, if using, and bake until golden brown, 15 to 20 minutes.

Remove from oven and, using a knife, carefully loosen torta from sides of pan. Place a large, ovenproof plate directly over the torta, and then—*carefully*—invert it onto the plate. (It should now be bottoms up!)

Let cool to desired temperature, and drizzle with additional olive oil prior to serving.

VARIATIONS

• Use meatless, or vegetarian, sausage.
• Use traditional pork sausage.
• Include small bits of ham (ham steak, boiled ham, prosciutto, pancetta).
• Use any combination of the following vegetables: spinach, kale, scallions, carrots, mushrooms, and broccoli.

Serves 4 to 6

Torta Rustica is very similar to an Italian frittata, or open-faced omelet.

ADDITIONAL SERVING RECOMMENDATIONS

• Serve this dish hot, with a mixed green salad.
• Serve this dish cold, as a snack.
• Cut into 2-inch squares, and serve bite-size tortas as hors d'oeuvres.

THE
BIG
BEEF

BIG FOOD ON BEEF (AND LAMB)

> "Vegetables are interesting but lack a sense of purpose when unaccompanied by a good cut of meat."
> —Fran Lebowitz, *Metropolitan Life*

Of all the various items that are available for purchase in bulk (underwear, shampoo, flour, shortening, cheese, laundry detergent, bell peppers), the beef cases always seem to draw the largest crowds. It's true. Everyone gathers round and mumbles to themselves as they stare at these giant, waist-high, open refrigerators and examine their contents, with completely stunned looks on their collective faces.

The next time you're shopping at a discount club or a large local grocery store, go ahead and get a gander at the lineup of people standing in front of the meat case, just gawking at its contents. What could they possibly be thinking as they gape at immense hunks of meat? The answer is clear. "How remarkable! How fabulous! But what the [bleep] am I going to do with it?"

These days, meat and certainly lamb can be an expensive proposition to have on your family's regular menu, so the necessity of learning how to buy good-quality meats at a lower price, store them, prepare them in any number of ways, and/or freeze them, is of (no pun intended) prime importance. But don't get me wrong: I'm not talking about making one gigantic meat loaf and having it for seven straight nights. What I *am* talking about is the *creative* use of these megalithic packages that make us all scratch our heads in bewildered awe, and send us running to the case with the packaged burgers or that box of 800 frankfurters. We needn't throw our hands up in dismay. All that's required is some modicum of patience, a little bit of humor, and a willingness to create leftover dishes that bear little resemblance to the primary dishes from whence they came. The results can be outstandingly delicious, and can be served to everyone from your lucky family to grateful guests who won't have the foggiest clue that the mouthwatering meal in front of them was born out of a previously cooked dish and is therefore the apex of frugality. Leftovers from inexpensive Wine-Braised Lamb Shanks can be reworked into neotraditional Pappardelle with Lamb Ragu; the leftovers from Pancetta-and-Rosemary-Wrapped Beef Tenderloin can be tossed with a light vinaigrette and served with mixed greens for an elegant twist on a traditional Venetian cold beef salad. In the world of BIG FOOD, the possibilities are endless.

BEEF BASICS

Meat, for reasons that I will never understand, seems to confound people. How much should they buy? If everyone is watching their fat intake, why do cooks always prefer fattier, or "marbled," cuts? Does meat have an indefinite shelf life? If I wrap something in that nice beige butcher paper, can I freeze it? (I always shudder when I answer that question in public.)

What's the difference between prime, choice, and select? (Do you really want to know?) Should I salt my meat before I eat it? (Not always.) Can I buy a cheaper cut and then tenderize it with salt? (Not unless you call your cardiologist first.) What's the difference between rump roast, top round, bottom round, blade steak, flatiron steak, flank steak, skirt steak, entrecote, and brisket? And what on earth is a spoon roast?

First, to debunk a few myths: the leanest of meat (like filet mignon) contains fat and cholesterol. There's no getting around that fact. But so does a porterhouse. So what's the difference? The marbling—a nice way of describing that beautiful, cherished white lace of fat that weaves its way throughout the meat. Fat provides taste and tenderness. Fattier meats can generally be grilled over higher heats for long periods of time without the risk of them turning into something with the consistency of a two-by-four (making them terrific for grilling over a hot, direct flame, or broiling). Unfortunately, since fat does not freeze nicely and can go rancid, fattier meats simply do not freeze as well or for as long as leaner

A WORD ABOUT E. COLI AND OTHER DANGEROUS BEEF-RELATED AILMENTS

E. coli, those lovely, unassuming little bacteria that lurk in hidden places (contaminated meat, for example), can be a deadly killer—every year, hundreds of people either get sick or die from ingesting food that was contaminated with the bugs. Meat seems to be a particular suspect, and so it is the USDA's suggestion that all meat be cooked to the point of no return—until you can drop it and it shatters. While most of us have very little control over where our meat actually comes from, we can practice good meat hygiene:

• Never *ever* defrost raw or cooked meat at room temperature. Defrost it in the microwave or in the refrigerator.

• Always wash utensils in hot, soapy water after they have come into contact with raw meat, and before they touch anything else.

• Know your meat: if it is packaged in bulk and has no label on it except for the store's bar code, dig into your wallet and buy a brand name.

cuts. But there is always a flip side, and here it is: leaner cuts, like the expensive and prized tenderloin, need to be fatted (or, in the old days, "larded" or "barded") so that they can be cooked without evolving into a baseball bat. Yet unlike their more marbled cousins, they do freeze a bit longer and are therefore worth purchasing in bulk. But marbled or not, you've got fat to deal with.

I love meat. In my youth, I tried in earnest to be a vegetarian, but it didn't take, and the day that I gave up eating sautéed wheat gluten and lentil nut loaf, I went out for a T-bone. But unfortunately, like many of us, I also have genetically high cholesterol, so I suggest that you do what I do: eat meat, like everything else, in moderation. A nice steak once in a blue moon will not kill you, but eating one every single night is not a good idea for *anyone*. Even if you can afford it.

BUYING MEAT IN BULK

When you go to a discount club or even a large supermarket these days, you'll always find hordes of people peering into the meat cases in shocked awe at the slabs and sides of beef that are staring back at them. Why? Because a side of beef or an entire tenderloin bears little resemblance to the steaks, roasts, and fillets that we're so used to seeing. Those individually wrapped steaks and roasts are usually more expensive, and, generally, the price per pound at a discount club is sharply lower than its more familiar supermarket counterpart—hence the awe. So, what to look for when you're buying meat in bulk?

• Know what you're looking at, and don't buy anything that is either unrecognizable to you or that

HOW TO MAKE SURE YOU'RE BUYING THE RIGHT BEEF CUT FOR THE RIGHT DISH

MEAT CUT	TENDERNESS	USE
Rib Eye Steaks	Very Tender	Broil or grill quickly.
Tenderloin: whole, and filet mignon	Very Tender	Roast quickly, with additional fat.
Sirloin Steaks	Very Tender	Grill or broil quickly.
Chuck Roasts: pot roast, ground beef, stew beef	Tough	Stew or braise; long cooking methods only.
Brisket	Tough	Stew or braise; long cooking methods only.
Flank Steak	Tough	Marinate and grill, broil, stew, or braise.
Top Round and Bottom Round: pot roasts, and stew beef	Tough	Stew, braise, or roast with additional fat; long cooking methods only.
Rump Roasts: pot roast, and stew beef	Tough	Stew, braise, or roast with additional fat; long cooking methods only.

UNDERSTANDING USDA GRADES AND STAMPS

The USDA (United States Department of Agriculture) has been charged with the watchdogging of safe meat processing and accurate labeling for a public that in the best or worst of times simply cannot get enough of meat. USDA grades fall into several categories.

• **Prime:** This is the Hummer limousine of beef, the sometimes quirky-looking (it's often not very red), sometimes dry-aged stuff that is the cream of the crop and priced accordingly. Tender, marbled, mouthwatering, and immensely flavorful, it is most often served in high-end restaurants and hotels, although a small proportion of the prime meat produced in this country winds up in supermarkets. On rare occasions, it will appear in discount clubs. When and if it does, and if you can afford it for a special event, avail yourself of it.

• **Choice:** This grade of beef is what most of us are used to buying at good supermarkets and discount clubs. Choice beef has less marbling than prime but is still of generally excellent quality. You will nearly always see this grade available in bulk.

• **Select:** Leaner and more uniform in color than either choice or prime meats, select is a good quality, but because it has less marbling and fat, it also may have less flavor and tenderness. (But there are ways to deal with that: Turn to Pancetta-and-Rosemary-Wrapped Beef Tenderloin, page 218.) This grade is always available in bulk.

• **Standard or commercial:** This grade of beef is usually "name brand"—sold to a specific supermarket and packaged under that store's label. It's of moderate to good quality.

• **Utility, cutter, and canner:** As a consumer, odds are you will never see this grade of meat for sale as roasts or steaks. Instead, this grade is generally made into ground beef or frankfurters—all the more reason to buy select (or above) grade hamburger meat and the best-quality frankfurters you can afford.

USDA STAMPS

• **Branded:** According to the Beef Board, beef can be either breed or location "branded" (Certified Angus Beef simply means that it comes specifically from Angus cattle; Japanese Kobe Beef comes from Kobe, Japan), company branded, or supermarket branded.

• **Unbranded:** This beef is USDA-approved and carries the generic name of the cut of beef on its label. It may be of any grade.

• **Certified Organic:** According to the Beef Board, Certified Organic Beef must meet strict USDA National Organic Program (NOP) standards: its cattle must be fed 100 percent organic feed and never given growth hormones or antibiotics. If you don't see the "Certified Organic" label on the packaging, the beef is not organic.

• **Natural:** The USDA defines Natural Beef as "minimally processed, containing no additives." All fresh beef found in the meat case that does not have an ingredient label (added if the product includes a marinade or solution) is Natural Beef. So if you find yourself paying more for something that calls itself Natural Beef, but it has an ingredient label on it, it's likely not what it says it is.

you won't know how to butcher once you get it home.

• Make sure that you're buying the right cut for the right dish.

• Understand the difference between the grades of beef available in bulk, which vary tremendously in terms of quality, flavor, and, of course, price. For example, if you see two separate cases of whole tenderloins priced differently per pound, odds are it's because their grades are different. That means that you have to choose whether you want to spend more for a better grade or less for a good but lower grade. Choosing the latter option is perfectly respectable (I did this recently for a barbecue), but know what you're looking at.

• Learn how to correctly store what you buy: the secret to storing beef for the long haul is knowing how to wrap it well to avoid any meat/air contact in the freezer. Double-wrap steaks individually in heavy-duty plastic, then wrap them once in heavy-duty aluminum foil, and then freeze them in a labeled, dated, heavy-duty freezer bag. You'll be glad you did.

LAMB BASICS

I'll admit it.

Somewhere in the recesses of

WELL-DONE, MEDIUM, RARE, OR BLACK AND BLUE?

Culinary trends come and go, but one that appears to be hanging on in more up-scale establishments these days is the cooking of lamb *so* rare that it appears to be raw inside. Traditionally, lamb isn't eaten rarer than medium-rare, which is how I certainly prefer it; Greek cooks, however, eat their lamb *done*—which for Americans can be translated to well-done. So if you find yourself in a Greek home or restaurant, ordering this delicacy, throw caution to the wind, keep your yammer shut, and eat it the way it's traditionally served by the people who are making it. The best way to determine the level of a lamb's doneness is by using an accurate digital thermometer, inserted into the thickest part of the meat but not touching the bone (if there is one). Lamb readings should be as follows:

- Very rare: 125 to 130°F
- Rare: 130 to 135°F
- Medium-rare: 140 to 145°F
- Medium: 145 to 150°F
- Well-done: 150 to 160°F

When you cook lamb (or beef or pork), use this basic rule of thumb: Cook the meat to its desired degree of doneness, remove from the heat, and let it rest for 10 minutes prior to serving.

If you want a perfectly medium-rare leg of lamb, remove the meat at the lower end of that temperature range; it will continue to cook while it rests.

---

my mother's main closet in New York lays a picture of me at 3 years old, my arms blissfully wrapped around a baby lamb so tiny, it was actually smaller than I was. I look as though I'm about to cry and mouthing the word *home*. It was clear: never mind Binky, my Schnauzer. I wanted to bring this lamb *home*. As a pet.

And that's the trouble with lamb, isn't it? So delicious. So tender and tasty. And so cute that you basically want to have yourself flogged for even thinking about eating it. To add insult to injury, the best lamb—*abbacchio*—is a baby lamb so young (under 13 pounds) that it hasn't even tasted grass yet. Over the years, I have had to come to terms with the fact that I am not a vegetarian; still, this lamb stuff is tough business. Which is why I always make sure that I have it only on special occasions; I even give thanks for it and maybe say a few words, just for the sake of karma. And then I go ahead and enjoy it in all its forms: chops, breast, stew, burgers, and—the king of lamb dishes—roast leg of lamb.

Lamb meat is very flavorful—sometimes too flavorful and even gamy for those of us who prefer our dishes mild. So if you find yourself dealing with an outsized cut (a very large leg, for example), make sure that you marinate it well in my favorite culinary trinity: extra virgin olive oil, lemon juice, and freshly minced garlic. If you happen upon ground lamb, season it with a little cumin and garlic before making it into BIG FOOD Burgers (page 222). The results are delicious.

PRIMARY

COLORADO SWEET STEAK

Contrary to the popular belief that salting meat prior to cooking will turn it into expensive shoe leather (the salt leeches the juices out of anything it's applied to), massaging a good piece of meat with the following rub is a great way of adding flavor without sauce. The result is juicy, tender, and immensely flavorful. This surprising recipe, which was adapted from a kitschy little grilling book called Patio Daddy-O, *can be used on nearly any grillable cut of beef.*

½	cup sugar	1	teaspoon onion powder
1	tablespoon kosher salt	1	(3- to 4-pound) slab top round, sirloin, or London broil, at least 1½ inches thick
½	tablespoon cayenne pepper		
1	teaspoon freshly ground black pepper		
1	teaspoon garlic powder		

Combine sugar, salt, cayenne pepper, black pepper, garlic powder, and onion powder in a bowl. Massage half of the mixture into one side of the meat, cover with plastic, and let rest on a platter at room temperature for 1 hour.

Preheat grill to high, or preheat broiler.

Turn the meat over and massage the remaining half of the mixture into the other side. Let rest, uncovered, at room temperature for 30 minutes.

Broil or grill over high heat for 6 minutes. Turn and cook 5 minutes longer. Remove to platter or slicing board and let sit, undisturbed, for 5 minutes. Carve against the grain and serve hot or cold.

VARIATIONS

- Slice and drizzle with fruit salsa for delicious tacos.
- Slice and serve as a base for poached eggs.
- Slice and combine with a drop of sesame oil, soy sauce, and ginger, and toss with cold spaghetti or soba noodles for an Asian twist.
- Slice and serve cold with BIG FOOD Aioli (page 35).

Serves 4 to 6

MASTERING THE POKE TEST

If you watch cooking shows on television (and who doesn't), chances are you've seen many a white-jacketed chef take his or her index finger and gently poke at a piece of cooking meat, chicken, or fish. If this has concerned you or ever left you scratching your head in confusion, it shouldn't: the Poke Test is an excellent way to determine the "doneness" of whatever it is you're cooking. (Just make sure your hands are clean.)

Mastering the Poke Test is easy. (Be brave—poking something quickly with your fingertip will not hurt, assuming that whatever you're poking is not on fire.) Using the tip of your index finger, gently *poke* your meat/chicken/fish. If it feels . . .

- Mushy and loose and offers no resistance, it's still raw
- Firmer but there is still give, it's rare
- Slightly springy, it's medium-rare
- Firm to your touch, it's done
- Hard to your touch, it's overdone, and can probably be snapped in half like a charcoal briquette

ADDITIONAL SERVING RECOMMENDATIONS

- Slice thinly on the bias and serve with Roman-Style Sautéed Greens (page 195).

SECONDARY DISHES

- *Steak sandwiches: Spread BIG FOOD Aioli (page 35) on grilled or toasted sourdough bread, and top with leftover sweet steak; a sliced, juicy tomato; and a round of red onion. Serve open-faced or closed.*
- *Wrap leftover steak in foil and heat gently in a low oven (300°F) for 8 minutes; toss with salad greens and Vinaigrette (page 92).*

WHAT TO DO WITH IT

- Unless you are faced with a mammoth tenderloin, roast the whole thing all at once.
- If you don't want or need to roast it in its entirety, slice away the portion that you don't want to use immediately, and cut it into individual 1½- to 2-inch-thick round filet mignons. Double-plastic-wrap each piece separately and freeze them in a labeled, dated, heavy-duty freezer bag for up to 6 months.

HOW LONG IT WILL LAST

- Odds are you won't have any left, but this dish will keep, double-plastic-wrapped and stored in a dated, heavy-duty freezer bag, in the refrigerator for up to 4 days.

SPECIAL TOOLS YOU'LL NEED

- All-cotton or linen kitchen twine

PRIMARY

PANCETTA-AND-ROSEMARY-WRAPPED BEEF TENDERLOIN

There is no greater way to treat meat lovers on a special occasion than to serve beef tenderloin. Lean and succulent, it is widely available at great prices at discount clubs, and I always take advantage and make it my holiday centerpiece, which poses one problem: how to keep the thing moist during the roasting process. What's the answer? A light, garlicky marinade, and then a wrap of heavenly pancetta—lean, uncured Italian bacon that is easy to find in any decent supermarket. The result is wildly delicious, tender, juicy, and so magnificent in its presentation that you may find yourself making excuses to have it instead of Thanksgiving turkey.

3	tablespoons extra virgin olive oil
3	garlic cloves, peeled and minced
½	teaspoon freshly ground black pepper
½	teaspoon grated lemon zest (see page 184)

1	(6- to 8-pound) beef tenderloin, trimmed of fat and silver skin
½	pound pancetta, thinly sliced
3	large whole sprigs rosemary

The night before serving:

In a small mixing bowl, combine oil, garlic, pepper, and zest; massage it into the tenderloin. (It doesn't matter if it feels greasy; that's okay.)

Triple-wrap meat in heavy-duty plastic wrap, set on a large cold-proof platter, and refrigerate for 8 hours, or overnight.

Remove meat from wrapping, set it on a large cutting board, and allow it to come to room temperature, approximately 2 hours.

Preheat oven to 450°F.

TRIMMED OR UNTRIMMED?

You can buy untrimmed beef tenderloin for a lower price than the trimmed version; this simply means that you have to take the time to remove its silvery skin and the layers of fat that may still surround it. My advice is to spend the extra dollar a pound and buy it trimmed—it'll save you work, and you won't risk slicing away some of the precious meat along with the fat.

The tenderloin will have a very thick end and a very thin end. Fold the thin end up as best you can and, using kitchen twine, tie it in place so that the whole tenderloin is of uniform thickness.

Lay pancetta slices atop the meat, overlapping them by ½ inch (they should look like intersecting Olympic rings). Tie each slice in place tightly with a 6- to 8-inch length of kitchen twine. Roll the tenderloin over onto its other side and repeat. Carefully tuck rosemary sprigs underneath the twine.

Place the tenderloin in a roasting pan, and roast for 7 to 8 minutes per pound for medium-rare (or to an internal temperature of 140°F, taken at the thickest part of the meat).

Remove from pan and let stand 10 to 15 minutes. Remove string, slice meat, and serve.

VARIATIONS

- Massage with BIG FOOD Herb Butter (page 33) prior to roasting.
- Drizzle with sweet Marsala wine or Madeira prior to roasting.
- Grill over indirect heat instead of roasting in the oven.

Serves 8 to 10

ADDITIONAL SERVING RECOMMENDATIONS

- Serve warm, with the traditional accompaniments: Brussels sprouts, pan-roasted new potatoes, and glazed carrots.
- Serve cold, with small side dishes: BIG FOOD Aioli (page 35), cornichons, toast points, and boiled and peeled baby onions.

SECONDARY DISHES

- *Drizzle leftover cold sliced beef with a vinaigrette of your choice, and serve with mixed greens.*

COOKING WITHOUT SALT: AN ITALIAN TRADITION

In some areas of Italy, it is a culinary tradition to add salty flavor to dishes *without* the addition of salt itself. Instead, some Italian cooks will use pancetta, prosciutto, bacon, or black olives to provide salty flavor, which is exactly what I've done here. So make sure you taste the finished dish before you ask for the salt!

TO LARD OR NOT TO LARD

Traditionally, tenderloin was "larded" or "fatted"—wrapped in caul fat (don't ask), smothered in butter, encased in suet, and/or wrapped in bacon strips—so that it would stay tender during the roasting process. Today, I wouldn't recommend caul fat, the birds can keep their suet, and wrapping in bacon is a sure way to smoke out your in-laws. Instead, marinate and then wrap in a lean, flavorful, thin-sliced specialty ham, like prosciutto or pancetta.

WHAT YOU HAVE ON HAND

- **Ground beef**
- **Ground pork**
- **Ground veal, turkey, or chicken**
- **Onions**
- **BIG FOOD Mediterranean Spice Blend (page 39)**

WHAT TO DO WITH IT

- Set aside ½ to ⅓ pound of each meat. Double-plastic-wrap the balance individually, and store in a dated, heavy-duty freezer bag for up to 3 days in the refrigerator, or up to 8 months in the freezer.
- Set aside 1 large onion for this recipe, and store the balance in a mesh bag in a cool, dark place, away from potatoes or fruit.

HOW LONG IT WILL LAST

- This meat loaf will last, double-plastic-wrapped and stored in a labeled, dated, heavy-duty freezer bag, for up to 4 days in the refrigerator.
- This meat loaf will freeze, wrapped as indicated above, for up to 6 months in the freezer.

PRIMARY

NOT MY MAMA'S MEAT LOAF

I have two memories of meat loaf from my childhood, and they involve ketchup and milk-soaked bread. So it was years before I realized that this lowliest of comfort foods can be as magnificent as caviar when made correctly, but boring as celery when made badly. This Italian-style recipe blends together three different meats, along with milk-soaked bread crumbs, onion, and herbs, and is a divine BIG FOOD dish. If you've made BIG FOOD Burgers (page 222) or Asian Noodles with Pork, Scallions, and Ginger (page 254), and you have leftover uncooked ground meats, use them here.

½	cup bread crumbs		2	garlic cloves, peeled and minced
½	cup milk		½	tablespoon BIG FOOD Mediterranean Spice Blend
1½	pounds ground meat: ⅓ each of pork, veal (or turkey), and beef		1	teaspoon kosher salt
1	large egg		1	teaspoon freshly ground black pepper
¼	cup ketchup			
1	large onion, peeled and minced			

Optional: *Baked potatoes, sour cream*

Preheat oven to 350°F.

In a small mixing bowl, soak bread crumbs in milk and set aside.

Using your (clean) hands, blend meats together in a large mixing bowl. Break the egg into the bowl and incorporate well. Add ketchup and mix well.

Drain bread crumbs in a fine mesh sieve and discard the milk. Add crumbs to meat along with onion, garlic, spice blend, salt, and pepper. Combine thoroughly.

Place meat mixture in a nonstick loaf pan. Alternatively, shape it into a rough loaf and set it in a nonstick roasting pan.

Bake for approximately 1 hour. Carefully pour hot fat out of pan prior to removing and slicing. Serve hot, with a traditional baked potato dolloped with sour cream, if desired.

VARIATIONS

- Replace the bread crumbs with saltine crumbs: pulverize the crackers in a food processor before soaking, and omit the salt from the recipe.
- Top the meat loaf with ketchup mixed with ¼ teaspoon cayenne pepper during the baking process.
- Add sliced raw mushrooms to the meat; the water expelled by them during the cooking process will add extra moisture.

Serves 4 to 6

THE PERFECT BAKED POTATO

We've all had soggy ones that have been steamed and overcooked ones that have gotten gummy. But the Perfect Baked Potato is easy to produce, thanks to this recipe that's been adapted from cooking great Jean Anderson. It makes an ideal accompaniment to any number of dishes and works brilliantly alongside meat loaf.

Allow one russet potato per person; poke it three times on all sides with a fork. Bake at 400°F for 1½ hours, or bake it with meat loaf at 350°F. Upon removing the meat loaf, increase oven temperature to 450°F, and bake potatoes for 10 more minutes.

LITTLE BIG FOOD

Busy parents, sleepy students, active adults . . . listen up! Why make dinner or "secondary" dishes from scratch (or semi-scratch) when you can make some of your favorite dishes in individual portions, and freeze them for those nights when you want something *really* quick and easy? A word to the wise: when stocking up on your kitchen supplies, go *small* as well as big. Buy a few inexpensive, individual-size baking pans (usually around 7 by 4 inches), and make a couple of smaller lasagnas rather than one big one. Smaller quiche tins allow for individual tortas (page 208); lovely little loaf pans are perfect for individual meat loaves. Make your BIG FOOD in smaller sizes, freeze it, and have it when the last thing you can think about is doing anything more than turning on the oven.

ADDITIONAL SERVING RECOMMENDATIONS

- Serve the meat loaf hot, with Roman-Style Sautéed Greens (page 195), steamed herbed rice, or the Perfect Baked Potato.
- Serve the meat loaf cold, on a Fromage Blanc Crouton (page 50) drizzled with extra virgin olive oil.

WHAT YOU HAVE ON HAND

- **Large packages of good-quality chopped beef**
- **Onions, red or white**
- **Mushrooms**
- **Cheese: American, Swiss, Gouda, Cheddar, blue, Monterey Jack, feta, mozzarella, or queso blanco**

WHAT TO DO WITH IT

- Set aside 3 pounds of ground meat for this recipe. Double-plastic-wrap the remainder, and freeze in labeled, dated, heavy-duty freezer bags for 6 to 8 months.
- Set aside 2 small onions for this recipe, and store the balance in a mesh bag in a cool, dark place, away from potatoes or fruit.
- Set aside ¹/₂ cup of mushrooms for this recipe, and sauté the balance for toppings.
- If you have leftover cheese, insert small ends and pieces into the burger rather than melting cheese on top.

BIG FOOD BURGERS

We all have favorites: you might like yours piled high with onions, relish, ketchup, and mayo, and I might like mine flat as a pancake and naked as a jaybird. You might like yours big; I might like sliders. The key to the BIG FOOD Burger is tenderness and a flavor imparted by herbs and the onions that give off their own liquid (which provides earthiness and moisture), not to mention 2 tablespoons of half-and-half or cream. If you're feeling particularly healthy, insert the tiniest pat of butter or cheese directly into the center of the burger, and form the patty around it.

3	pounds good-quality ground beef	¹/₂	tablespoon fresh thyme, chopped, or 1 teaspoon dried
2	tablespoons half-and-half or heavy cream	1	teaspoon kosher salt
2	small onions, peeled and finely minced	1	teaspoon freshly ground black pepper
¹/₂	cup button mushrooms (or any wild variety), cleaned and pulverized in a food processor		

Optional: *¹/₂ stick unsalted butter, sliced into thin pats; ¹/₂ pound cheese, cut into 1-inch cubes*

MODERATION BEGINS WITH PORTION SIZE

Horrified, are you? A hamburger recipe that calls for the addition of cream and, possibly, butter? Gentle reader, take heart (literally). Thus begins a short lecture on the importance of moderation and portion size. Yes, this recipe does call for either half-and-half or cream. The good news is that it calls for 2 tablespoons of it spread out among 3 pounds of beef. Very often, we lose sight of exactly how much bad stuff we'll be ingesting when we hear what it is. Keep in mind that you will *not* be eating the entire amount of hamburgers that this recipe makes. You'll be eating *one*. If you're particularly concerned, omit what worries you. Otherwise, go ahead and enjoy your burger however you like it . . . just make a pact with yourself to eat well the next day, and limit your meat and dairy intake for the rest of the week.

Preheat grill to medium.

On a large plastic cutting board, spread the meat out so it's flat, like a rectangular pancake. Drizzle half-and-half over it, then onions, mushrooms, thyme, salt, and pepper.

Fold the meat together with your (clean) hands, kneading it as you would bread, until well combined, about 2 minutes.

Divide into 6 patties of equal size, inserting a pat of butter or a cube of cheese into the center of each, if using. Do not compress patties with your hands, or you will have hockey pucks, not food.

Place patties on grill and cook to desired temperature (see chart, page 212). Serve immediately.

VARIATIONS

- Combine beef with chopped pork and veal for additional flavor.
- Substitute ground turkey or chicken for beef.
- Add the following: minced garlic; finely grated carrots; finely chopped celery; frozen spinach, thawed and finely chopped.
- Substitute lamb for beef, and add Middle Eastern spices: cumin, ginger, coriander, garam masala.
- Grill on rye bread with Swiss cheese for a classic patty melt.
- Instead of forming into patties, combine the herbed chopped meat with an additional roughly chopped small onion, 1 cup fresh or frozen chopped vegetables, and 1 (16-ounce) can of crushed tomatoes. Top with mashed potatoes and bake at 350°F for 35 to 40 minutes. What have you got? Hamburger pie.

Serves 6

HOW BIG IS TOO BIG?

Very often, chopped meat comes in immense—really immense—packages, anywhere up to 8 pounds. Unless you're feeding an army or the local Boy Scout troop, you will never need that much meat. However, if the price is too good to resist, go ahead, but promise yourself that you will:

- Break the package into 1-pound portions, and freeze them in labeled, dated, heavy-duty freezer bags.
- Make a variety of burgers (some with cheese, some without), and freeze them, *uncooked*, for up to 6 months in clearly marked bags.

HOW LONG IT WILL LAST

- Hamburgers are best when eaten hot, directly from the grill, oven, or stove.
- Leftover hamburgers will keep in the refrigerator, double-plastic-wrapped and stored in dated heavy-duty freezer bags, for up to 3 days.
- Leftover hamburgers will freeze, double-plastic-wrapped and stored in labeled, dated, heavy-duty freezer bags, for up to 8 months, or 6 months if there is cheese involved.

ADDITIONAL SERVING RECOMMENDATIONS

- Serve these burgers on excellent-quality sourdough rolls that have been lightly brushed with extra virgin olive oil and toasted under the broiler or grilled.
- Serve with the following toppings:
  - BIG FOOD Barbecue Sauce (page 37)
  - BIG FOOD Aioli (page 35)
  - Arugula or similar bitter greens
  - Sliced tomato
  - Sliced raw or sautéed red onion
  - More cheese
  - Sliced, sautéed mushrooms
  - Sliced, pickled jalapeño peppers
  - Bread-and-butter pickles

WHAT YOU HAVE ON HAND

- **6 pounds of beef stew meat or top round**
- **2-liter bottle of dry red wine, preferably Pinot Noir**
- **Onions**
- **Carrots**
- **Mushrooms**

WHAT TO DO WITH IT

- Set aside 2 pounds of beef for this recipe; double-plastic-wrap the balance, and store in a labeled, dated, heavy-duty freezer bag for up to 8 months in the freezer. Or, grind the balance in a food processor and use in Sweet-and-Sour Stuffed Cabbage (page 234), Not My Mama's Meat Loaf (page 220), or BIG FOOD Chili con Carne (page 238).

- Use enough wine to cover the meat; cork the bottle tightly, and store the balance in the refrigerator for up to 14 days.

- Set aside 2 large onions for this recipe; store the balance in a mesh bag in a cool, dark location, away from potatoes or fruit.

- Set aside ½ pound of mushrooms for this dish; store the balance in a perforated bag in your salad crisper.

PRIMARY

BEEF BOURGUINON

Many years ago, I was lucky enough to spend Christmas at the home of my dear friend, and an exceptional cook, Stevie Romanoff, and her husband, Porter Boggess, in Lake Forest, Illinois. Her family came from miles around, climbing mountains and fording streams for one reason: her Beef Bourguinon. Velvety and rich, it is the quintessential BIG FOOD dish because: 1) it requires inexpensive stew meat; 2) it takes a BIG quantity of relatively inexpensive wine; and 3) it can freeze for months and be reheated on the Night Before Christmas. Adapted from Narcissa and Narcisse Chamberlain's ancient The Flavor of France in Recipes and Pictures, *certain modern conveniences have been employed that would make a Burgundian chef wince. But not I.*

2	tablespoons butter		1	package low-sodium dried onion soup mix
2	tablespoons extra virgin olive oil, divided		2	large onions, peeled and coarsely chopped
2	pounds stewing beef, cut into 1½ inch cubes		2	large carrots, peeled and cut into 2-inch pieces
1	tablespoon flour		2	shallots, peeled and chopped
1	teaspoon freshly ground black pepper		2	garlic cloves, peeled and minced
½	teaspoon kosher salt			Bouquet garni*
1	bottle dry red wine, preferably Pinot Noir (or Burgundy)		½	pound raw mushrooms, sliced

Optional: *1 tablespoon brandy, plus 4 tablespoons Madeira*

* *To make a bouquet garni, tie the following together with kitchen twine: 3 stalks fresh flat-leaf parsley, 1 sprig fresh thyme, and 1 bay leaf.*

Melt butter and 1 tablespoon of the oil in a large, heavy Dutch oven or saucepan over medium heat, until rippling but not smoking. (Do not let the butter burn.)

Brown the meat in batches, approximately 8 to 10 minutes per batch. Once all of the meat is brown, return it all to the pot, cover with flour, add pepper and salt, and mix well. Add enough wine to cover the meat completely, and blend in the soup mix.

Heat the remaining 1 tablespoon of oil in a small sauté pan, until rippling but not smoking. Add onions and cook until they just begin to take on color, about 8 minutes.

Add onions to the meat, along with carrots, shallots, garlic, and bouquet garni. Cover and let simmer for 3 hours.

At this point, the dish can be cooled completely and stored in the freezer for up to 6 months.

Add mushrooms, blend gently, and continue to cook for 1 hour. Add brandy and Madeira, if using. Remove herbs prior to serving. Serve hot.

VARIATIONS

- Make this dish with a combination of water and wine, using only 1½ cups of red wine and water to cover meat.
- Substitute beef stock for the water.
- Add the following vegetables at the same time as the carrots: peeled turnips, cut into ¼-inch dice; celery, cut into 2-inch pieces; parsnips, peeled and cut into 2-inch pieces.

Serves 6

HOW LONG IT WILL LAST

- Stored in a tightly sealed container in the refrigerator, this dish will last up to 4 days.
- Stored in a dated, heavy-duty freezer bag, this dish will freeze up to 6 months.

ADDITIONAL SERVING RECOMMENDATIONS

- Serve Beef Bourguinon over steamed or boiled rice.
- Serve it over lightly buttered egg noodles dusted with freshly ground pepper.

SECONDARY DISHES

- *Beef Stroganoff: Gently warm the leftover meat and sauce, and add sliced mushrooms and a dollop of sour cream. Blend well, and serve as above.*

- **6 to 8 pounds of brisket**
- **Onions**
- **Bag of carrots**
- **Celery**
- **Large cans of Italian-style plum tomatoes**
- **Coca-Cola**
- **Leftover dry red wine**

WHAT TO DO WITH IT

- Cook the entire piece of meat; it will shrink during the braising process, and leftovers can be cooled and then frozen.
- Set aside 3 large onions for this dish; store the balance in a mesh bag in a cool, dark place, away from potatoes and fruit.
- Set aside 4 to 5 carrots for this dish; store the balance in your salad crisper, in a heavy-duty plastic bag poked with a few holes.

PRIMARY

NEW YEAR'S BRISKET

Every faith and ethnicity has at least one dish attached to it that conjures up images of families gathering together around the table and celebrating, and this one is mine. Often what is most important is that we're together and we've asked others who might otherwise be alone to eat with us, in the most civilized of hospitable traditions. I make this delicious and filling dish on the Jewish New Year (Rosh Hashanah), and for no other reason than my family adores it. The leftovers are arguably better than the original meal, and its sweetness suggests our hope for a sweet New Year.

1	(8-pound) brisket	4	carrots, peeled and cut into 4-inch pieces
3	garlic cloves, 2 peeled and sliced into slivers, 1 peeled and sliced in half	3	celery stalks, cut into 3- to 4-inch pieces
1/2	teaspoon kosher salt	1 1/2	cups dry red wine
1/2	teaspoon freshly ground black pepper	1/4	cup Heinz chili sauce
1/4	tablespoon Hungarian paprika	1	cup canned crushed Italian-style plum tomatoes
2	tablespoons canola oil	1	can Coca-Cola
3	large onions, peeled and sliced into thin rings		

COOKING WITH COCA-COLA

That's right. Coca-Cola. Miss Fancy "I Cook Only with Good Wine" cooks with Coca-Cola (which, I should add, I *don't* drink). In fact, many good home cooks (especially in the South) understand that once you heat Coca-Cola or ginger ale, what you are left with is a caramel-like basting liquid derived from the drink's heavy sugar content. Whenever you want to add sweetness and a *gloss* to a savory food that is going to be long-cooked, this is the way to do it. Try it here, in a slow-cooked smoky barbecue, or over a Southern-style ham.

A BIG TSIMMES

When I was a child and prone to hyperbole, my grandmother would shake a finger at me and say, "Elissa, don't make such a big *tsimmes*!" What *is* a tsimmes? A prolonged job or procedure, a trouble, a mess—which is what a good tsimmes is meant to look like. So if it's not the most attractive thing you've ever made, don't worry.

Using a long, thin knife, carefully make ½-inch slits all over the meat, and insert the garlic slivers. Take half of the remaining garlic clove and rub it all over the meat. Mince the other half, and reserve.

Season the meat on both sides with salt, pepper, and paprika.

Preheat oven to 325°F.

Heat oil in a large Dutch oven or large, heavy-duty roasting pan set over 2 burners, over medium-high heat, until rippling but not smoking. Brown the meat on one side, approximately 5 minutes, turn over, and repeat. Remove from pan and set aside.

Reduce heat to medium. Add onions, carrots, celery, and reserved minced garlic to the pan. Cook until vegetables begin to soften, about 8 minutes, taking care not to let onions burn.

Add brisket back to pan; spoon half of the vegetables on top of it. Add wine, chili sauce, tomatoes, and Coca-Cola. Bring to a low boil and cook for 5 minutes.

Cover the pan tightly (if you're using a roasting pan, cover with heavy-duty aluminum foil and make sure you have a good seal), place in oven, and cook for 3 hours, spooning the sauce over the meat at half-hour intervals during the cooking process.

Remove the meat from the pan and slice thinly on the bias, against the grain. Return it to the pan, spoon sauce over it, cover, and continue to cook for another hour.

Remove from oven and let brisket cool for approximately 45 minutes. Refrigerate for at least 8 hours or overnight. (If you cannot take the time to refrigerate this dish overnight, invest in a fat separator, and use it for the gravy.)

The next day, skim the fat from the meat and the gravy, cover, and reheat in a 325°F oven for 1 hour. Serve hot.

VARIATIONS

- Make this dish sweet-and-sour by adding a handful of golden raisins and a splash of red wine vinegar during the second hour.
- Omit the chili sauce and add 2 tablespoons of strong instant coffee for a fuller-bodied sauce.
- Add 1 package of dried onion soup mix or 1 cup of leftover French Onion Soup (page 54), onions included.
- Add sliced dried prunes, figs, and apricots (make sure they are not candied) to the sauce.

Serves 6

HOW LONG IT WILL LAST

- Ideally, sliced brisket should be refrigerated the day it is cooked, then reheated and served the following night. Beyond that, cooked brisket and its gravy will last for up to 4 days refrigerated, sealed in an airtight container.
- Sliced brisket and its gravy can be frozen (separately), both for up to 4 months. Double-plastic-wrap and seal the brisket in a labeled, dated, heavy-duty freezer bag; freeze the gravy in a heavy-duty freezer bag.

ADDITIONAL SERVING RECOMMENDATIONS

- Refrigerate brisket the night it's been cooked; the next day, skim the fat off of it, reheat the brisket, and serve on a platter accompanied by sliced raisin challah (Jewish egg bread), the vegetables that have cooked with the meat, gravy, steamed broccoli, and Roman-Style Sautéed Greens (page 195).

SECONDARY DISHES

- *Day after New Year's* Tsimmes*: Lay the leftover meat in a roasting pan or Dutch oven, and spoon the softened vegetables and gravy over it, mashing the vegetables to a heavy pulp. Bake until heated through.*

WHAT TO DO WITH IT

- Divide the meat in half; double-plastic-wrap the balance, and store in a dated, heavy-duty freezer bag in the refrigerator for up to 3 days, uncooked, or in the freezer for up to 6 months.

- Set aside a large onion for this dish, and store the balance in a mesh bag in a cool, dark location, away from potatoes and fruit.

- Set aside the peppers for this dish, and store the balance in the salad crisper or freeze (page 171).

HOW LONG IT WILL LAST

- This dish will last, stored in the refrigerator in a tightly sealed container, for up to 4 days.

- This dish will last, stored in the freezer in a dated, heavy-duty freezer bag, for up to 3 months.

PRIMARY

STIR-FRIED BEEF WITH VEGETABLES

As a student in Boston (and then as an underemployed college grad), I ate my weight in this simple, easy-to-prepare standby that has for decades provided wholesome goodness to the time-and-money-strapped among us. Make this dish with either fresh, uncooked meat, or leftovers that were originally cooked on the medium-rare side. Toss the leftovers with Chinese-style noodles, a knob of chopped fresh ginger, and a splash of spiced soy sauce, and call it another meal.

2	pounds flank, blade, or sirloin steak, sliced thinly into strips, against the grain
1	tablespoon soy sauce or nam pla (Vietnamese fish sauce)
1	tablespoon peanut oil
2	garlic cloves, peeled and minced
1	tablespoon fresh ginger, peeled and sliced into rounds
1	large onion, peeled and coarsely chopped
1	large red bell pepper, seeded, ribbed, and cut into strips
1	large green bell pepper, cored and cut into strips
¼	teaspoon red pepper flakes
	Juice of 1 lime

Place beef in a large, nonreactive bowl and toss with the soy sauce. Set aside.

Set a large sauté pan or wok over medium-high heat until very hot, 2 to 3 minutes. Add peanut oil, carefully swirling to coat the pan.

Add garlic, ginger, onion, peppers, and red pepper flakes, and stir until softened, 6 to 8 minutes.

Add the beef and soy sauce, and stir until the meat is cooked through.

Remove from heat, drizzle with lime juice, and serve immediately.

Because it is cooked at a high heat, this dish tends to create a lot of smoke. Do not be tempted to reduce the heat, or the vegetables will steam rather than fry.

Note: If the finished dish appears to be dry, add an additional $\frac{1}{2}$ tablespoon of soy sauce or nam pla to the dish.

VARIATIONS
- Add $\frac{3}{4}$ cup of raw, unsalted peanuts to the vegetables.
- Add the zest of 1 lime.
- Add $1\frac{1}{2}$ cups bok choy greens.
- Add 1 cup of broccoli florets.
- Add 1 packed cup of basil.
- Substitute any of the following for the beef (and adjust cooking time as needed): white meat chicken, shrimp, or firm tofu.

Serves 4 to 6

WHEN MEAT IS ON THE RISE
In today's world of high prices, shopping for meat in bulk can still be cost prohibitive. What to do? Look for alternative cuts that will allow you to prepare the same sorts of dishes for less money. Replace flank steak with blade steak, skirt steak, or top round; use bottom round in place of brisket. If stewing meat seems unreasonably expensive, buy bottom round, sharpen your chef's knife, and cube it yourself. And if you have leftover raw meat and see some hamburgers or chili in your future, cube your leftovers and run them through the food processor.

ADDITIONAL SERVING RECOMMENDATIONS
- Serve this dish over thinly sliced cabbage.

SECONDARY DISHES
- *Spicy Beef Lo-Mein: Toss the leftovers with Chinese-style noodles.*
- *Spicy Beef Chow Fun: Toss the leftovers with wide-cut rice noodles.*
- *Spicy Mu Shu Beef: Serve the leftovers along with small flour tortillas and a dollop of packaged hoisin sauce.*
- *Spicy Beef Salad with Bean Sprouts and Carrots: Toss the leftovers with a splash of rice wine vinegar, bean sprouts, and shredded carrots.*

WHAT YOU HAVE ON HAND

- 6 to 8 pounds of flank, blade, or sirloin steak
- Balsamic vinegar
- Cherry tomatoes
- Parmesan cheese

WHAT TO DO WITH IT

- Set aside approximately 2 pounds of steak; double-plastic-wrap the uncooked balance, and store in a dated, heavy-duty freezer bag in the refrigerator for up to 3 days. Wrapped the same way, it will keep in the freezer for up to 6 months.
- Buy the best-quality balsamic vinegar you can afford, and store it in a cool, dark location.
- Use cherry tomatoes in place of larger tomatoes in any dish.
- To stew surplus cherry tomatoes, sauté them in olive oil with a bit of garlic, salt, sugar, and black pepper.

HOW LONG IT WILL LAST

- This dish will last up to 4 days in the refrigerator, tightly sealed in plastic wrap and placed in a labeled, dated, heavy-duty freezer bag.

PRIMARY

BALSAMIC MARINATED FLANK STEAK WITH GREENS, PARMESAN, AND CHERRY TOMATOES

A modern, economical twist on traditional Bistecca alla Fiorentina *(which calls for a very thick, very expensive porterhouse), this simple and exceptionally delicious recipe uses flank steak but can also be made with 1-inch-thick blade steak, an unsung, highly flavorful, marbled cut that costs virtually nothing. Either way, marinate the steak for as long as 3 hours, grill or broil it quickly, and let it rest before slicing it thinly against the grain.*

½   cup balsamic vinegar

3   tablespoons honey

4   garlic cloves, peeled and smashed

1   tablespoon freshly ground black pepper

Kosher salt

2   pounds flank or blade steak

15–20   cherry tomatoes

1   bunch of fresh arugula or similar tender salad greens, washed and dried

Extra virgin olive oil, hunk of fresh Parmesan cheese, and fresh lemon juice for garnish

Combine vinegar, honey, garlic, pepper, and salt to taste in a medium-size, non-metallic bowl. Pour into a heavy-duty, gallon-size, ziplock freezer bag.

Add meat to bag, tightly zip closed (pressing air out), toss to coat meat with marinade, and refrigerate for 3 hours. Remove steak from marinade and pat dry; discard marinade.

Preheat grill to medium or set oven at broil. If using broiler, set rack 3½ to 4 inches from heat before preheating; if grilling, cook over direct heat. Grill or cook steak 3 minutes per side for rare, or 4 minutes per side for medium-rare. Move to a lower rack or to a cooler part of the grill, and continue to cook for 1 more minute.

Transfer to a cutting board and let sit for 5 minutes before slicing. In the meantime, place cherry tomatoes into a grill basket or broiler pan and grill or cook, shaking the pan frequently, until they begin to blister and soften, about 5 minutes.

Slice steak thinly against the grain, and arrange atop arugula. Sprinkle cherry tomatoes on top of meat and drizzle with oil. Using a vegetable peeler, shave thin strips of Parmesan onto meat. Squeeze lemon juice over all. Serve immediately.

Serves 4 to 6

WHERE TO USE BALSAMIC VINEGAR
- Drizzled onto fresh berries
- Heated and drizzled onto vanilla ice cream
- Painted onto large, grilled, portobello mushrooms
- Drizzled, with lemon juice, onto salad greens in place of vinaigrette
- Drizzled onto roasting chicken

ADDITIONAL SERVING RECOMMENDATIONS
- Slice on the bias against the grain, and serve at room temperature.

SECONDARY DISHES
- *Toss sliced meat with scallions, minced garlic, and any spaghetti-like pasta or soba noodles. Drizzle with rice vinegar, grated ginger, a drop of soy sauce, and a squeeze of lime.*
- *Toast rounds of crusty, country-style white bread, and drizzle with olive oil. Top with sliced leftover steak and a poached egg. Season carefully with kosher salt, freshly ground black pepper, and dried or fresh parsley.*

WHAT YOU HAVE ON HAND

- **6 to 8 pounds of sirloin or top round, cut into cubes**
- **Onions**
- **Cherry tomatoes**
- **Eggplant**
- **Bell peppers**
- **Canned pineapple chunks**
- **Fresh mango**
- **Any other firm-fleshed fruit or vegetable**

WHAT TO DO WITH IT

- This dish is perfect for a crowd, so cube the meat, invest in big skewers, and cook it all.
- Prepare the skewers the night before if you are in a rush: let the meat marinate overnight.

HOW LONG IT WILL LAST

- Beef Kebabs are best when eaten immediately. However, if you have leftovers (and you will), remove everything from the skewers, place in a dated heavy-duty freezer bag, and refrigerate for up to 4 days.

PRIMARY

BEEF KEBABS FOR A CROWD

The credo of BIG FOOD is not only to use what you bring home in bulk but also to do it as simply as possible, and kebabs are about as simple a recipe as one could hope for. They can be assembled in advance, marinated overnight, and cooked on the grill, on the stove top, or under the broiler after a busy day at work. They can be made with nearly any cut of leaner beef and any kind of firm vegetable, and even some fruit, in any combination. This recipe calls for sirloin that you've cubed yourself, but feel free to buy lean stewing meat or even use leftover steak cut into cubes.

³/₄	cup extra virgin olive oil	1	pound whole cherry tomatoes
3	garlic cloves, peeled and minced	6	pounds beef (sirloin or top round), cut into 1-inch cubes
1	teaspoon kosher salt		
½	tablespoon coarsely ground fresh pepper	2	large eggplants, cut into 1-inch cubes
	Juice of 1 lemon	4	large bell peppers, seeded, ribbed, and cut into large squares
4	large onions, peeled and cut into eighths		

Optional: Mango, cut into cubes; seedless grapes; canned pineapple chunks

THE ART OF GETTING SKEWERED

There is no party dish that is more fun to cook than kebabs. But it is the wise person who knows his own skewers: unsoaked bamboo skewers can and will catch fire, and metal skewers can get as hot as branding irons. How to solve this problem?

- Marinate your kebabs on bamboo skewers.
- If you're not marinating your kebabs, soak your bamboo skewers in water for 30 minutes before loading them up with meat and vegetables and putting them on the grill.

If you must use metal skewers, place the ingredients that don't retain heat well closest to the handle: onions, tomatoes, and other vegetables will not hold heat as well as denser vegetables, such as eggplant, and will likely allow the skewer handle to be cool enough to touch with a gloved hand shortly after being removed from the heat source.

In a small bowl, whisk oil, garlic, salt, pepper, and lemon juice together. Using long bamboo skewers, thread together kebabs in this fashion:

• Onion	• Peppers
• Tomato	• Beef
• Beef	• Tomato
• Eggplant	• Onion

Repeat. If using fruit, skewer as close to the meat as possible.

Place skewers in a large roasting pan, drizzle with marinade, double-plastic-wrap tightly, and refrigerate for 8 hours or overnight.

Preheat grill to medium. Lay the skewers down over direct heat, turning every 5 minutes until meat and vegetables are cooked through, 8 to 10 minutes. If you find that the vegetables are cooking more quickly than the meat, move the skewers off of direct heat, and continue to cook until the meat is thoroughly cooked.

VARIATIONS
• Replace beef with chicken, swordfish, tuna, shrimp, pork, cooked ham steak, or lamb.

Serves 8 to 10

ADDITIONAL SERVING RECOMMENDATIONS
• The possibilities are endless:
  • Serve them buffet style: give everyone a skewer, and let guests—young and old—assemble their own kebabs from ingredients placed on different platters. They'll hand the uncooked kebabs to you for grilling or broiling.
  • Serve them Middle Eastern–style: wrap the skewer in a warm flatbread, and then pull the skewer out, leaving you with a sandwich of sorts.
  • Serve with rice, vegetables, and a side of Stuffed Tomatoes (page 90).
  • Serve with BIG FOOD Aioli (page 35).

SECONDARY DISHES
• *Use the leftover kebabs in a version of Grilled Vegetable Salad with Chicken and Pine Nuts (page 88).*
• *Toss warmed leftover kebabs with penne or any tubular pasta.*

PRIMARY/SECONDARY

SWEET-AND-SOUR STUFFED CABBAGE

This dish, which can be made with ground veal, beef, chicken, pork, or a combination of all four, is worth the time and effort; it's delicious served immediately, but even better after a day of sitting in the refrigerator or a month in the freezer. Small hands are perfect for helping to roll up the cabbage; give the little ones a bowl of the meat mixture and some cabbage leaves, and put them to work. Adapted from a prized family recipe created by stuffed-cabbage-maker extraordinaire Pauline Schwartz, it is a delicious mélange of sweet and savory tastes and textures.

1	medium onion, peeled and diced
½	teaspoon sweet paprika
2	pounds ground beef
2	tablespoons long-grain rice
1	tablespoon lemon juice
1	large head cabbage
½	cup red wine vinegar

1	(28-ounce) can crushed Italian-style plum tomatoes, divided
1	cup golden raisins
½	cup sugar
	Kosher salt and freshly ground black pepper
	Crusty bread or steamed rice

Fill a large stockpot with water, cover, and bring to a boil.

Place onion into a separate large saucepan with a cover; add water to cover by 2 inches. Drizzle in paprika and bring to a very low simmer, uncovered.

Meanwhile, combine beef, rice, and lemon juice in a large mixing bowl. Blend well and set aside.

When the water in the stockpot has come to a boil, add the entire head of cabbage (and open your windows), cover, and boil for 10 minutes. Remove, let cool on a platter, core, and carefully pull off the leaves, flattening them with your hands and taking care not to tear them.

Add the vinegar and half of the tomatoes to the pot with the onion, stir, and continue to simmer.

Place $1/4$ cup of the meat mixture in the middle of each cabbage leaf (slightly less if leaves are small) and roll up, tucking in the ends as you go. Repeat until all of the mixture is used.

Place stuffed cabbages into simmering onion mixture; it's preferable to do it in one layer, but should you have to go to two, that's fine.

Pour the remaining tomatoes over the cabbage rolls and add the raisins. Cover, bring to a boil, and cook for 10 minutes. Reduce to a simmer and continue to cook for 2 hours. Add sugar, season with salt and pepper to taste, and serve in shallow soup bowls with thick slices of crusty bread, or on a bed of steamed rice.

VARIATIONS

- Replace beef with ground turkey, chicken, pork, or veal, or any combination of these ground meats.

Serves 6

HOW LONG IT WILL LAST

- Sweet-and-Sour Stuffed Cabbage will last up to 4 days in the refrigerator, stored in an airtight container.

- Stored the same way, Sweet-and-Sour Stuffed Cabbage will last up to 4 months in the freezer.

WHAT YOU HAVE ON HAND

- **Fresh ground beef, pork, or a combination of the two**
  or
- **4 to 6 pounds of inexpensive blade, skirt, or flank steak**
- **Salt pork, pancetta, or thickly sliced prosciutto**
- **Canned Italian-style plum tomatoes**
- **Milk**
- **Carrots**
- **Onions**
- **Celery**

WHAT TO DO WITH IT

- Set aside 2 pounds of meat for this dish; double-plastic-wrap the balance, and refrigerate in a dated, heavy-duty freezer bag for up to 4 days, or freeze for up to 6 months.
- Set aside 1 medium onion for this dish; store the balance in a mesh bag in a cool, dark location, away from potatoes or fruit.

PRIMARY

TRADITIONAL BOLOGNESE SAUCE

Falling squarely into the "if it ain't broke, don't fix it" category, this simple-to-prepare BIG FOOD Bolognese Sauce hails from the glorious Emiliga Romagna region of Italy and blends milk, meat, wine, cured pork, tomatoes, and herbs for a delicious sauce that freezes incomparably well. This BIG FOOD lifesaver can be tossed with freshly cooked pasta and a little grated cheese; frozen in bulk in small containers and hauled out for an individual lasagna; or made with all ground beef, all ground pork, or a combination of the two.

2	tablespoons extra virgin olive oil
¼	pound thickly sliced pancetta or prosciutto, diced
1	medium onion, peeled and finely minced
2	carrots, peeled and finely minced
2	celery stalks, finely minced
2	pounds coarsely ground beef, preferably lean
1	(12-ounce) can crushed Italian-style plum tomatoes with their juices

1	cup dry white wine
2	tablespoons tomato paste
2	bay leaves, crushed
2	cups milk
	Kosher salt and freshly ground black pepper
	Hot cooked pasta
	Parmesan cheese

WHERE TO USE CHEAPER CUTS OF MEAT

This sauce—a classic Italian ragu, or meat sauce—is effectively a *braise*, or a long-cooking way to tenderize tougher, cheaper, more sinewy (and nearly always more flavorful) cuts of meat . . . even if they've been ground. Arguably, this rustic peasant style of cooking is one of the most utilitarian ways of stretching a dollar (or a euro). If a recipe calls for ground meat but you want one that's both packed with flavor and low in cost, look for less expensive cuts. Shoulder of veal, pork butt, and skirt, flank, and blade steak are all relatively inexpensive and can be ground at home in the food processor. (See page 254 for more instructions.) To save your shekels in the meat department, do the following:

- Look at your recipe and see what kind of meat is called for.
- Go to the cuts-of-meat charts (pages 213 and 214), and see what you should use for that recipe and which less expensive alternatives are suitable.

Heat oil in a large saucepan or Dutch oven over medium-high heat, until rippling but not smoking. Add pancetta, reduce heat to medium, and sauté until meat has rendered its fat into the pan, about 6 minutes. Remove with a slotted spoon and reserve.

If more than 2 tablespoons oil and fat have accumulated in the pan, wipe some of it out with a paper towel held by your longest tongs, leaving about 2 tablespoons in the pan.

Add onion, carrots, and celery, and sauté until translucent, about 10 minutes. Add beef and continue to cook, stirring frequently, until meat loses its redness but is still moist, about 8 minutes.

Add tomatoes, wine, tomato paste, bay leaves, and reserved pancetta. Stir, partially cover, reduce to a low simmer, and continue to cook for 30 minutes.

Add milk, stir well, return partial cover, and cook until most of the milk has been absorbed, about 1½ hours. The finished sauce should be a little thinner than a traditionally thick stew.

Season with salt and pepper to taste, serve over hot pasta (try a ribbony variety, such as tagliatelle, or a tubular pasta), and top with Parmesan; or cool completely and store.

VARIATIONS

- Substitute the following for meat: ground pork, ground veal, ground turkey, or a combination of these.
- Substitute dry red wine for white wine.
- Sauté the pancetta or prosciutto in half butter, half extra virgin olive oil.
- Substitute cubed leftover ham for the pancetta or prosciutto.

Yields approximately 1 quart

HOW LONG IT WILL LAST

- Traditional Bolognese Sauce will last up to 4 days in the refrigerator, stored in an airtight container.
- Traditional Bolognese Sauce will freeze for up to 6 months, stored in a dated, labeled, airtight container.

SECONDARY DISHES

- *Lasagna Bolognese: Layer sauce with lasagna sheets, and top each layer with grated Pecorino Romano cheese.*
- *Ladle Traditional Bolognese Sauce onto warmed slices of Italian bread, top with cheese, and bake until cheese has melted.*

- Ground or leftover uncooked beef, pork, veal, chicken, or turkey
- Canned beans: black, kidney, white, cranberry, Adzuki, red, navy, or pinto beans; black or white soybeans; but *not* baked beans
- Canned crushed Italian-style plum tomatoes
- Onions
- Cider vinegar

WHAT TO DO WITH IT

- Increase the size of the recipe proportionally so that you can make as much as you bring home ingredients for.
- If you're working with unground beef, chicken, veal, pork, or turkey: set aside 1½ pounds of it, double-plastic-wrap it, chill in freezer (but do not freeze) and grind in a food processor according to the instructions on page 254.
- Use any combination of beans.
- Set aside 3 onions for this dish, and store the balance in a mesh bag in a cool, dark location, away from potatoes or fruit.

PRIMARY/SECONDARY

BIG FOOD CHILI CON CARNE

Another way to use up all of that extra meat, chicken, pork, or beef that you bring home from your discount club shopping excursions, this recipe calls for beef but can be easily adapted to utilize any of the above. A highly personalized twist on everyone's favorite one-pot dish, it also calls for any variety of canned beans that you have lurking in your larder, with only a few exceptions. Make it as hot or as mild as you like, and break out the storage containers, because it freezes magnificently for the long haul.

2	tablespoons extra virgin olive oil	1½	pounds ground beef
3	medium onions, peeled and chopped	1	(28-ounce) can crushed Italian-style plum tomatoes
2	garlic cloves, peeled and minced	3	(16-ounce) cans beans and their liquid (see "What You Have on Hand" for bean types)
⅓	cup chili powder		
2	bay leaves, crushed	4	tablespoons cider vinegar
1½	teaspoons dried cumin		Kosher salt
1	teaspoon dried oregano		

BUYING CHILI POWDER

Not all chili powders are alike: some are made from very mild chilies, and some from incendiary chilies that can stand your hair straight up. What to do? Avoid purchasing "generic" chili powder that labels itself as such; instead, look at the description. Here's a short guide.

- **Ancho chili powder:** Made from ancho chilies, which are, in fact, dried red poblanos. I once thought poblanos were mild, but my aunt, who was crying over a bowl of soup I had made her (in which they were an ingredient), assured me otherwise. On the BIG FOOD heat scale, ancho chili powder falls squarely in the middle.
- **Cayenne pepper:** This is not chili powder. Never use it as a substitute, or you will be very sorry.
- **Chipotle chili powder:** Made from dried and smoked jalapeños, these chilies are hot, flavorful, dark, and smoky. A personal BIG FOOD favorite.
- **Pasilla chili powder:** Dark and chocolatey in color and flavor, pasillas are used most often as one of the many ingredients in mole, the great Mexican delicacy. Medium-hot.
- **Habanero chili powder:** Run, do not walk, from this petite little chile that is just to the right of combustible.

Heat oil in a large saucepan or Dutch oven over medium heat, until rippling but not smoking.

Add onions and garlic. Stir to coat with oil and cook until translucent, 6 to 8 minutes. Add chili powder, bay leaves, cumin, and oregano. Reduce heat to low, cover, and cook until flavors blend, about 10 minutes.

Add meat and cook, stirring frequently to break up chunks, until no longer pink, about 8 minutes. Add tomatoes and beans, and simmer gently, uncovered, for 1 hour.

Stir in vinegar and salt to taste, adjusting seasonings if necessary. Simmer for 30 minutes. Season with salt to taste and serve hot.

VARIATIONS

- Use cubed beef, chicken, pork, or turkey instead of ground.
- Experiment with different strengths of chili powder (but not on your family).

Serves 6

THICKENING SOUPS, STEWS, AND GRAVIES

If you're making chili and it's a little thin for your liking, use a large spoon to ladle out some of the liquid and place it in a small bowl, add a tablespoon of masa harina or flour, and blend well. Return the liquid mixture to the chili and stir. Follow the same rule for all soups, stews, and gravies.

HOW LONG IT WILL LAST

- Stored in an airtight container, BIG FOOD Chili con Carne will keep for up to 4 days in the refrigerator or up to 6 months in the freezer.

ADDITIONAL SERVING RECOMMENDATIONS

- Serve BIG FOOD Chili con Carne over rice or on a warm tortilla, topped with any of the following: diced, raw red onion; shredded Monterey Jack cheese; low- or full-fat sour cream, blended with fresh or dried chives; your favorite hot sauce, if you have a death wish; and/or chopped tomatoes.

SECONDARY DISHES

- *Chili Tacos:* Ladle leftover reheated BIG FOOD Chili con Carne into packaged crisp corn tortillas.
- *Chili con Carne con Huevos:* Top leftover, reheated BIG FOOD Chili con Carne with poached eggs, or blend it into an omelet, for a spicy brunch dish.

WHAT YOU HAVE ON HAND

- 1 (8-pound) leg of lamb, bone in
- Garlic
- Eggs
- Packaged beef stock, or leftover stock or consommé from Pot-au-Feu (page 48)
- Lemons
- BIG FOOD Mediterranean Spice Blend (page 39)

WHAT TO DO WITH IT

- Trim the meat of excess fat.
- Set aside the appropriate amount of garlic for this dish, and store the balance in a cool, dark location.
- The basting sauce calls for 6 eggs: store the balance in the coldest part of your refrigerator (not the door).

HOW LONG IT WILL LAST

- Greek-Style Leg of Lamb will last in the refrigerator, sliced off the bone, double-plastic-wrapped and stored in a heavy-duty freezer bag, for up to 4 days.
- Greek-Style Leg of Lamb can be frozen for up to 3 months. Double-plastic-wrap, then wrap in a layer of aluminum foil and store in a labeled, dated heavy-duty freezer bag.

PRIMARY/SECONDARY

GREEK-STYLE LEG OF LAMB WITH EGG AND LEMON SAUCE

In this traditional dish, the leg of lamb is marinated slowly in herbs, and then roasted on a bed of sliced potatoes. The result is itself cause for festivity; the leftovers, for starting the party all over again.

MARINADE:

½	cup extra virgin olive oil	3½	teaspoons BIG FOOD Mediterranean Spice Blend
	Juice of 1 whole lemon	1	teaspoon lemon zest
6	garlic cloves, peeled and minced	½	teaspoon freshly ground black pepper
1½	tablespoons white wine vinegar		

LAMB:

1	(8-pound) leg of lamb, bone in, trimmed of excess fat		Kosher salt and freshly ground black pepper
10	garlic cloves, peeled and minced	2	tablespoons extra virgin olive oil, divided in half
3	tablespoons BIG FOOD Mediterranean Spice Blend	4	Idaho potatoes, peeled and sliced into ¼-inch rounds
1½	teaspoons lemon zest	½	cup dry white wine

EGG AND LEMON SAUCE:

6	egg yolks	¼	cup leftover or packaged beef stock
	Juice of 1 lemon		

FOR THE MARINADE:

Combine oil, lemon juice, garlic, vinegar, spice blend, zest, and pepper. Pour into an oblong baking dish big enough to hold lamb. Set lamb on top of marinade, and turn until coated. Wrap lamb in the pan with plastic and refrigerate 8 to 12 hours (do not marinate for more than 12 hours). Rotate frequently to ensure even coating.

FOR THE LAMB:

Preheat oven to 375°F.

Remove lamb from marinade, and discard marinade. Thoroughly mix garlic, spice blend, and zest in a mixing bowl to create a paste; add salt and pepper to taste. Spoon mixture over the entire surface of lamb. Pat with 1 tablespoon oil; set aside.

Place potatoes in a roasting pan large enough to hold the lamb. Drizzle with remaining 1 tablespoon oil and season with salt and pepper. Set lamb on top of potatoes and pour wine around it. Roast for 30 minutes.

FOR THE SAUCE:

While lamb is roasting, beat egg yolks together with lemon juice in a mixing bowl. Heat stock in a small saucepan over low heat until warm. Slowly drizzle in egg mixture, whisking quickly to prevent eggs from cooking. Remove from heat.

Using a pastry brush, baste lamb every 10 to 15 minutes with generous amounts of sauce.

Continue roasting until an instant-read thermometer inserted at the thickest part of the meat reads 140°F to 145°F for medium, or 145°F to 150°F for well-done. The lamb should be well browned and the potatoes cooked through. Let lamb rest for 10 minutes before carving. Serve atop the potatoes.

VARIATIONS
• Add a pinch of cumin to the paste.

Serves 6

ADDITIONAL SERVING RECOMMENDATIONS

• Grill over indirect heat and serve at room temperature, with a side of BIG FOOD Aioli (page 35), Marinated Black Olives with Garlic and Red Pepper (page 116), and Tapenade (page 118).

SECONDARY DISHES

• *Turkey Shepherd's Pie (page 202)*
• *Lamb Kebabs (page 232)*
• *Lamb Pockets: Cut packaged dough into 4-inch squares, coarsely grind the leftover lamb, and dollop a tablespoonful into the center of each square. Brush the edges with water, fold over, and bake at 350°F until golden brown, about 10 to 15 minutes.*

GOING BONELESS

Once a rarity in chain supermarkets and discount clubs, lamb is now widely available and often of excellent quality (which it should be, because it is also often quite expensive, by BIG FOOD standards). Most stores carry petite legs that have been boned and rolled; they are usually packaged in an elasticized mesh bag, which can be removed if the leg is to be stuffed. I generally leave it on the meat— and suggest you do too—when I roast it because it holds the rolled meat together while it is cooking. This causes some consternation among my culinary colleagues, and for no reason. Traditionally, Greek-style leg of lamb is cooked on the bone: The meat remains tender, the flavor is arguably better, and it's simply easier to turn in the roasting pan (just grab hold and turn). If you do go boneless, decrease your roasting time so that the meat doesn't burn. The best way to do this is to invest in a good digital thermometer, which will cost $15 to $30 and allow you to keep precise track of cooking temperatures.

WINE-BRAISED LAMB SHANKS

In the world of BIG FOOD, resourcefulness knows no bounds. Lamb shanks were always considered "throwaway" meat by fancy types who sipped their wines and savored their foie gras while their peasant brethren scrounged for scraps. Or so they thought. This long-cooking, rustic, one-pot dish is made from possibly the least expensive cut of meat you will ever see anywhere (I've seen lamb shanks in my supermarket for as little as $2.50 a shank) and probably the most delicious. In this dish, the juices from the lamb shank meld beautifully with the wine and the vegetables to create a very rich sauce, so rich, in fact, that you might not be able to finish it. Just pull the meat off the bone, mix it back into the sauce, and reheat the next day with a can of whole Italian-style tomatoes for a magnificent pasta sauce.

2	tablespoons unbleached, all purpose flour	2	large carrots, peeled and diced
1	teaspoon kosher salt	2	large celery stalks, diced
$\frac{1}{2}$	teaspoon freshly ground black pepper	1	large onion, peeled and diced
4-6	medium-size lamb shanks	1	garlic clove, peeled and minced
2	tablespoons extra virgin olive oil	$\frac{1}{2}$	tablespoon dried rosemary
			Dry red wine, to cover
			Hot cooked egg noodles

Preheat oven to 300°F.

Place flour, salt, and pepper in a large, heavy-duty freezer bag, zip closed, and shake.

Add shanks (one at a time if necessary), zip closed, and toss to coat with flour mixture. Remove, shake off excess flour, and set aside.

Heat oil in a large ovenproof saucepan or Dutch oven over medium heat, until rippling but not smoking. Add shanks, in batches if necessary, and brown well on all sides, approximately 8 to 10 minutes per batch, removing browned shanks to a plate as you go. Add carrots, celery, and onion, and cook, stirring occasionally until translucent, about 8 minutes. Do not let them take on any color. Stir in garlic and rosemary, and continue to cook for 5 minutes. Return shanks to pan (a tight fit is okay).

Add wine to cover, stir once, cover, and place in the oven. Cook, spooning sauce over shanks frequently, until meat is falling off the bone and sauce is fragrant and flavorful, 2½ to 3 hours.

Serve hot, on a bed of egg noodles.

VARIATIONS

• Add additional carrots or peeled turnips, parsnips, or rutabaga to the dish.

Serves 4 to 6

ADDITIONAL SERVING RECOMMENDATIONS

• Serve this dish on a bed of egg noodles (yolk-free, if you must).
• Serve this dish on a bed of soft-cooked, instant polenta.
• Serve with a side of Roman-Style Sautéed Greens (page 195).

SECONDARY DISHES

• *Simple Pappardelle with Lamb Ragu: Pull the leftover cooked meat off the bone and throw it back into its sauce, along with a 16- or 28-ounce (based on how much meat you have leftover) can of crushed Italian-style plum tomatoes. Simmer for 45 minutes, and toss with wide-cut pasta.*

IN A PIG'S EYE

BIG FOOD ON PORK

> "Eternity is two people and a ham."
> —Irma S. Rombauer, *The Joy of Cooking*, 1930

Mrs. Rombauer was right (as she was in most things culinary) when she uttered those words. You can just see her, can't you? Maybe her kids had left home, and she and the husband were sitting around on a late Sunday afternoon, having just finished an early dinner. There they were, staring at a huge piece of ham, wondering how long it would take for the two of them to finish the whole thing without eating ham sandwiches, ham salad, and ham loaf every day for the next month.

As far back as 1930, the doyenne of American home cooking was faced with the same BIG FOOD issues that we are today: just like meat, chicken, and fish, pork products beckon us to buy them in bulk because, odds are, they're less expensive that way. But who wants to eat the same thing for an eternity? What Mrs. Rombauer may or may not have considered at that time was the fact that, as with meat, poultry, and fish, ham (and pretty much any pork product) can be used to create luscious secondary dishes that bear little resemblance to the original from whence they came. And now, with pork being as healthy and lean as it is (and religious or cultural restrictions not withstanding), there is simply no reason not to enjoy it on a regular basis.

Thankfully, gone are the days when eating pork was like eating blowfish (you never knew what you were getting); today, most of the pork produced in this country is of exceptionally good quality—so good, in fact, that that nasty disease that many of our mothers and grandmothers remember, trichinosis, has been all but eliminated, along with the need to cook the stuff until it was carbonized or had the texture of Styrofoam. These days, pork—while it still should not be eaten rare—can be that follow, however, recommend that you cook them until the meat is just white, juicy, and tender, as opposed to gray and leathery. But however you choose to cook it, today's pork and pork products are succulent, lean, flavorful, relatively inexpensive, easy to cook, and easy to rework into secondary dishes, such as a modern twist on Brazilian Feijoada, a heavenly stew consisting of leftover pork that has been cubed and then tossed with canned posole, black beans, lime, chicken stock, and chili. So the next time you see those immense packages of pork chops in your discount club's meat case, or you find yourself scratching your head while staring at a pork roast the size of a Volkswagen, go ahead and buy this perfect BIG FOOD protein: help is on the way.

BUYING PORK IN BULK

Like beef, pork is now available in massive quantities that demand we know how to store them well and understand when to use certain cuts as opposed to others: lean pork tenderloins are often packaged two or three together; chops—boneless or not—are often packaged 8 or 10 together. Shoulders and Boston butts are often so enormous that they're overwhelming to the eye. The great news is that the pork of today is quite a bit leaner than the pork of yore, so the meat actually freezes better and longer than it used to. So, what to look for when you're buying pork in bulk?

eaten a little on the pink side, which is how you might enjoy it if you were dining, say, in Italy, overlooking the lush, green Po Valley in Lombardy.

Ultimately, of course, how well done you cook your pork is your choice; the recipes in the pages

HOW TO MAKE SURE THAT YOU'RE BUYING THE RIGHT PORK CUT FOR THE RIGHT DISH

PORK CUTS	TENDERNESS	USAGE
Loin: roasts, rib chops, loin chops	Very Tender	Roast, pan-sear, or grill quickly.
Tenderloin	Very Tender	Roast, pan-sear, or grill quickly.
Ham, fresh and cured	Tender	Roast, bake, or braise.
Boston Butt: shoulder roast	Tough	Use in long-cooking stews, braised roasts.

- Know what you're looking at, and don't buy anything that is either unrecognizable to you or you won't know how to butcher once you get it home.

- Make sure that you're buying the right cut for the right dish.

STORING AND USING PORK SAFELY

Pork should be stored similarly to beef and chicken: frozen pork can be double-plastic-wrapped, sealed in a heavy-duty freezer bag, and stored in your freezer for up to 6 months. Uncooked pork that's brought home should be used within 3 days. Cooked pork will generally freeze for 2 to 3 months, depending on what it has been prepared with. Pork products—bacon and sausage, for example—can be frozen for up to 2 months when packaged well. And like all other meats, poultry, and fish, never ever defrost uncooked pork and then refreeze it.

MUSTARD-GLAZED PORK TENDERLOIN WITH OVEN-ROASTED APPLES

WHAT YOU HAVE ON HAND

- **2 large pork tenderloins**
- **Apples: any crisp variety**

WHAT TO DO WITH IT

- Remove both tenderloins from their package. Set aside 1 for this recipe; dry and double-plastic-wrap the second, then wrap again in heavy-duty aluminum foil and freeze for up to 6 months, or store in the refrigerator for up to 3 days.

- Set aside 4 apples for this dish; store the balance in your crisper, away from onions or potatoes.

HOW LONG IT WILL LAST

- Cooked pork tenderloin will last up to 3 days in the refrigerator, double-plastic-wrapped and stored in a heavy-duty freezer bag; it will keep for up to 3 months in the freezer, wrapped the same way.

Luscious, tender, lean, and simple to prepare, pork tenderloins cook very quickly, making them perfect for busy households wanting to get dinner on the table as quickly as possible. But the fact of their leanness means that they can also overcook very quickly, leaving you with something that has the consistency of a short baseball bat. The way around this is to quickly marinate the meat in a combination of spices and extra virgin olive oil, and then sear it in a hot pan on top of the stove prior to popping it into a hot oven; the sear locks the flavorful juices into the meat. Served with oven-roasted apples, this is a healthy, light, and tasty weeknight dinner.

1	garlic clove, peeled and finely minced	1	pork tenderloin (about 1 pound)
1	teaspoon dry mustard	4	large crisp apples, cored, peeled, and cut into $\frac{1}{2}$-inch cubes
1	teaspoon dried thyme	2	tablespoons fresh lemon juice
1	teaspoon dried sage	1	tablespoon cider vinegar
1	teaspoon freshly ground black pepper	$\frac{1}{2}$	teaspoon dried sage
$\frac{1}{2}$	teaspoon kosher salt		
3	tablespoons extra virgin olive oil, divided		

In a small bowl, blend together garlic, mustard, thyme, sage, pepper, salt, and 2 tablespoons of the oil. Transfer mixture to a large heavy-duty freezer bag, add the tenderloin, zip closed, and shake to coat well. Refrigerate for 30 minutes, or up to 4 hours. Remove tenderloin from bag; discard marinade.

Preheat oven to 400°F.

In a nonreactive roasting pan large enough to later add the tenderloin, toss apples with lemon juice, vinegar, and sage, combining well. Bake uncovered, stirring frequently, for 5 minutes. Reduce the heat to 350°F and continue to bake, stirring frequently.

Heat the remaining 1 tablespoon of oil in a large, nonstick sauté pan over medium heat, until rippling but not smoking. Add the tenderloin, and brown on all sides.

Set tenderloin in the roasting pan, on top of the apples. Cook until a thermometer inserted into the thickest part of the tenderloin reads 145°F, about 10 minutes.

Remove from oven, and let tenderloin rest for 10 minutes prior to slicing. Spoon apples and their liquid onto a serving platter. Place sliced tenderloin on top of the apples, and serve.

VARIATIONS

- Replace the dry mustard with honey mustard or spicy German mustard.
- Substitute boneless pork chops for the tenderloin and prepare the same way, adjusting cooking time accordingly.
- Supplement the apples with ripe pears, chopped dried apricots (not candied), chopped dried pitted plums, and/or raisins, in any combination.

Serves 4

Owing to their leanness, pork tenderloins are a wonderful way to incorporate healthy protein into a low-carb diet.

BUYING MARINATED MEATS

Don't do it. Ever. Sure, we've all seen those marinated port tenderloins just waiting for us to take them home and pop them into the oven. Two reasons to avoid them: salt and other preservatives. Packaged marinated meats are invariably packed to the brim with sodium and other preservatives that kept the marinade from "turning" during the shipping process. Steer clear.

ADDITIONAL SERVING RECOMMENDATIONS

- For a fancier presentation, spread the apples on a platter, set the pork directly on top, and slice at the table.
- Serve with Roman-Style Sautéed Greens (page 195) and Smashed New Potatoes: baby potatoes that have been steamed in their skins, tossed with a dollop of cream cheese, and then "smashed" with a wooden spoon.

SECONDARY DISHES

- *Brazilian Feijoada (page 250)*
- *Asian Noodles with Pork, Scallions, and Ginger (page 254)*
- *Cold medallions of pork with BIG FOOD Aioli: Slice cold leftover tenderloin into approximately 1/4-inch rounds; serve with BIG FOOD Aioli (page 35), cornichons, and toast points.*

SECONDARY

BRAZILIAN FEIJOADA

This rich and delicious traditional Brazilian pork stew gets a modern makeover with the use of leftover, cubed boneless pork (from a tenderloin or leftover Italian-style pork roast that's been cut off the bone). Or you can make it with fresh, cubed pork. Made with canned beans, canned posole (also called hominy, and found in the canned bean aisle), packaged stock, and spices, it is one of the most perfect BIG FOOD leftover meals I know of; it travels well, stores well, and is better a day or so after its preparation.

2	tablespoons extra virgin olive oil		1	(28-ounce) can posole, drained
2	pounds leftover cooked pork roast, tenderloin, or chops, cut into 1½-inch cubes		1	cup leftover BIG FOOD Basic Chicken Stock or packaged stock
2	medium onions, peeled and coarsely chopped			Juice of 2 limes, divided
1	jalapeño pepper, seeded and chopped		⅓	cup chopped fresh cilantro
1	(28-ounce) can black beans or white beans, with their liquid			Kosher salt and freshly ground black pepper

Optional: *1 (16-ounce) can crushed Italian-style plum tomatoes, for a more soup-like result*

RLOIN

Heat oil in a large Dutch oven or saucepan over medium-high heat, until rippling but not smoking. Add pork and brown on all sides, approximately 5 minutes. Remove with a slotted spoon and set aside.

Add onions and cook until translucent, 6 to 8 minutes. Add jalapeño and cook until softened, about 5 minutes. Add tomatoes, if using, and cook until they've softened and their liquid is released, 8 to 10 minutes.

Add beans, posole, stock, and half of the lime juice. Increase heat to high, and bring to a boil for 5 minutes. Reduce to a lively simmer, and return pork to the pot. Cook until liquid is reduced by a third, about 15 minutes.

Add cilantro and remaining lime juice. Season to taste with salt and pepper. Blend well, simmer for 5 minutes more, and serve hot.

VARIATIONS
Make this dish with:
• Leftover white-meat chicken
• Leftover white-meat turkey
• Leftover steak

Serves 4 to 6

ADDITIONAL SERVING RECOMMENDATIONS
• Serve in deep bowls as a stew, with steamed rice or a warm flour tortilla. Garnish with cilantro and slices of fresh lime.

WHAT YOU HAVE ON HAND

- **1 pork roast, on the bone, approximately 6 to 8 ribs**
- **Garlic**
- **Lemon**
- **Fennel**

WHAT TO DO WITH IT

- Make sure that you're buying a roast that has its "chine bone" cracked, otherwise you will not be able to slice it into individual chops.
- Set aside 3 garlic cloves for this recipe, and store the balance in a cool, dark location.

HOW LONG IT WILL LAST

- Double-plastic-wrapped and set on a platter, this dish will last for approximately 3 days in the refrigerator. BIG FOOD suggestion: Slice the meat from the bone immediately after serving, cube it, and store for up to 3 days in preparation for making Brazilian Feijoada (page 250).

ITALIAN-STYLE PORK ROAST WITH FENNEL, GARLIC, AND RED PEPPER

Adapted from chef Mario Batali, this Sunday roast is a throwback to the days when families came home from church and sat down to a meal lovingly prepared by a senior member of the family, who had been slaving away at it all day. The good news is that this roast—which can easily serve as the centerpiece at an important meal involving your future in-laws, your boss, or your intended—falls into the "fix it and forget it" category and can be proportionally increased or decreased based on the size of the roast you bring home.

3	fennel bulbs, leafy ends (fronds) cut off and reserved	1	(3- to 4-pound) pork roast, on the bone, chine cracked
3	garlic cloves, peeled and finely minced	2	carrots, peeled and sliced on the bias into 2-inch pieces
1	teaspoon kosher salt	2	celery stalks, sliced on the bias into 2-inch pieces
1	teaspoon red pepper flakes	1	large onion, peeled and sliced into 1/4-inch rounds
4	tablespoons extra virgin olive oil, divided	1/2	cup dry white wine
	Grated zest of 2 lemons, divided		

Chop fennel fronds finely and place in a small mixing bowl. Add garlic, salt, pepper flakes, 3 tablespoons of the oil, and half of the lemon zest. Blend to create a thick paste.

Preheat oven to 375°F.

Rub pork roast all over with the fennel paste, massaging it into the meat. Drizzle with the remaining 1 tablespoon of oil.

Slice fennel bulbs lengthwise in half and in half again. Place in a roasting pan, along with carrots, celery, and onion. Set pork roast on top of vegetables, and roast for 30 minutes.

Reduce heat to 350°F, pour the wine directly over the top of the roast, add the remaining lemon zest, and return to oven, basting frequently with the pan juices, until a digital thermometer inserted into the thickest part of the meat reads 145°F, about 1 hour.

Remove from oven, set roast on a cutting board, and let stand for 10 minutes. Slice and serve, surrounded with the roasted vegetables. Alternatively, serve whole roast and vegetables on a platter, slicing roast into individual chops at the table.

VARIATIONS

- Increase the spice: add additional red pepper flakes.
- Replace fennel bulbs with lemon quarters.
- Use a boneless pork loin; cook to 140°F.

Serves 4 to 6

WHAT YOU HAVE ON HAND

- **2 pounds ground pork, fresh or leftover that you've ground in the food processor**
- **Asian-style noodles, like soba**

WHAT TO DO WITH IT

- If you're starting with leftover pork, cube the meat and pulse it in the food processor until it is coarsely ground. If you have more than 1 pound, double-plastic-wrap and freeze the remaining cooked portion in a labeled, dated, heavy-duty freezer bag for up to 2 months. Freshly ground pork should be handled similarly; it will freeze for up to 4 months.

SECONDARY

ASIAN NOODLES WITH PORK, SCALLIONS, AND GINGER

Another well-loved BIG FOOD dish that's easy to prepare, stick with the traditional scallions, or add as many vegetables to this dish as you wish: asparagus, bell pepper, summer squash, snow peas, string beans, and grated carrots work perfectly here, too.

1	pound Asian-style noodles		1	teaspoon black bean paste
2	tablespoons peanut oil		1	teaspoon chili paste
2	garlic cloves, peeled and minced		¼	cup packaged chicken stock
1	tablespoon peeled and minced fresh ginger		1	pound coarsely ground pork (fresh, or from leftover cubed pork)
3	scallions, chopped			
2	tablespoons soy sauce or nam pla (Vietnamese fish sauce)			

Optional: *Extra chopped scallion greens and ground, unsalted, raw peanuts for garnish*

BIG FOOD'S BEST FRIEND: THE FOOD PROCESSOR

I used to be a purist in the kitchen, which meant that I never did with a food processor what I could do with my knife. That changed when I realized that I could do a lot more than chop an onion in my food processor: in fact, I could grind meat, which made me very happy when I began to buy my food in bulk.

When you divide a large roast—be it pork, beef, or even veal—as I recommend you do in most of these recipes, consider immediately grinding up the balance in your food processor and freezing it for use in Italian-Style Turkey Meatballs (page 204), BIG FOOD Burgers (page 222), Not My Mama's Meat Loaf (page 220), Mexican Tortilla Pie (page 198), or Traditional Bolognese Sauce (page 236).

To grind meat in your food processor:

- Chill your meat in the freezer, but do not let it actually freeze.
- Slice into large cubes.
- Process a few cubes at a time.
- Store in dated, labeled, heavy-duty freezer bags in the freezer, according to that particular meat's timetable.

Fill a large stockpot with salted water, and bring to a boil. Cook noodles until al dente (tender, but still slightly firm to the bite). Drain and toss with ice water in their colander. Set aside.

Heat oil in a large skillet or wok over medium heat, until just beginning to smoke. Add garlic and ginger, and sauté, stirring quickly, until aromatic and beginning to take on color, about 6 minutes. Add scallions and continue to cook until wilted, 3 to 4 minutes.

Add soy sauce, bean paste, chili paste, and stock. Cook 5 to 7 minutes. Add pork, breaking it up as it cooks; if using fresh pork, cook until it is no longer pink. If using leftover pork, cook until heated through.

Add reserved noodles, cover, and gently shake pan to combine. Serve hot with extra scallion greens and peanuts, if using.

VARIATIONS
• Substitute beef, chicken, or tofu for the pork.
• Add 1 teaspoon of curry paste blended with ¼ cup coconut milk to the cooking liquid.
• Add hot red pepper flakes to the dish.
• Add cubed fresh mango to the garlic-and-ginger stir-fry.
• Pork Fried Rice: In place of noodles, in a separate pan set over high heat, fry leftover white rice in 1 teaspoon of peanut oil. Add the pork mixture directly to the rice.

Serves 4

PRIMARY/SECONDARY

SPINACH COLCANNON WITH GROUND PORK

Colcannon is rustic food attributed to those among our ancestors who had to stretch every dollar to its limit. Therefore, some may sneer at the addition of meat to this classic, unsung Irish recipe. But not I. Make this dish when you're cleaning out your cold storage and have uncovered boxes of frozen spinach clogging up your freezer, or enormous bags of it in your crisper, along with those nearly sprouted potatoes you're just itching to toss.

2	tablespoons extra virgin olive oil
1	large onion, peeled and coarsely chopped
1	pound ground pork from previously cooked, cubed pork, or 1 pound fresh ground pork
4	large potatoes, peeled or unpeeled (your choice) and cut into eighths (once lengthwise, then across four times)
½	teaspoon nutmeg
3	(9-ounce) packages frozen spinach, thawed, drained, and chopped; or 3 (16-ounce) bags fresh spinach, woody stems removed, boiled, drained, and chopped
1	teaspoon freshly ground black pepper
½	teaspoon kosher salt

Preheat oven to 350°F.

Heat oil in a large, deep, cast-iron pan over medium-high heat, until rippling but not smoking. Add onion and sauté until translucent, about 6 minutes.

Add pork, heating it through if you are using leftovers, and cooking it through until no longer pink if it is fresh, 8 to 10 minutes. Add potatoes, pressing them into the surface of the pan with the back of a spoon until golden and crisp, about 10 minutes. Add nutmeg, and stir to blend well.

Add spinach, blend well, and continue to cook, stirring frequently, until liquid has released and evaporated, about 10 minutes. Add pepper and salt.

Place in oven, and cook until potatoes are browned and crisp, about 35 minutes. Serve hot.

VARIATIONS

- Substitute for the spinach: kale, chard, mustard greens, or collard greens, parboiled for 10 minutes and drained.
- Substitute for the pork: ground beef, crumbled sausage meat, ground chicken or turkey, or ground lamb.

Serves 6

ADDITIONAL SERVING RECOMMENDATIONS

- Serve hot, with a mixed green salad.
- Serve hot, topped with a poached or fried egg.

SAUSA

WHAT YOU HAVE ON HAND

- Immense packages of sausages, of any kind (including frankfurters)
- Large bottles of dark beer
- Red onions

WHAT TO DO WITH IT

- Set aside 6 large red onions for this dish; store the remainder in a mesh bag in a cool, dark location, away from potatoes and fruit.

HOW LONG IT WILL LAST

- Porter's Brats are best served immediately, and hot. Leftovers can be double-plastic-wrapped and stored in a heavy-duty freezer bag in the refrigerator for up to 3 days.

ADDITIONAL SERVING RECOMMENDATIONS

- Fish the boiled red onions out of the beer, and serve them as a topping.
- Serve as you would hot dogs, with the following accompaniments: raw onion, cooked red onion (see above), relish, ketchup, mustard (the spicier the better), and/or BIG FOOD Chili con Carne (page 238).

SECONDARY DISHES

- *Rigatoni Baked with Pork Sausage (page 268)*

PRIMARY

PORTER'S BRATS

From the hills of the northern Midwest comes a recipe designed to make you think differently about all of those immense packages of sausage—brats, kielbasa, pork, chicken, meatless, and turkey sausages—that are available in bulk. This simple dish, which came to me from my dear friend and wonderful home cook, Porter Boggess, requires the boiling of sausage in dark beer with sliced red onion (parents, take note: the alcohol burns off), and then finishing the sausage on the grill. Made in quantity, they're perfect to serve to a hungry crowd, even if the Green Bay Packers aren't playing.

6	(16-ounce) bottles dark beer	2	pounds sausages: bratwurst, knockwurst, or frankfurters, or chicken, turkey, pork, veal, or meatless sausage
6	large red onions, peeled and thinly sliced		Warm frankfurter rolls
1	tablespoon juniper berries		
1	tablespoon caraway seeds		
1	tablespoon whole black peppercorns		

Bring beer to a low boil in a large stockpot over medium-high heat. Add onions, juniper berries, caraway seeds, and peppercorns. Reduce to a low simmer, cover, and cook for 45 minutes.

Prick sausages with a fork on two sides, and add 4 or 5 links to the pot. Cover and simmer for 30 minutes.

Preheat grill to medium-hot.

As sausages finish cooking, immediately place on grill and cook until well-browned and crispy. Serve hot, on warm frankfurter rolls.

Serves 4 to 6

ALSATIAN CHOUCROUTE GARNI

As a BIG FOOD shopper, you have likely come home from your shopping trips lugging your weight in sausages—chicken, turkey, meatless, pork, veal, bratwurst, knockwurst, and everyone's favorite: the frankfurter. In this country, we are sausage-happy. They are delicious, filling, generally inexpensive, and easy to cook, and kids love them. And if you're like me, you always have some lurking around in the back of the freezer. Choucroute Garni—stick-to-the-ribs Alsatian peasant food—combines sausage with sauerkraut to produce a dish that's smoky, succulent, and easy to make. Make this in bulk and freeze the sauerkraut in one dish, the sausages in another.

1	tablespoon unsalted butter	2	teaspoons caraway seeds
1	tablespoon canola oil	2	bay leaves
2	large white onions, peeled and sliced	1	teaspoon whole black pepper-corns
4	pounds packaged sauerkraut	8	mild sausage links: chicken, turkey, pork, veal, beef
3/4	cup dry white wine		
1	tablespoon dried juniper berries		

Optional: *Spicy mustard and cornichons*

Heat butter together with oil in a large saucepan or Dutch oven over medium-high heat, until foam just begins to subside. Add onions, stir, and cook until softened, about 6 minutes.

Drain sauerkraut of its liquid and add it to the pot, stirring to blend well with onions; discard liquid. Add wine, bring to a boil, and cook 5 minutes.

Reduce to a slow simmer. Add juniper berries, caraway seeds, bay leaves, and pep-percorns. Cover and cook for 1 hour (check frequently for dryness, adding 2 to 3 additional tablespoons of wine, if necessary).

Bury links in the sauerkraut, making sure they are completely covered. Replace cover and continue to cook for an additional hour. Serve hot with spicy mustard and cornichons, if using.

Serves 4 to 6

WHAT YOU HAVE ON HAND

- **Sausages: mild boudin blanc, chicken sausage, turkey sausage, knockwurst, bratwurst, frankfurters (pork or beef), fresh, or leftover**
- **Canned or otherwise packaged sauerkraut**

WHAT TO DO WITH IT

- Set aside approximately 8 links for this recipe; freeze the balance in a dated, heavy-duty plastic freezer bag or use in BIG FOOD Cassoulet (page 260).

HOW LONG IT WILL LAST

- Stored in a tightly sealed con-tainer in the refrigerator, Alsatian Choucroute Garni will last up to 4 days. Freeze the sauerkraut and links separately for up to 3 months.

SECONDARY DISHES

- *BIG FOOD Cassoulet (page 260)*

WHAT YOU HAVE ON HAND

- Mild sausage: preferably pork, but chicken, turkey, and veal will work
- Leftover sausage from Alsatian Choucroute Garni (page 259)
- Leftover pork from Italian-Style Pork Roast with Fennel, Garlic, and Red Pepper (page 252) or Mustard-Glazed Pork Tenderloin with Oven-Roasted Apples (page 248)
  or
- Leftover lamb from Greek-Style Leg of Lamb with Egg and Lemon Sauce (page 240) or leftover lamb meat from Wine-Braised Lamb Shanks (page 242)
- Bread crumbs
- Large cans of white beans
- Salt pork, bacon, or pancetta
- Beef stock or consommé from Pot-au-Feu (page 48)

WHAT TO DO WITH IT

- Set aside 1 pound of fresh sausage for this dish; double-plastic-wrap the balance, and freeze it in a dated heavy-duty freezer bag for up to 6 months.
- Set aside 2 to 3 leftover links from Alsatian Choucroute Garni for this dish.
- Cut leftover pork and leftover lamb into ½-inch cubes for this dish.

PRIMARY/SECONDARY

BIG FOOD CASSOULET

In certain regions of France, hordes of people lay claim to the reigning king of long-cooking dishes, cassoulet. Some make it with duck; others make it with four or five different kinds of pork. But wherever you're from, you will almost always see it made with white beans, sausage of some type, and topped by a golden brown crust. Julia Child, who this author considers a national gift to hungry Americans, published a cassoulet recipe that took somewhere in the neighborhood of 3 days to make. Desirous of a version that anyone could make with a few cans of beans and a couple of varieties of meat—some leftover—I give you BIG FOOD Cassoulet.

1	pound fresh mild sausage plus ½ pound leftover cooked sausage, if available (or 1½ pounds of all fresh, or all cooked)	1	teaspoon kosher salt
½	pound pancetta, prosciutto, or salt pork, cut into ½-inch cubes	1	teaspoon freshly ground black pepper
		1	tablespoon dried parsley
2	shallots, peeled and finely minced	3	cups leftover cubed pork or lamb, or a combination of the two
2	garlic cloves, peeled and finely minced	2	cups packaged beef stock or leftover consommé from Pot-au-Feu
4	(16-ounce) cans white beans, with their liquid	1	cup bread crumbs
		1	tablespoon unsalted butter

Preheat oven to 350°F.

Heat a medium (4-quart) Dutch oven with lid over medium heat. Add sausage and brown on all sides, about 8 minutes. (Sausage renders its own fat, so it should not need oil. If using very lean sausage, add 1 tablespoon of extra virgin olive oil to the pan prior to adding the sausages.) Remove and drain on paper towels. When cool, slice into 2-inch pieces.

Add pancetta and cook until fat is rendered, about 8 minutes. Remove with a slotted spoon and drain on paper towels.

Remove pan from heat and, using tongs and a balled-up paper towel, wipe out all but 2 tablespoons fat. Return to medium heat, add shallots and garlic, and sauté until translucent, about 5 minutes. Using a slotted spoon, transfer shallot mixture to a small bowl.

Arranging ingredients in layers, as you would a lasagna, add a half an inch of white beans and their liquid to pot, followed by a sprinkle of the salt and pepper. Then add a third of the pancetta, followed by a third of the shallot mixture, followed by a sprinkle of parsley. Add a layer of pork, followed by the sausage pieces. Repeat until you have filled the pot.

Pour the stock over the beans (don't be alarmed if it looks as if it might overflow), sprinkle with bread crumbs, and dot with butter. Set pot on a baking sheet, cover, place in oven, and cook for 2 hours.

Remove cover, increase heat to 400°F, and bake until top is browned, about 25 minutes more. Serve hot.

VARIATIONS

- Replace the pork and pork products with duck and duck sausage, beef and beef sausage, lamb and lamb sausage, chicken and chicken sausage, or meat substitute and vegetarian sausage.
- Replace the pancetta, prosciutto, or salt pork with leftover cubed ham.

Serves 6

HOW LONG IT WILL LAST

- Stored in an airtight container in the refrigerator, BIG FOOD Cassoulet will keep for up to 4 days; it will freeze for up to 2 months.

ADDITIONAL SERVING RECOMMENDATIONS

- Ideally, make this dish in a beautiful Dutch oven that you can bring straight from the oven to the table. Serve in bowls, along with a mixed green salad, followed by a dessert of fresh fruit.
- Double the ingredients in this dish and serve buffet-style.

SECONDARY

OVEN-BARBECUED PORK SPARERIBS

Ribs are a glorious summertime treat, designed to be eaten outdoors (where the neighborhood dog can clean up what's been dropped on the lawn). But when you don't have the time to sit around for 5 hours, maintaining a steady 200°F on your smoker, what to do? Make this oven-based version, which calls for a dry rub, a few cups of BIG FOOD Barbecue Sauce, and a baking sheet, and that's all: the result is lip-smackingly good, and the leftovers, even better.

3	cups BIG FOOD Dry Rub	3	cups BIG FOOD Barbecue Sauce or your favorite packaged brand
3–4	racks pork ribs		

Generously massage rub into ribs, coating well. Place in a large roasting pan, double-plastic-wrap it, and refrigerate 8 hours, or overnight.

Preheat oven to 350°F.

Remove racks from the refrigerator, and brush off any excess rub. Paint liberally with 2 cups of the barbecue sauce, and place side by side in roasting pan. Cover tightly with aluminum foil, reduce heat to 300°F, and bake for 3 hours, basting frequently with the remaining 1 cup of barbecue sauce. Serve hot.

VARIATIONS

- Substitute beef ribs for pork ribs.
- Add chopped fresh mangoes or peaches to the remaining cup of barbecue sauce prior to basting with it.

Serves 4 to 6

ADDITIONAL SERVING RECOMMENDATIONS

- Serve as you would traditional *cue:* with sides of boiled corn, coleslaw, biscuits, and plenty of napkins.

SECONDARY DISHES

- *Oven-Barbecued Pulled Pork: tear the meat from the bones, chop it into long strips, and serve on soft rolls, with additional BIG FOOD Barbecue Sauce (page 37).*

PRIMARY/SECONDARY

SLOW-ROASTED PORK, PORTUGUESE STYLE

The big daddy of flavor and the crown prince of frugality, tenderness, and taste, Boston butt—otherwise known as pork butt, shoulder butt, and shoulder picnic—wins the prize on delicious BIG FOOD utilitarianism. Always huge, and nearly always cheap, this cut, when cooked slowly at a low temperature, is nothing short of miraculous. This recipe, which sprang from a friend's attic recipe file, has been adapted to include tomatoes, black olives, and garlic. It yields voluminous quantities of remarkably tender leftover meat.

1	(6- to 7-pound) Boston butt	2	large onions, peeled and sliced
2	tablespoons extra virgin olive oil	1	(28-ounce) can crushed Italian-style plum tomatoes with their juices
2	tablespoons BIG FOOD Mediterranean Spice Blend		
1½	teaspoons freshly ground black pepper	2	cups dry red wine
1	teaspoon kosher salt	½	cup pitted black and green olives, mixed
3	garlic cloves, peeled and thinly sliced		

Preheat oven to 450°F.

Place pork on a cutting board, trim off excess fat, and massage well with oil, spice blend, pepper, and salt. Using a long, thin knife, make several narrow, 1-inch slits in the meat. Insert 1 slice garlic in each.

Place onions in a large roasting pan, and set the pork on top of them. Pour tomatoes and wine directly over the meat, and cover the pan with aluminum foil, sealing edges tightly.

Place pork in oven, reduce heat to 250°F, and roast until the meat is falling off the bone, about 5 hours. Add olives, replace foil, and continue to cook for another half hour.

Serve hot.

VARIATIONS

- In place of the Mediterranean spices, rub the Boston butt with Worcestershire sauce and brown sugar.
- Line the bottom of the roasting pan with sliced, raw potatoes seasoned with salt and pepper, and let them roast with the butt.

Serves 6

ADDITIONAL SERVING RECOMMENDATIONS

- Slice and serve with pasta, rice, or on a sandwich.

SECONDARY DISHES

- *BIG FOOD Cassoulet (page 260)*
- *Pork Fried Rice (page 255)*
- *Asian Noodles with Pork, Scallions, and Ginger (page 254)*

WHAT TO DO WITH IT

- Unwrap the ham and, if it is of a lesser brand or you suspect that it is highly salted, fill your kitchen sink with cold water, and set the ham in it to soak for 1 to 3 hours. Alternatively, fill your largest stockpot with milk, and soak the ham in it for 1 to 3 hours.

HOW LONG IT WILL LAST

- Cooked ham will last up to 5 days in the refrigerator, double-plastic-wrapped and stored in dated, heavy-duty freezer bags.
- Cooked ham can last up to 3 months in the freezer, wrapped as above, but its consistency will get mealy, owing to its water content. Therefore, frozen cooked ham should only be used chopped and added to soups and stews.

PRIMARY

BIG FOOD HAM

Around Christmas and Easter, hams of every size begin to appear in food stores across our country: most have been cooked, and every one of them promises ease of serving. Likewise, every family I know of has their own version of "What to Do with It" once they bring it home (and the results are often cloyingly sweet). I like to coat mine with the kind of spice that cuts through the richness, and I use a surprise ingredient that comes by way of Aretha Franklin. Holiday or not, ham is always good to have kicking around your cold storage: it makes for great leftovers and (while it's not a perfect substitute for them) can be used wherever pancetta or prosciutto is called for in BIG FOOD. Buy your ham on the bone, and save that golden bone to add smoky flavor to soups and stews.

1	(8- to 10- pound) cooked ham (not canned)		1	cup orange juice, packaged or freshly squeezed, but not from concentrate
½	cup brown sugar		2	tablespoons honey
2	tablespoons dry mustard		1	tablespoon soy sauce
1	tablespoon ground ginger		1	(12-ounce) can ginger ale
½	teaspoon red pepper flakes			

Remove ham from its outer wrapping, and soak if necessary (see "What to Do with It").

Preheat oven to 350°F.

Blend sugar, mustard, ginger, and pepper flakes together in a medium-size bowl. Add orange juice, honey, and soy sauce, and whisk to combine. Set aside.

Thoroughly dry the ham and, using a sharp knife, gently score the surface, first on the diagonal in one direction, then on the diagonal in the other, to make a diamond-shaped pattern.

Using your largest roasting pan with rack, line pan with heavy-duty aluminum foil. Place ham on rack and set into pan. Cover ham and seal pan tightly with additional foil. Roast until the internal temperature of the ham reaches 120°F, 15 to 20 minutes per pound.

Remove foil, baste liberally with the reserved glaze, and pour entire can of ginger ale over the meat. Return to oven and continue to cook, uncovered, basting every few minutes, until ham's internal temperature reaches 140°F, about 20 to 25 minutes more. Allow ham to rest for 15 minutes before slicing and serving.

VARIATIONS

- Instead of preparing your own glaze, brush the ham with packaged chutney, gauged to your own spice preference.
- Crushed fresh pineapple, peaches, or apples—or all of them—can be added to the pan and then basted onto the ham, with the glaze, during the last 20 minutes of cooking.

Serves 8 to 10

FREEZE THE BONE

If you have a ham bone left over but no immediate plans to use it, freeze it in a heavy-duty freezer bag for up to 2 months, and use it to flavor soups and stews.

FRESH HAM VERSUS COOKED HAM

Never confuse these two cousins: anything labeled "Fresh Ham" is an *unsmoked, uncooked* leg of pork, while cooked ham has been smoked and cured. Fresh ham can be prepared the same way as cooked ham, but it should be roasted to an internal temperature of 160°F before serving.

ADDITIONAL SERVING RECOMMENDATIONS

- Slice and serve Southern style, with sides of Roman-Style Sautéed Greens (page 195), biscuits, Mature Mac and Cheese (page 270), and Smashed New Potatoes (page 249).

SECONDARY DISHES

- *Make ham sandwiches with Maple Horseradish Mustard (page 38).*
- *Cube leftover ham and add to soups, salads, omelets, and Torta Rustica (page 208).*
- *Blend cubed leftover ham with mayonnaise and dill, and serve on black bread.*

WHAT TO DO WITH IT

- If you are using leftover pork sausages, cut them on the bias into 1½- to 2-inch pieces and set aside. If using fresh pork sausages, poke a few holes into each one, and gently simmer them in water for 5 minutes. Let cool, and proceed as above.

- Defrost 3 cups of BIG FOOD Marinara Sauce.

- Cut 1 pound of mozzarella into ½-inch cubes, and set aside.

- Spoon 12 ounces of ricotta into a bowl, and blend with 1 egg and ½ teaspoon of nutmeg, cover, and refrigerate until needed. Store the remainder in its original container.

SECONDARY

RIGATONI BAKED WITH PORK SAUSAGE

For those adults among us who love the foods of our childhood (namely, SpaghettiOs), think of this dish as the grown-up version of something we adore when life gets a little bit tough. Easy to make, it can be first mixed together in one big lasagna pan, then baked in separate, smaller pans for reheating individual portions later. Hungry mouths—young or old—will love this after a hard day's work at the office or on the playground.

12	ounces ricotta cheese	6	cooked Italian pork sausages, sliced on the bias
1	egg, lightly beaten	1	pound mozzarella, cut into ½-inch cubes, or 1 (16-ounce) package shredded
½	teaspoon nutmeg		
½	tablespoon freshly ground black pepper	1	pound rigatoni, cooked 1–2 minutes short of being done
1	tablespoon extra virgin olive oil		
3	cups BIG FOOD Marinara Sauce or packaged sauce		

VERY GOOD, TO VERY GREAT

This lovely dish—and many just like it—is very, very good. But it becomes *great* when made with the best ingredients you can find: if you happen to live near an Italian butcher who makes his own sausages, try them. Likewise, if you can get top-notch, freshly made mozzarella, try it, at least once. You'll notice the difference immediately.

Preheat oven to 350°F.

Mix together ricotta with egg, nutmeg, and pepper in a small bowl.

Grease a lasagna pan with oil, and ladle in enough sauce to just coat the bottom. Add a layer of sausage, followed by a third of the ricotta, then a third of the mozzarella. Cover with a layer of pasta and a liberal ladle of sauce. Repeat three times, ending with the mozzarella.

Bake until the top is golden brown, 35 to 40 minutes.

VARIATIONS

For the pork sausage, substitute cooked:

• Chicken sausage

• Turkey sausage

• Meatless sausage

• Ground pork, turkey, or beef

Serves 6 to 8

HOW LONG IT WILL LAST

• Rigatoni Baked with Pork Sausage will last, double-plastic-wrapped, in the refrigerator for up to 4 days; wrapped the same way and then covered with a layer of heavy-duty aluminum foil, and labeled, it will freeze for up to 3 months.

ADDITIONAL SERVING RECOMMENDATIONS

• Serve hot, in bowls, along with a mixed green salad or Roman-Style Sautéed Greens (page 195).

• Serve buffet-style or bring to a potluck.

WHAT YOU HAVE ON HAND

- **Tubular pasta: penne, ziti, gemelli, elbows, or shells**
- **Firm cheeses: Cheddar, Asiago, Parmesan, queso blanco, Swiss, Gruyère, Emmentaler**
- **Prosciutto or leftover ham**
- **Frozen peas**

WHAT TO DO WITH IT

- Grate 2 cups of the cheese; double-plastic-wrap the balance and store in a dated, heavy-duty freezer bag in the refrigerator for up to 5 days. Or make Fromage Fort (page 34).
- Cube ³/₄ cup prosciutto or leftover ham. Double-plastic-wrap the balance, and store in a heavy-duty freezer bag in the refrigerator for up to 4 days.

PRIMARY/SECONDARY

MATURE MAC AND CHEESE

I grew up, as many of you did, thinking that macaroni and cheese was grown in a box and mixed on top of the stove, along with a silvery envelope of powdered orange cheese "food" that needed to be blended with a little milk or water to be edible. The good news is that if you have any of it left in your pantry, it'll still be edible in 30 or 40 years. This "mature" version calls for prosciutto (but you can use any sort of leftover ham), any three firm cheeses (one should be extra-sharp), and any kind of tubular pasta. What makes this robustly flavored version different—what gives it a little "edge"—is the addition of truffle oil (an admitted splurge, but one that can be had relatively inexpensively), nutmeg, and a hint of hot red pepper.

1	teaspoon nutmeg	1	tablespoon white truffle oil
¹/₂	teaspoon red pepper flakes	2	cups grated Cheddar, Asiago, Emmentaler, Gruyère, and/or Parmesan, in any combination
3	cups milk (low-fat or full-fat)	1	pound tubular pasta, cooked al dente (tender, but still slightly firm to the bite)
4	tablespoons unsalted butter, divided		
3	tablespoons unbleached, all-purpose flour	¹/₂	tablespoon kosher salt
³/₄	cup cubed prosciutto or leftover ham	³/₄	cup bread crumbs

Optional: ³/₄ cup frozen peas

Preheat oven to 375°F.

In a mixing bowl, add nutmeg and pepper flakes to milk, and whisk together.

Melt 3 tablespoons of the butter in a medium saucepan over low heat, until just beginning to foam. Using a wooden spoon, sprinkle in flour, a little at a time, stirring well after each addition, until all of the flour is incorporated and the mixture just begins to take on some color, about 4 minutes.

Add milk mixture in a slow and steady stream, stirring constantly, until the consistency becomes that of a thick, lump-free cream.

Add prosciutto and peas, if using, along with truffle oil; stir well to incorporate. Fold in cheeses and stir well to combine.

Combine cheese sauce and pasta in a large mixing bowl, and season with salt. Grease a rectangular baking pan with the remaining 1 tablespoon of butter, pour in the noodle mixture, and sprinkle with bread crumbs.

Bake until the top is golden brown, 20 to 25 minutes. Serve hot with a small mixed green salad.

VARIATIONS
- In place of ham, substitute chopped, boiled shrimp; leftover crabmeat; leftover lobster meat; or good-quality canned tuna.
- Add sliced mushrooms.

Serves 4 to 6

HOW LONG IT WILL LAST
- Sealed in an airtight container in the refrigerator, this dish will last up to 4 days; stored the same way, it will last in the freezer for up to 3 months.

SECONDARY DISHES
- *Fromage Fort (page 34)*

BIG FOOD ON WINE

"Wine is bottled poetry."
—Robert Louis Stevenson

True enough: there is perhaps no greater match for food than the appropriate wine with which to pair it. (Even *pizza* tastes better when paired with the right wine.) One makes the other sing, and neither has to be particularly fancy nor expensive.

But navigating one's way around a wine shop or department in a large supermarket or discount club can quickly turn grapes of joy to grapes of wrath. Without *any* instruction as to what kind of wine to buy and why, one is sunk. On the flip side, too much undivided direction from a wine salesman can quickly border on intrusive, confusing the shopper and often winding up costing him a lot more than it should have.

I believe that shopping for wine doesn't have to be confusing, stressful, time consuming, or even expensive, and with a few hints about what to buy and why, your next wine shopping trip will be painless.

First: Set your price limit, and stick with it. When shopping at a discount club, a supermarket wine department, or even a fancy wine store, you can easily find delicious wines for $15 and under, and in some cases, under $10. *Never* allow yourself to be steered towards anything that you feel is out of your price range, whatever it may be. If you are buying a case of wine (12 bottles), inquire about a case discount, which is usually 10% off the total amount spent. When you walk into a wine department, remember who the boss is: you. Don't be afraid to express your opinion, desires, and needs to the wine salesman. If he or she can't or won't oblige, leave.

Second: Think about what you are going to be serving the wine with. Fish? Poultry? Pork? Beef? Pasta? Snacks? Will your food be spicy and bold, or mild and delicate? Italian-style, or Asian? Are

WINE MATCHING TIPS

Although I am a firm believer in drinking what you *like*, here are some basic guidelines to help you navigate the wine aisles. None of the recommended wines sells for more than $15 at the time of this printing.

DRY WHITE WINE

Pair with:

- Egg dishes—omelets, frittatas, poached eggs
- Lighter pasta dishes
- Lighter chicken dishes—grilled, roasted, sautéed, or in a salad
- Vegetarian dishes

Styles include:

- Dry Malvasia
- French-style Chardonnay, Semillion blend
- Pinot Grigio or Italian Pinot Gris
- Alvarinho, used in Portuguese Vino Verde
- Spanish Torrontes

Try:

- Bonny Doon Ca'Del Solo Mavasia Bianca: dry, tart, citrus flavor, made in California by Randall Graham.
- Beringer Knights Valley Alluvium Blanc: fruity and herbal, soft and lightly buttery while remaining distinctly dry, made in California.
- Ecco Domani Pinot Grigio: lingering tastes of apricot and citrus, very light in color and weight. A good summertime barbecue wine, made in Italy.

FRUITY WHITE WINES

Pair with:

- Asian-style dishes, specifically spicier Thai and Chinese food
- Spicier vegetable-based soups
- Compound salads including chicken or fish

Styles include:

- California, Oregon, and Alsatian-style (not German) Riesling
- Italian Tocai from Friuli (not Hungarian Tokay)
- California Chardonnay

Try:

- Turning Leaf Riesling: round, fruity, and creamy California Riesling that pours slightly syrupy.
- Bonny Doon Pacific Rim Riesling: tastes of honey and apple in a perfect match for spicy Asian food.
- Colutta Dry Tocai Friulano: hints of hazelnut, vanilla, and winter fruit in a richly fragrant and aromatic wine.
- Amberhill Chardonnay: mild oak flavor balances the subtle fruitiness of this very inexpensive, top-value wine.

FULL-BODIED DRY RED WINE

Pair with:

- Heavy stews and roasts, usually beef or game
- Grilled dishes
- Pasta in heavy red sauce
- Rich, heavier foods

Styles include:

- "Super Tuscan"—unspecified combination of Sangiovese, Nebbiolo, and Chianti
- Syrah
- Zinfandel
- Cabernet Sauvignon
- Bordeaux
- Merlot

Try:

- Primitivo A Mano: a heavily tannic, rustic-style, inexpensive Italian wine filled with the flavor of ripe berries, peppery spice, and leather.
- Apollonio Salice Salentino: smoke and black currant flavors abound in this long-finishing, easy drinking Italian wine. Let it breathe for 45 minutes before pouring it.
- Woodbridge Mondavi Syrah: Jammy and rich with hints of licorice.
- Fetzer Valley Oaks Cabernet: Well-blended flavors of chocolate and blackberries make this wine an excellent value at (usually) under $10.
- Cline California Red Truck: easy to drink, this is a blend of 6 different grapes (Mourvedre, Syrah, Cabernet Sauvignon, Cabernet Franc, Pinot Noir, and Alicante Bouschet). The result is teeming with earthy, cherry flavors.
- Rosenblum Vintners Cuvee Zinfandel: remarkably round, full-bodied, and heavily textured with the essence of dark jam and black pepper.

LIGHTER-BODIED RED WINES

Pair with:

- Salads
- Rich, fattier fish (salmon, bluefish)
- Pizza

Styles include:

- Pinot Noir
- Beaujolais
- Tempranillo
- Dolcetto
- Nero d'Alvola
- French Burgundy (Expensive)

Try:

- Estancia Pinnacles Pinot Noir: an outstanding bargain wine from California, full of the flavor of sweetened oak, black cherry, and dried flowers.
- Borsao: ridiculously inexpensive, this Spanish red has all the subtle power of the most expensive Burgundies costing 10 times as much. Spicy, velvety, and soft, this is a keeper if you like lighter-bodied reds.
- Dolcetto D'Alba Cavallotto: soft, flowery, with the flavors of anise, minerals, and bright fruit.

you looking for something to sip while sitting on the deck with friends and enjoying some cheese? Gone are the days when white wine *had* to be served with fish and chicken, and red with beef. There are heavier and lighter styles of both red and white grapes, so it's okay to throw out the "official" rule book. Drink what you like, but generally, pair spicy wines with spicy foods, and lighter wines with lighter foods. Likewise, if the dish you're serving has been cooked with red wine, serve red wine with it; if you've cooked with white wine, serve white wine with it.

Third: Be willing to experiment. Good wines don't necessarily have to come from California, Italy, France, or Germany. These days, reasonably priced bottles hail from South Africa, Australia, New Zealand, New York, Virginia, Chile, and Hungary.

Fourth: Don't be afraid of the box or the screw-top. Some of the world's finest wine writers admit to keeping a box of good-quality wine in their fridge because it is generally perfect for everyday drinking, and lasts longer than it will in a bottle. Screw-top caps (also known as Stelvin Closures) have also entered the big leagues: California wine-maker Randall Graham of Bonny Doon Vineyards also swears by them to keep wine fresher, longer.

AN INEXPENSIVE WAY TO TASTE

The best way to learn about what you like and what you don't is to taste, so invite five or six friends over. Let them know in advance what the theme of the evening will be (for example, Zinfandel). Have each person bring a different bottle of that variety of wine, within a strict price range; open them all at the same time, let them breathe for 10 minutes, and then taste them in clean glasses (not plastic, which can actually affect the flavor of the wine). Compare notes, close your eyes, and let your taste buds tell you what they will.

HOW LONG WILL IT LAST?

	REFRIGERATE	FREEZE
SOUPS		
Pot-au-Feu	3 days	6–8 months
Mushroom and Barley Soup	3–4 days	6 months
Elena's Ukrainian Beef Borscht	5 days	6 months
French Onion Soup	3 days, no cheese	6–8 months, no cheese
Traditional Jewish-Style Chicken Soup	4 days, no noodles	6 months, no noodles
BIG FOOD Basic Chicken Stock	3 days	6 months
Tortellini en Brodo	3 days, no pasta	6–8 months, no pasta
Asian Chicken Soup	4 days	6 months
Mexican Chicken Soup	3–4 days	6 months
BIG FOOD Rustic Tomato Soup	3–4 days	6–8 months
White Bean Soup	3–4 days	6–8 months
Tuscan Bread Soup	3–4 days	6 months, no bread
Pasta e Fagiole	3–4 days	6 months
Oven-Roasted Tomato Soup	3–4 days	6–8 months
Traditional Gazpacho	3–4 days	6–8 months
Corn and Crabmeat Chowder	2–3 days	3–4 months
Cold Potato Soup	4–5 days	3 months
SALADS		
Panzanella	2–3 days	NA
Spicy Southwestern Corn, Crab, and Black Bean Salad	3–4 days	NA
Curried Salmon Salad	2–3 days	NA
Chopped Cobb Salad	2–3 days	NA
Grilled Vegetable Salad with Chicken and Pine Nuts	3–5 days	NA
Stuffed Tomatoes	3 days	NA
Warm Spinach Salad	NA	NA
Warm Grilled Chicken Salad	2–3 days	NA
Asian Fresh Tuna Salad	2 days	NA
Mediterranean White Bean Salad with Tuna	3 days if canned tuna; 2 days if fresh tuna	NA
Tuna Salad Niçoise	3 days, not dressed	NA
APPETIZERS		
Spicy Corn and Black Bean Cakes	3–4 days	6 months
Chicken Liver Crostini	3 days	6 months for spread
Sicilian Eggplant Salad	1 week	6 months
Baked Ricotta	2 days	NA
White Bean Hummus	4 days	NA
Traditional Hummus	5 days	6 months
Fried Rice Balls	3 days	NA
Marinated Black Olives	3 days	NA
Tapenade	7–10 days	NA
Pan Bagnat	2 days	NA
Pigs in Blankets	4 days	3–6 months
FISH		
Gravlax	1 week	NA
Wine-Poached Salmon Fillet	4 days	NA
Oven-Roasted, Tamari-Glazed Salmon	3 days	NA
Salmon Burgers	3 days	3 months
Penne with Vodka, Cream, and Smoked Salmon	2 days	NA
Smoked Salmon and Asparagus Frittata	2 days	NA
Mediterranean Tuna	2 days	NA
Pan-Fried Spicy Crab Cakes	3 days	4 months
Brandade	3 days	NA
New England–Style Codfish Cakes	4 days	4 months
Houston Street Whitefish Salad	5 days	NA
Risotto with Baby Shrimp and Peas	3 days	NA
Spiced Shrimp in Black Beer	2 days	NA

	REFRIGERATE	FREEZE
POULTRY		
BIG FOOD Herb-Roasted Chicken	4 days	4 months
Apricot-Glazed Roasted Chicken	4 days	3 months
Wine-and-Herb-Poached Chicken Breasts	3 days	3–6 months
Pan-Braised Chicken with Lemon, Thyme, and Black Olives	3 days	4–6 months
Chicken Braised with Figs, Honey, and Red Wine	4 days	4–6 months
Asian Chicken-Stuffed Lettuce Rolls	3 days, chicken only	NA
Chicken Sausage and Peppers	4 days	6 months
Chicken Saltimbocca	3 days	3 months
Chicken Potpie	3 days	8 months
Chicken Croquettes	4 days	8 months
Balik Fish	3 days	6 months
Fool's Chicken	4 days	NA
Oven-Barbecued Pulled Chicken	4 days	6 months
Quesadilla of Chicken, Chilies, Tequila, and Lime	3 days	NA
Fettucine with Lemon Chicken, Parmesan, and Wine	4 days	NA
Pappardelle with Chicken Ragu	4 days	6 months, sauce only
Chicken Sliders	Made from leftovers, 3 days; from fresh chicken, 4 days	LO, 3 months; from fresh, 6 months
Hunter's Chicken	4 days	6 months
Paella	4 days	NA
Chicken Gumbo	4 days	6 months
Chicken Fajitas	1–2 days	NA
Mexican Tortilla Pie	4 days	2–3 months
Turkey Hash	3 days	NA
Turkey Shepherd's Pie	4 days	3–4 months
Italian-Style Turkey Meatballs	4 days	3 months
Chicken Chili Stew	4 days	3 months
Torta Rustica	3 days	NA
BEEF & LAMB		
Colorado Sweet Steak	4 days	NA
Pancetta-and-Rosemary-Wrapped Tenderoin	4 days	NA
Not My Mama's Meat Loaf	4 days	6 months
BIG FOOD Burgers	3 days	8 months
Beef Bourguinon	4 days	6 months
New Year's Brisket	4 days	4 months
Stir-Fried Beef with Vegetables	4 days	3 months
Balsamic Marinated Flank Steak	4 days	NA
Beef Kebabs for a Crowd	4 days	NA
Sweet-and-Sour Stuffed Cabbage	4 days	4 months
Traditional Bolognese Sauce	4 days	6 months
BIG FOOD Chili con Carne	4 days	6 months
Greek-Style Leg of Lamb	4 days	3 months
Wine-Braised Lamb Shanks	3 days	Sauce: 3 months
PORK		
Mustard-Glazed Pork Tenderloin	3 days	3 months
Brazilian Feijoada	4 days	4 months
Italian-Style Pork Roast	3 days	NA
Asian Noodles with Pork, Scallions, and Ginger	3 days	NA
Spinach Colcannon	4 days	3 months
Porter's Brats	3 days	NA
Alsatian Choucroute Garni	4 days	3 months, sauerkraut and sausages frozen separately
BIG FOOD Cassoulet	4 days	2 months
Oven-Barbecued Spareribs	3 days	NA
Slow-Roasted Pork, Portuguese Style	4 days	3 months, sliced
BIG FOOD Ham	5 days	3 months, sliced
Rigatoni Baked with Pork Sausage	4 days	3 months
Mature Mac and Cheese	4 days	3 months

BIG FOOD ACTION CHART

	DISH	POULTRY	BEEF	LAMB	PORK	SMOKED MEAT/ BACON/SAUSAGE	EGGS	FISH	BROTH/STOCK	TOMATOES (FRESH OR CANNED)	ONIONS	GARLIC	CARROTS	
BASICS	BIG FOOD Infused EVOO											X		
	BIG FOOD Compound Butter													
	Fromage Fort											X		
	BIG FOOD Aioli											X		
	Wasabi Mayonnaise													
	Southwestern Mayonnaise													
	BIG FOOD Cocktail Sauce													
	BIG FOOD Barbecue Sauce													
	Maple Horseradish Mustard													
	Honey Mustard													
	Wasabi Mustard													
	Herb Mustard													
	BIG FOOD Mediterranean Spice Blend													
	Asian Spice Blend													
	BIG FOOD Dry Rub													
	BIG FOOD Marinara Sauce										X	X	X	X	
SOUPS	Pot-au-Feu	X	X								X	X	X	
	Mushroom and Barley Soup								X		X	X	X	
	Beef Borscht		X			X			X	X	X	X	X	
	French Onion Soup								X		X	X		
	Traditional Jewish-Style Chicken Soup	X									X		X	
	BIG FOOD Basic Chicken Stock	X									X	X	X	
	Tortellini en Brodo								X					
	Asian Chicken Soup with Greens	X							X		X	X		
	Mexican Chicken Soup with Vegetables, Chili, and Lime	X							X	X	X		X	
	BIG FOOD Rustic Tomato Soup								X	X	X	X	X	
	White Bean with Escarole and Sausage					X			X	X	X	X	X	
	Tuscan Bread Soup								X	X		X		
	Pasta e Fagiole								X	X	X	X	X	
	Oven-Roasted Tomato Soup								X	X	X			
	Traditional Gazpacho									X	X	X		
	Corn and Crabmeat Chowder					X		X	X		X			
	Cold Potato Soup with Roasted Garlic and Rosemary								X			X		

278 BIG FOOD ACTION CHART

CELERY	MUSHROOMS	MISCELLANEOUS VEGETABLES	MAYONNAISE	EVOO	CONDIMENTS	BUTTER/MILK/SOUR CREAM	RICE/GRAINS/PASTA	BREAD/TORTILLA/FROZEN DOUGH	CANNED BEANS/POSOLE	POTATOES	CHEESE	LEMONS/LIMES	SPICES/HERBS	WINE MATCH
				X								X	X	
						X						X	X	
											X	X		
			X									X		
			X		X									
			X									X	X	
					X							X	X	
					X								X	
					X									
					X									
			X		X									
													X	
													X	
													X	
													X	
X				X									X	
X		X											X	4
X	X	X		X			X						X	4
X		X							X				X	3
											X			3
X		X					X						X	1
X														NA
							X				X		X	1,4
		X					X						X	2
		X						X	X			X	X	Beer
							X				X		X	1,4
X		X	X						X				X	4
			X					X			X		X	1,4
X			X				X		X		X		X	1,4
			X								X		X	4
		X	X		X							X	X	1
		X				X							X	4
		X		X		X				X				2,4

WINE KEY: (1) Dry, crisp white; **(2)** Fuller-bodied, fruity white; **(3)** Full-bodied, heavier red; **(4)** Lighter-bodied, earthier red

DISH	POULTRY	BEEF	LAMB	PORK	SMOKED MEAT/ BACON/SAUSAGE	EGGS	FISH	BROTH/STOCK	TOMATOES (FRESH OR CANNED)	ONIONS	GARLIC	CARROTS
SALADS												
Panzanella									X		X	
Spicy Southwestern Corn, Crab, and Black Bean Salad							X		X	X		
Curried Salmon Salad with Grapes and Walnuts							X			X		
Chopped Cobb Salad	X				X				X	X		
Grilled Vegetable Salad with Chicken and Pine Nuts	X									X	X	
Stuffed Tomatoes									X			
Warm Spinach Salad with Mushrooms and Bacon					X					X		
Warm Grilled Chicken Salad with Herbs	X									X	X	
Asian Fresh Tuna Salad							X			X	X	X
Mediterranean White Bean Salad with Tuna							X			X	X	
Tuna Salad Niçoise						X	X			X	X	
APPETIZERS												
Spicy Corn and Black Bean Cakes						X						
Chicken Liver Crostini alla Toscana	X							X				
Sicilian Eggplant Salad									X	X	X	
Baked Ricotta						X						
White Bean Hummus											X	
Traditional Hummus												
Fried Rice Balls with Mozzarella						X						
Marinated Black Olives with Garlic and Red Pepper											X	
Tapenade												
Pan Bagnat						X	X		X	X	X	
Pigs in Blankets					X							
FISH												
Gravlax							X					
Wine-Poached Salmon with Herbes de Provence							X					
Oven-Roasted Tamari-Glazed Salmon							X					
Salmon Burgers						X	X			X	X	
Penne with Vodka, Cream, and Smoked Salmon							X		X			
Smoked Salmon and Asparagus Frittata						X	X			X		
Mediterranean Tuna with Black and Green Olives							X		X	X	X	
Pan-Fried Spicy Crab Cakes						X	X			X	X	
Brandade							X				X	
New England–Style Codfish Cakes						X	X					
Houston Street Whitefish Salad							X			X		
Risotto with Baby Shrimp and Peas							X	X		X		
Spiced Shrimp Boiled in Black Beer							X					
POULTRY												
BIG FOOD Herb-Roasted Chicken	X							X		X		X
Apricot-Glazed Roasted Chicken	X											
Wine-and-Herb-Poached Chicken Breasts	X											
Pan-Braised Chicken with Lemon, Thyme, and Black Olives	X							X			X	
Chicken Braised with Figs, Honey, and Red Wine	X				X			X			X	
Asian Chicken-Stuffed Lettuce Rolls	X									X	X	
Chicken Sausage and Peppers	X				X				X	X	X	
Chicken Saltimbocca	X				X			X				

CELERY	MUSHROOMS	MISCELLANEOUS VEGETABLES	MAYONNAISE	EVOO	CONDIMENTS	BUTTER/MILK/SOUR CREAM	RICE/GRAINS/PASTA	BREAD/TORTILLA/FROZEN DOUGH	CANNED BEANS/POSOLE	POTATOES	CHEESE	LEMONS/LIMES	SPICES/HERBS	WINE MATCH
				X	X			X					X	1,4
		X							X			X	X	2
X			X									X	X	2
		X		X							X	X		1,4
		X		X									X	1,4
		X		X			X				X		X	1,4
	X	X		X										4
X		X		X	X								X	1,4
		X			X							X	X	2
		X		X					X			X	X	1
		X		X	X					X			X	1
		X						X	X				X	2
				X		X		X						3
		X		X									X	1
											X		X	1,4
				X					X			X	X	2
				X	X				X			X	X	2
							X	X			X		X	1,4
				X								X	X	4
				X	X							X	X	4
		X		X	X			X					X	1,4
								X						1,4
					X								X	1
					X	X							X	1,4
					X							X	X	2
				X	X								X	1,4
		X			X	X	X						X	1
		X			X						X		X	1,4
		X		X								X	X	1,4
X		X	X	X	X	X		X					X	2
				X	X	X				X			X	1,4
					X			X					X	1,4
X			X					X				X	X	1
		X			X	X	X				X		X	1
					X								X	1 or Beer
				X								X	X	1,4
				X	X							X	X	4
													X	1
				X	X							X	X	4
				X	X							X	X	3,4
		X			X							X	X	2
		X		X									X	3,4
				X		X						X	X	4

WINE KEY: (1) Dry, crisp white; **(2)** Fuller-bodied, fruity white; **(3)** Full-bodied, heavier red; **(4)** Lighter-bodied, earthier red

(CONTINUED)

DISH	POULTRY	BEEF	LAMB	PORK	SMOKED MEAT/ BACON/SAUSAGE	EGGS	FISH	BROTH/STOCK	TOMATOES (FRESH OR CANNED)	ONIONS	GARLIC	CARROTS
POULTRY												
Chicken Potpie	X							X		X		X
Chicken Croquettes	X					X		X		X		
Papa's Balik Fish	X					X				X	X	X
Fool's Chicken	X	X			X							
Oven-Barbecued Pulled Chicken	X											
Quesadilla of Chicken, Chiles, Tequila, and Lime	X											
Fettucine with Lemon Chicken, Parmesan, and Wine	X							X			X	
Pappardelle with Chicken Ragu	X							X	X	X	X	X
Chicken Sliders with Mediterranean Herbs	X									X		
Hunter's Chicken	X				X				X	X	X	
Paella	X				X		X	X	X	X	X	
Chicken Gumbo	X				X			X	X	X	X	
Chicken Fajitas	X									X		
Mexican Tortilla Pie	X									X		
Turkey Hash	X				X					X	X	
Turkey Shepherd's Pie	X							X		X		X
Italian-Style Turkey Meatballs	X								X	X	X	
Chicken Chili Stew with White Beans and Posole	X							X		X	X	
Torta Rustica					X	X				X	X	
BEEF & LAMB												
Colorado Sweet Steak		X										
Pancetta-and-Rosemary-Wrapped Tenderloin		X			X						X	
Not My Mama's Meatloaf	X	X		X		X				X		
BIG FOOD Burgers		X								X		
Beef Bourguinon		X						X		X	X	X
New Year's Brisket		X							X	X		X
Stir-Fried Beef with Vegetables		X								X	X	
Balsamic Marinated Flank Steak		X							X	X	X	
Beef Kebabs		X							X	X	X	
Sweet-and-Sour Stuffed Cabbage		X							X	X	X	
Traditional Bolognese Sauce		X			X				X	X		X
BIG FOOD Chile con Carne		X							X	X	X	
Greek-Style Leg of Lamb			X			X		X			X	
Wine-Braised Lamb Shanks			X							X	X	X
PORK												
Mustard-Glazed Pork Tenderloin				X							X	
Brazilian Feijoada				X				X		X		
Italian-Style Pork Roast				X						X	X	X
Asian Noodles with Pork, Scallions, and Ginger				X				X		X	X	
Spinach Colcannon with Ground Pork				X						X		
Porter's Brats					X					X		
Alsatian Choucroute Garni					X					X		
BIG FOOD Cassoulet			X	X	X			X		X	X	
Oven-Barbecued Pork Spareribs				X								
Slow-Roasted Pork, Portuguese Style				X					X	X	X	
BIG FOOD Ham					X							
Rigatoni Baked with Pork Sausage					X	X						
Mature Mac and Cheese					X							

CELERY	MUSHROOMS	MISCELLANEOUS VEGETABLES	MAYONNAISE	EVOO	CONDIMENTS	BUTTER/MILK/SOUR CREAM	RICE/GRAINS/PASTA	BREAD/TORTILLA/FROZEN DOUGH	CANNED BEANS/POSOLE	POTATOES	CHEESE	LEMONS/LIMES	SPICES/HERBS	WINE MATCH
X	X	X			X			X		X			X	1,4
					X	X		X				X	X	1
X					X			X					X	1
					X	X							X	1,4
					X								X	1,4
					X			X			X	X	X	1,4
				X	X		X				X	X	X	1,4
X				X							X		X	1,4
					X			X			X		X	4
		X		X	X								X	3
	X	X		X			X						X	1,4
		X											X	2,3
X		X											X	2,4
		X			X			X					X	2,4
		X			X			X			X		X	2,4
		X								X			X	4
X	X	X											X	4
					X			X			X		X	4
				X					X			X	X	2,4
		X								X	X		X	1,4
					X								X	3
				X	X							X	X	3
					X	X		X					X	4
	X				X	X					X		X	4
	X			X	X								X	3,4
X					X								X	4
		X			X							X	X	2,4
		X			X							X	X	3,4
		X		X	X							X	X	4
		X			X		X					X	X	4
X				X	X						X		X	3
				X	X				X				X	3
					X					X		X	X	2,4
X				X	X								X	3
				X	X							X	X	4
				X	X				X			X	X	4
X					X							X	X	1
		X			X		X						X	2
		X		X	X					X			X	4
					X								X	2 or Beer
		X			X	X							X	2
					X			X	X				X	3
					X								X	4
				X	X								X	4
					X								X	1,4
				X	X						X		X	3
		X			X			X			X			4

WINE KEY: (1) Dry, crisp white; **(2)** Fuller-bodied, fruity white; **(3)** Full-bodied, heavier red; **(4)** Lighter-bodied, earthier red

INDEX

Underscored page references indicate boxed text, charts, and marginalia.